SO-COP-563

Hands-On
Mosaic™

A Tutorial for Windows™ Users

David Sachs and Henry Stair

Prentice Hall PTR, Englewood Cliffs, NJ 07632

Library of Congress Cataloging in Publication Data

Sachs, David.
    Hands-on mosaic: a tutorial for windows users / David Sachs and
  Henry Stair.
        p.   cm. --
    Includes index.
    ISBN 0-13-17231-9
    1. Mosaic (Computer file) 2. Internet (Computer network)
  3. Hypertext systems. 4. Interactive multimedia I. Stair, Henry H.
  II. Title.
TK5105.875.I57s32   1994   94-23495
005.04--dc20   CIP

Editorial/production supervision: *Camille Trentacoste*
Interior graphic design: *Gail Cocker-Bogusz*
Cover design: *Gryphon Three Design*
Manufacturing manager: *Alexis Heydt*
Acquisitions editor: *Mary Franz*
Editorial Assistant: *Noreen Regina*

© 1995 by Prentice Hall PTR
Prentice-Hall, Inc.
A Simon & Schuster Company
Englewood Cliffs, New Jersey 07632

The publisher offers discounts on this book when ordered in bulk quantities. For more information, contact: Corporate Sales Department, Prentice Hall PTR, 113 Sylvan Avenue, Englewood Cliffs, NJ 07632, Phone: 800-382-3419 Fax: 201-592-2249, E-mail: dan_rush@prenhall.com

NCSA Mosaic™ and the associated logo are trademarks owned by the University of Illinois. All other product names mentioned herein are the trademarks of their respective owners.

Printed in the United States of America
10 9 8 7 6 5 4 3 2 1

ISBN 0-13-17231-9

Prentice-Hall International (UK) Limited, *London*
Prentice-Hall of Australia Pty. Limited, *Sydney*
Prentice-Hall Canada Inc., *Toronto*
Prentice-Hall Hispanoamericana, S.A., *Mexico*
Prentice-Hall of India Private Limited, *New Delhi*
Prentice-Hall of Japan, Inc., *Tokyo*
Simon & Schuster Asia Pte. Ltd., *Singapore*
Editora Prentice-Hall do Brasil, Ltda., *Rio de Janeiro*

About the Authors

David Sachs is Professor of Office Information Systems and Assistant Dean in Pace University's School of Computer Science and Information Systems. He has been actively involved in the development and teaching of computer science courses since 1984. He has co-authored *Discovering Microsoft Works, Mastering Microsoft Works,* and *Hands-On Internet.* Dr. Sachs is particularly interested in the field of telecommunications and its impact upon our world. His interests include racquetball and downhill skiing.

Henry (Pete) Stair is a senior consultant with Mycroft Information in New Canaan, Connecticut, where he specializes in high-performance global telecommunications and computer networking. He co-authored the post-graduate textbook *Megabit Data Communications* and *Hands-On Internet.* He is a registered professional engineer (CA) and a member of the IEEE and the Internet Society. His interests included demystifying technology, cross-country skiing, consciousness research, and classical music.

Dedication

Hands-On Mosaic is dedicated to my mother, Norma, my brother, Robert, and the memory of my father, Monroe, for all of their care and support. There are no words which can convey the depth of my gratitude. And to my wife, Linda, as always, thanks for your love and friendship; I am wonderfully blessed.

—*David Sachs*

Hands-On Mosaic is dedicated to Lorrine: *l'amour, toujours l'amour.*

—*Henry Stair*

Contents

PART ONE: MOSAIC READY

PART TWO: MOSAIC SET

Part Three: MOSAIC GO!

APPENDICES

Acknowledgments

As with all books, this one is the product of many hands. Our gratitude goes out to all of you for support and encouragement. We must, however, single out just a few special thanks.

At PTR Prentice Hall, Mary Franz has been our shepherd, spur and steadfast supporter. Camille Trentacoste, Production Editor, and Gail Cocker-Bogusz, have worked hard to guide us through the maze of graphics publishing. And Noreen Regina has done a wonderful job of keeping all of the many pieces of paper headed in the right direction.

Our copy editor, Martha Williams, has been wonderful. Her attention to detail has been superb and her caring suggestions about how to improve the clarity of writing have been gratefully accepted.

We have been particularly fortunate to have had a wonderful group of technical reviewers, including Paul Bingman, Alison Brown, Ryan Grant (from NCSA), Brian Kelly, Michael Kelsey, Craig Rosenberg, Bob Williams (from NetManage, Inc.), and Darian Woodford (from NCSA). Our technical reviewers have kept us from straying and their suggestions have added much to our presentation. Even with the best of their help, we and we alone, are responsible for any remaining goofs, glitches, and gaps.

—David Sachs and Henry Stair

Introduction: What Is Mosaic and What Can It Do?

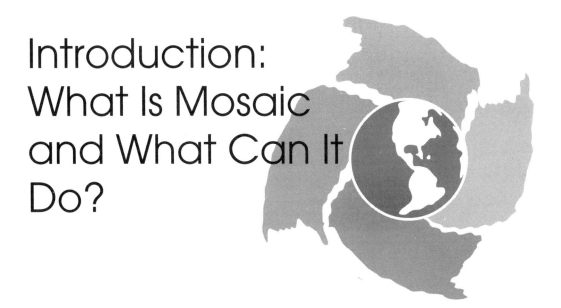

Mosaic[1] is an information browser with a very user-friendly, windows-like appearance. It was developed at the National Center for Supercomputing Applications (NCSA) at the University of Illinois at Urbana-Champaign. Mosaic allows you to rove the Internet's world of multimedia information without having to learn or remember the many commands that have always made the Internet a little uncomfortable for beginners.

Using this extremely friendly and powerful tool, you will be able to do all of the traditional Internet activities, such as E-mail, ftp, and telnet. In addition, the multimedia aspect of Mosaic means that you will be able to find and use art work, maps, satellite photos, and music!

Figure I-1 shows you the NCSA home page you will see when you log in to Mosaic. If you are already familiar with the traditional Internet interfaces, you will immediately recognize how different Mosaic looks from the character-based interfaces you have used until now.

---

1. NCSA Mosaic™ is an Internet browser written at the National Center for Supercomputing Applications at the University of Illinois, Urbana-Champaign.

Figure I-1
NCSA Home Page

WHY HAVE WE WRITTEN THIS BOOK FOR THE WINDOWS PC USER?

Users of Microsoft® Windows™ are used to having a friendly, powerful interface for their software. Many commands can often be invoked by pointing and clicking at them. Until now, this has not been true for most Windows PC users who have been Internet users as well. If you have been using what is known as terminal access, then the interface you have had to use is one filled with many UNIX commands, a command-line interface, and no ability to have color, sound, or graphics. Using Mosaic as your multimedia navigator for the Internet will change all that.

Mosaic is freely available on the Internet. However, even if you have heard about Mosaic, you may not know where to get it. And, even if you have downloaded a copy, you may have been somewhat perplexed as to what to do next. Suddenly, you encountered discussions about SLIP and PPP connections (we will explain them shortly) as well as something known as a TCP/IP stack of software. All of this can be very confusing, at least at first.

We believe that NCSA Mosaic for Microsoft Windows is an extremely powerful multimedia tool with which Windows users can navigate the Internet. We have written this book to show you how you can have access to this multimedia software and the global Internet on your Windows PC.

INTRODUCTION

Welcome to *Hands-On Mosaic*. This book contains everything you need to explore the world's greatest network of networks—the Internet—using Mosaic. In a series of online sessions, you learn how to

1. establish the special type of Internet connection that is needed to use Mosaic

2. install the special type of software (included with this book) that is needed to use Mosaic

3. download your own copy of Mosaic

4. use Mosaic to navigate the multimedia Internet

All of the software and instructions you will need to do this are contained in this book.

FOR WHOM IS THIS BOOK INTENDED?

Beginning Internet Users

This book has been written with the Internet user in mind. Therefore, if you are truly a beginning Internet user, we suggest that you begin elsewhere and then return to *Hands-On Mosaic* once you have some fundamental Internet skills under your belt. If this description applies to you, you might wish to start with *Hands-On Internet* by Sachs and Stair.

Internet Users with Terminal Accounts

If you have been using the Internet for some time, using a terminal account, and a traditional UNIX environment but have been wishing for more ease-of-use and power, this book is definitely for you. *Hands-On Mosaic* will teach you about the special type of Internet service provider connection you need to use Mosaic. We then help you install the special type of software required by Mosaic. Finally, we teach you all about the many powerful opportunities Mosaic can provide. All of these will enable you to learn how to access the Internet using a Windows environment. In addition, you will have the ability to quickly and efficiently download and use multimedia files of all shapes and sizes.

Experienced Internet Users

If you are an experienced Internet user who would like to significantly upgrade your Internet capabilities, *Hands-On Mosaic* is definitely for you. Change your terminal account to SLIP or PPP and install the Chameleon™ Sampler from NetManage,™ Inc., that is included with this book. Then you will be able to do all of the usual Internet activities (E-mail, ftp, and telnet) far more easily. In addition, you will then find that you have access to a whole array of multimedia resources that were previously unavailable.

How Is This Book Organized?

In the text and graphics that follow, we will guide you hands-on through three parts: "Mosaic Ready," "Mosaic Set," and "Mosaic Go!"

Mosaic Ready

To use Mosaic, two preliminary conditions must be met. First of all, your computer must have a SLIP or PPP connection that provides you with a direct connection to the Internet. Second, you must have installed a TCP/IP stack of software. We teach you how to do both of these in "Mosaic Ready." First, we help you to find an Internet service provider who can provide you with SLIP or PPP access. Next, we teach you how to install NetManage's Chameleon Sampler, which contains the TCP/IP stack of software. By the end of this part, you will truly be Mosaic ready!

Mosaic Set

In "Mosaic Set," we use Chameleon Sampler to help you to download Mosaic. With Chameleon Sampler, you will be able to

1. use ftp to download the compression and virus protection software you will need before downloading Mosaic

2. use ftp to download a copy of Mosaic

Finally, you learn how to install Mosaic on your Windows PC and to test it.

Mosaic Go!

In "Mosaic Go!" we lead you through many hands-on sessions, including ones that show you how to install and use Mosaic. We introduce you to concepts such as hypertext and hypermedia, which are exciting new English language ways to navigate the Internet. Finally, we show you how to use Mosaic to find your own treasures. Not only will be you able to find text files, but you will also be able to find an enormous array of multimedia software, including art work, maps, satellite photos, voices, and music!

CONVENTIONS USED THROUGHOUT THE BOOK

Sessions—There are nine sessions in this book, each of which is intended to be done online and hands-on, so you can work along with us as you first put your Windows PC directly onto the Internet and then install your own copy of Mosaic.

Overviews—As you will see, once you have Mosaic up and running, home pages will provide you with an overview of the options awaiting you each step of the way.

Hands-On Activities—In each session, you will find many hands-on activities in which we lead you carefully through the steps that are necessary to complete each activity successfully.

Pointers—From time to time, there are suggestions about ways to make particular activities flow more smoothly.

HeadsUp!—There are times when what you are about to do will be somewhat complicated, or more technical, than you may have experienced previously. We would like you to be fresh, alert, and paying close attention when we get to these activities.

Tips—Sometimes we provide some commentary about what may have just happened.

WHAT WILL YOU NEED?

1. First, you need to have an IBM personal computer or compatible capable of running Microsoft Windows 3.1 (or higher) in enhanced mode. That is, you need what is known as an 80386 (or higher) processor and 640 kilobytes of conventional memory, plus at least 4 megabytes of extended memory.

2. In addition, you need a $3\frac{1}{2}$" floppy disk drive and a minimum of 2 megabytes of free hard disk space for the Chameleon Sampler diskette that is provided with *Hands-On Mosaic.*

3. In addition, we suggest you have at least 6 megabytes of free disk space for the information you will be receiving from your travels with us about the Internet.

4. To communicate with an Internet service provider, you need a modem and a telephone line connected to your computer. We strongly recommend a high-speed modem (14,400 bits per second or higher) due to the amount of multimedia information you will be receiving once you are using Mosaic. (The faster your modem, the quicker the information will be transferred to your computer.)

You do *not* need any other software. The Chameleon Sampler diskette included with this book is all you need to establish a direct Internet connection so you can run Mosaic. Once Chameleon Sampler has been installed, we show you how to acquire your own copy of Mosaic from the Internet.

HOW TO USE THIS BOOK

If You Presently Have a Terminal Connection to the Internet

If you presently have a terminal connection to the Internet, you should proceed through this book in the order in which it is written. You need a SLIP or PPP connection and an installed TCP/IP stack of software. You learn how to do both of these in "Mosaic Ready." You need to download compression and virus protection software and Mosaic. You do all of this in "Mosaic Set." Finally, you will want to have an opportunity to explore much of the power of Mosaic. You have that opportunity in "Mosaic Go!"

If You Presently Have a SLIP/PPP Connection and Installed TCP/IP Software

In this case, you should move directly to Part Two, "Mosaic Set." You will have to download compression and virus protection software, as well as a copy of Mosaic. Then, in "Mosaic Go!" you will have the opportunity to explore many of the multimedia capabilities of Mosaic.

Let's get started!

Overview

Mosaic Ready will prepare your Windows PC for running Mosaic. To do so, you will need to learn about the special Internet connections that are required, as well as about the special software (included with *Hands-On Mosaic*) that must be installed.

In **Session One**, you will learn about the TCP/IP protocols, and SLIP and PPP connections, as well as how to find the Internet Service Providers who provide such connectivity.

In **Session Two**, you will learn how to install Chameleon Sampler, using either the pre-configured files provided by NetManage, or by writing your own configuration files. If need be, you will learn how to edit the SLIP.INI file.

In **Session Three**, you will connect to the Internet using Chameleon Sampler. In addition, you will Ping several Internet hosts, and you will use Chameleon Sampler's Telnet.

By the end of **Mosaic Ready**, you will be completely ready to install Mosaic on your Windows PC.

How To Use Mosaic Ready

If you do not presently have a SLIP or PPP Internet Service connection, and you do not presently have a TCP/IP stack of software installed on your Windows PC, then you should work through all of the sessions and activities in **Mosaic Ready**.

If you already have a SLIP or PPP connection to the Internet, and a TCP/IP stack of software installed on your Windows PC, then you may wish to continue to **Part 2 -- Mosaic Set**.

PART 1

SESSION 1

PCs on the Internet

This first session is extremely important. There is a lot of information contained here that is vital if you are to understand all that we will do in the remainder of the book.

If you have been using the Internet for some time and already have an Internet service provider, then you may find that some of the information contained in this session is familiar to you. If that is the case, then the most important decision will be to decide which Internet service provider you would like to use for your SLIP or PPP connection to the Internet. With luck, it will be the one you already have. If not, then feel free to skip to Activity 1 to retrieve a current copy of *PDIAL* or Activity 2 to retrieve *NIX-Pub*. We do, however, urge you to read the information about the TCP/IP protocol because that may be new to you.

Please be aware that copies of *PDIAL* and *NIXPub* are included in the Appendix to this book. If you do not presently have an Internet service provider and wish to call one immediately, there should be enough current information in the Appendix to enable you to do that.

WHAT IT MEANS TO BE "ON THE INTERNET"

According to a recent article in *Internet Society NEWS* (vol. 3, no. 1, November, 1994), there are four types of Internet access. We will focus on three of them.

Method One: Gateway Access

If you have America Online®, CompuServe®, Genie®, or Prodigy®, you already have an Internet connection available to you. You may have an easy-to-use Windows-type interface to your service provider. However, even with one of these connections, you will be unable to get information directly to your computer by using file transfer protocol (ftp), or to sign on directly into other computers using telnet. You may have an E-mail address and what is known as an Internet ID and be able to communicate with those on the Internet through what is known as a *gateway*. But, you are not really on the Internet (See Figure 1-1.)

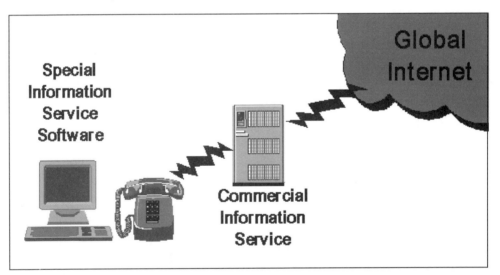

Figure 1-1
Information Services

Method Two: Terminal Access

You may be connected to an Internet service provider by using a dial-up modem line. You may be using simple asynchronous communications software such as ProComm® or SmartComm® or Telix™ that lets you connect to a host computer on the Internet by having your personal computer emulate a "dumb terminal," such as a VT-100. You may have been struggling with strange typed commands to use the Internet. Binary files can be moved to your computer only through additional file transfer steps or encoding schemes. You can use ftp, telnet, and E-mail, but, again, you are not really on the Internet. (See Figure 1-2.)

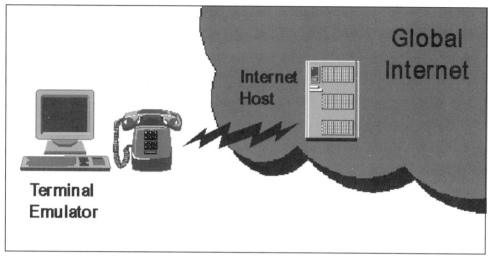

Figure 1-2
Terminal Emulation

Method Three: Host Access

Host access assumes that you have a computer and software that can support TCP/IP protocols (we will explain this shortly) and potentially provide the full range and power of Internet services, limited only by the capability of your computer. Host access is the focus of this book. Once you have correctly installed the Chameleon Sampler, you will be on the Internet.

YOUR PC MUST HAVE THREE THINGS _____

To have host access, and to REALLY be on the Internet, your PC must have three things:

1.   A communications program called TCP/IP

2.   An Internet protocol or IP address

3.   A connection to an Internet gateway or provider.

If you have these three things, you are really on the Internet and can be part of all of the information, excitement, resources, and tools now available. In this book, we will focus on one marvelous new Internet tool called NCSA Mosaic. You have to be on the Internet in order to use NCSA Mosaic. (See Figure 1-3.)

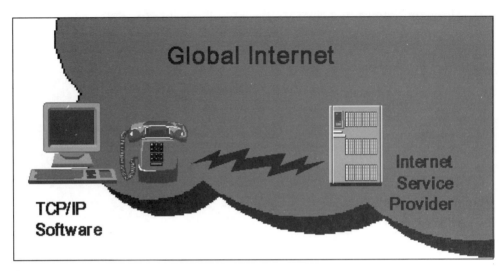

Figure 1-3
On the Internet

Let's look at these three elements, one at a time.

Heads Up!

If you have been using the Internet for some time, you may know some of the following information. However, it is possible that some of it will be new to you.   Feel free to skim the information that follows.

THE TCP/IP PROGRAM

A communications program called TCP/IP runs on every computer on the Internet. Actually, the Internet is made up of all of the interconnected computers running some version of this program. It's really a whole set of programs that goes by the name TCP/IP. *TCP/IP* is an acronym that stands for *Transmission Control Protocol/Internet Protocol.*

Now, a *protocol* can be thought of as a way of reaching agreement. TCP/IP does just that. It lets all of the interconnected computers in the world talk to each other. We call that group of computers the Internet.

Think of it as similar to what is referred to as "business English." Most business people in the world speak just enough English to communicate with each other. They know a limited set of words that permits them to work together. The basic set of words allows people of many different languages to talk. That's what TCP/IP does for all different kinds of interconnected computers.

We don't know why TCP/IP came to be the common tongue, any more than we know why English became the common business language. Partisans for each claim many reasons, but for our purposes it is sufficient to know that they both function similarly. If you know business English, you can conduct business all over the world, and if your computer knows TCP/IP, it can communicate with all of the other computers on the Internet.

So, to make your PC talk to all the other Internet computers in the world, we have to teach it to talk TCP/IP. We have made doing that (relatively) easy for you. The diskette that comes with this book includes a TCP/IP communications program known as the *Chameleon Sampler.*

There are lots of TCP/IP programs. Some can work on the big mainframe computers behind the glass walls. Some run on supercomputers and high-power workstations. Our Chameleon Sampler TCP/IP program runs on PCs running Microsoft's Windows.

TCP/IP is more than just a communications program; it also includes a number of applications (programs) and tools. The Chameleon Sampler that is included with this book contains a number of these programs.

WHAT TCP DOES

TCP (Transmission Control Protocol) makes sure, to the best of its ability, that your information passes through the Internet complete and undamaged. TCP sets up *sessions* with other TCP programs across the Internet. This is very similar to a telephone call. Typically, you call another party, and when the connection is made, you talk. TCP does this with your data.

The TCP programs on the two different connected computers work to assure you of good communications. TCP tries to keep your information clean from telephone line errors and makes sure that all of the information is there.

WHAT IP DOES

IP (Internet Protocol) takes information from TCP and tries to get it across the Internet. Unlike TCP, IP just sends its datagrams into the network and hopes that they will arrive. This is like a postal system. You put the letter in the postal box and hope that it gets to its destination. If the datagram gets lost, IP doesn't worry; it has tried its best.

This may seem risky, but it works amazingly well. IP may lose an occasional datagram, but TCP assures you that the information will get through. TCP does this by getting a return receipt for all of its data. If IP loses some data, TCP will send it again. This means that if a line breaks, or a computer in the network fails, that data will still get through. It's a lovely combination.

INTERNET ADDRESSES

Once you are running TCP/IP, there has to be a way to make your PC unique in the Internet world. As humans, we have learned how to find individuals by a complex system of names, addresses, and telephone numbers. This works, most of the time, because there are a lot of people to ask.

However, with computers, it's more difficult because the computers don't really know how (or whom) to ask. The solution is for each computer on the Internet to have a consistent, world-wide computer address. The address is called the *Internet protocol address* or *IP address*. Once a computer has been given an *IP address*, it should be unique in the world. This means that no other computer should have that address.

Another convention we will use is to refer to the Internet computers as *hosts*. It's just a convention. The computer can be any size from the mainframes to your PC, but we will call them all hosts. This means that the *IP address* is also referred to as the *host address*.

The IP address is really just a binary number made up of ones and zeros. This system makes it easy for the host (computer) but tough on humans. To simplify the human problem, we have a way of talking about the addresses. We do this by converting the ones and zeros into four sets of numbers. Then, we can just say four numbers, and that's the IP address.

So when humans do talk about IP addresses, they say

> One-ninety-two **dot** sixteen **dot** forty-one **dot** twelve

after they have read

> `192.16.41.12`

The numbers that are used for each of the sets of numbers which make up the IP addresses can range from zero (0) to two-fifty-five (255). This means that the lowest number we will use is

> `0.0.0.0`

and the largest number we will use is

> `255.255.255.255`

For at least the next few years, IP addresses will continue to look like this, and we will continue to say them this way.

INTERNET NAMES

While the hosts use IP addresses to find each other, this convention is often hard for humans. To make it easier, each host also has a name. Here's how the Internet uses names:

1. Your host (your own PC) can have any name which is acceptable to your Internet service provider.

2. That host name then becomes part of what is called a *sub domain* and a *top domain* (sort of like a family tree). There can be one or several parts to the whole name.

Let's look at some sample names to understand how it's done.

    a. `panix.com`

    b. `uiuc.edu`

    c. `ncsa.uiuc.edu`

    d. `microsoft.com`

    e. `internic.net`

If we examine each of these, we can see that they are (almost) self-explanatory.

    a. *panix.com* is the host address of an Internet service provider (Panix). The last part (.com) tells us that the address is a commercial enterprise.

    b. *uiuc.edu* is not so easy, unless you have been to the University of Illinois at Urbana-Champaign (uiuc). You can also now guess that it's an educational institution (.edu).

c.   *ncsa.uiuc.edu* is a host at UIUC which is used by the National Center for Supercomputer Applications (NCSA). NCSA is the developer of NCSA Mosaic.

d.   *microsoft.com* should be pretty easy to decode. Microsoft is a commercial (.com) company, so that extension is pretty obvious.

e.   *internic.net* refers to the interNIC, which is a shorthand name for the Internet Network Information Center (NIC). It has a number of functions, including giving out IP addresses and registering names, so it's part of a network (.net).

The last part of each name (.gov or .edu or .com) is called the *highest level domain*. When the entire host name is used, it is called the *fully qualified domain name (FQDN)*.

The final thing to notice about names is that we have printed them all in lowercase with no spaces. This is the usual convention in the Internet community, as many of the hosts treat upper- and lowercase letters differently. Although your PC treats upper- and lowercase letters the same, many hosts do not. So, you will find that many addresses use only lowercase.

This means that when you pick a name for your host (subject to the agreement of your Internet service provider), it will look something like this (notice the underline and dash to prevent spaces):

```
my_host.some-domain.provider.net
```

and is pronounced as we did the addresses, with a *dot* between each part. If you have been using America Online or CompuServe or Prodigy for E-mail, you will recognize the name forms

aol.com

compuserve.com

prodigy.com

Once you have an Internet service provider, you will give your PC a name. It can be your own name, or any kind of a (polite, we hope) name you wish. Since you may want to reserve your own name (Sally, Sam, or Smith) for your E-mail, the name you give your host could be different.

At this point, you may be asking how the Internet name and the Internet address relate to each other. That's a very good question. The answer is important and will be needed in the next session. Here's how it works.

Domain Nameservers

There are some special hosts all around the Internet called *nameservers*. Their function is to know the current IP address of each name.

This allows people to specify Internet names, which are easier for people to use and remember. And it allows hosts to use Internet addresses, which are faster for host computers to use.

That leads to the question: How does your host know the address of the nameserver? The answer is: You will learn the address of the nameserver from your Internet service provider, and you will tell your host when we set up your Chameleon Sampler.

Now, we are ready to talk about the third necessary element which is required for you (and your computer) to be on the Internet—a connection.

AN INTERNET GATEWAY OR PROVIDER CONNECTION ___

In earlier days on the Internet, universities and research labs banded together to connect to each other using TCP/IP. What they built has evolved into today's Internet. Now, more than half of the domains on the Internet are commercial. As such, a number of companies now offer Internet connectivity for a fee. We next describe how to find and sign up with one of these Internet service providers.

When you select an Internet service provider, you will need to use two acronyms to tell the provider what kind of Internet connection you want. The acronyms are *SLIP* (which stands for *Serial Line Interface Protocol*), and *PPP* (which stands for *Point-to-Point Protocol*). (There's that protocol word again.) You will need one or the other of these to become a full part of the Internet. We'll explain them in a moment.

Many Internet providers, including many of the smaller services, offer only the so-called "shell" accounts. We described this earlier as the VT-100 terminal emulator kind of service. While this is satisfactory for many things, it won't work with NCSA Mosaic or the other common graphic user interfaces (GUI, pronounced gooey). These more user-friendly and Windows-like screens make the Internet much less intimidating and much easier to use.

There are also Internet providers who use their own proprietary GUI interface programs for your PC. While these provide many of the Internet capabilities, most cannot use the common tools such as NCSA Mosaic.

You will want to select a provider that offers either SLIP or PPP accounts.

SLIP AND PPP

Earlier we discussed the fact that protocols are used to communicate between hosts on the Internet. Two of these are important to us here. These are *SLIP (Serial Line Interface Protocol)* and *PPP (Point-to-Point Protocol)*. SLIP or PPP will be the protocol you will choose to connect to your Internet service provider. Some providers offer PPP and almost all providers offer SLIP.

SLIP is the older of the two and it is really not a standard protocol. It sort of happened and a lot of people started to use it. Later, the Internet community decided that a better and more complete standard should be used. They developed PPP and many providers, but not all, use it. What you really need to know is that there are two protocols, and you will have to choose one of them.

Actually, there really are three protocols. SLIP comes in a type called compressed, and therefore is called *CSLIP* which stands for *compressed SLIP*. Unfortunately, some providers who use CSLIP call it SLIP. We'll help you through these little differences.

That's really all you need to know about SLIP, PPP, and CSLIP.

FINDING SLIP AND PPP SERVICE PROVIDERS

Every month, more providers are providing Internet connectivity. Since these providers exist all over the world, it could be tough finding them. Fortunately, some volunteers have decided to keep and distribute lists for the rest of us. We all owe them a debt of gratitude. Before we show you how to get the most current lists, we will highlight some of the best known providers. They break basically into two groups: big or nationwide and small or local.

You will want to find the one or ones best suited to your purposes. There are several ways to select among them. After we describe them and show you how to find the latest lists, we'll point out some differences.

The Biggest Providers

The following list includes many of the largest Internet service providers. It's produced by InterNIC Information Services of General Atomics and is reprinted here and in the Appendix with permission.

Later in this session, we will show you how to get the latest list if you already have E-mail or an Internet service. If you do not, we have included it in the Appendix.

These are, in general, large commercial service providers, many of whom also offer services to individuals. Detailed contact information can be found in the Appendix.

Important: The Chameleon Sampler included with this book comes with preconfigurations for 25 Internet service providers. A list of these (as well as some other providers) is presented in Table 1-1. Configurations and help files are provided for each one. They will be installed on your hard drive when you install Chameleon Sampler. Information about them will be included in the README file. We have put an asterisk (*) in the Included column next to the name of each one of the service providers for which a preconfiguration file is included on Chameleon Sampler.

Table 1-1: Internet service providers

Provider Name	Included with Chameleon Sampler	Service Area
AlterNet	*	US and International
ANS	*	US and International
BARRNet		Northern/Central California, Nevada (CA, NV)
CERFnet	*	Western US and International

Table 1-1: Internet service providers (Continued)

Provider Name	Included with Chameleon Sampler	Service Area
CICnet	*	Midwest US (MN, WI, IA, IN, IL, MI, OH)
CO Supernet		Colorado (CO)
CONCERT		North Carolina (NC)
CSUnet		California (CA)
HoloNet		North America
IACNet		Cincinnati Area (KY, IN, OH)
ICNet		Michigan, Northern Ohio (MI, OH)
Interaccess	*	Chicago (IL)
International Connections Mgr.		International
Internetworks		US and Pacific Rim
Interpath		North Carolina (NC)
JVNCnet	*	US and International
Los Nettos		Los Angeles Area (CA)
MCSNet		Greater Chicago (IL)
MichNet/Merit		Michigan (MI)
MIDnet		Mid US (NE, OK, AR, MO, IA, KS, SD)
MRNet	*	Minnesota (MN)
MSEN		Michigan (MI)
NEARNET		Northeastern US (CT, MA, ME, NH, NJ, NY, RI, VT)
NETCOM		US
netILLINOIS		Illinois (IL)

Table 1-1: Internet service providers (Continued)

Provider Name	Included with Chameleon Sampler	Service Area
NevadaNet		Nevada (NV)
NorthwestNet		Northwestern US (WA, OR, ID, MT, ND, WY, AK)
NYSERNet		New York (NY)
OARnet		Ohio (OH)
PACCOM		Hawaii (HI) and Australia, Japan, Korea
PREPnet		Pennsylvania (PA)
PSCNET		Eastern US (PA, OH, WV)
PSINet	*	US and International
Sesquinet		Texas (TX)
SprintLink		US and International
SURAnet		S. East US (WV, VA, SC, NC, TN, KY, LA, MS, AL, GA, FL, DC, MD, DE), South America, Puerto Rico
THEnet		Texas (TX)
VERnet		Virginia (VA)
Westnet		Western US (AZ, CO, ID, NM, UT, WY)
WiscNet		Wisconsin (WI)
WVNET		West Virginia (WV)

Some Smaller Providers

In the last several years, a number of smaller regional or local providers have begun to offer services. There are two available publications, *NIXPub* and *PDIAL* that try to keep track of them all. We present some of these smaller providers in Tables 1-2 and 1-3 and include a full list in the Appendix. Again, we will show you how to get the latest lists if you have E-mail or an

Internet connection. If you do not, don't worry; the lists in the Appendix will get you started. Later, you can get the current lists and shop around to find the best deal for yourself.

Table 1-2 presents a few examples from *NIXPub*. The actual list contains much more detail about the services, access numbers, and costs. There are, of course, many more providers in the full list. *NIXPub* is produced by BUX Technical Services and is reproduced here and in the Appendix by permission.

Table 1-2: *NIXPub* Service Provider Examples

Name	Location		Included With Chameleon Sampler
panix	New York City	NY	*
ddsw1	Chicago	IL	
telerama	Pittsburgh	PA	
indirect	Phoenix	AZ	
fullfeed	Madison	WI	
crash	San Diego	CA	
blkbox	Houston	TX	
dircon	London	UK	

PDIAL is another list showing many other Internet service providers. Like *NIXPub*, *PDIAL* includes much more information about each provider and many more are listed. *PDIAL* is produced by Peter Kaminski and is in Table 1-3 and in the Appendix by permission.

Table 1-3: *PDIAL* Service Provider Examples

name	Anomaly—Rhode Island's Gateway to the Internet
local access	RI: Providence/Seekonk Zone
name	Communications Accessibles Montreal
local access	QC: Montreal, Laval, South-Shore, West-Island

Table 1-3: *PDIAL* Service Provider Examples (Continued)

name	Clark Internet Services, Inc. (ClarkNet)
local access	MD: Baltimore; DC: Washington; VA: Northern VA
name	connect.com.au pty ltd
local access	Australia: Melbourne, Sydney
name	Evergreen Communications
local access	AZ
name	CyberGate, Inc
local access	South Florida, expanding in FL
name	HookUp Communication Corporation
local access	Ontario, Canada
name	IEunet Ltd., Ireland's Internet Services Supplier
local access	Dublin, Ireland
name	The John von Neumann Computer Network—Dialin' Tiger
local access	Princeton and Newark, NJ; Philadelphia, PA; Garden City, NY; Bridgeport, New Haven, and Storrs, CT; Providence, RI
name	Texas Metronet
local access	TX: Dallas, Fort Worth
name	MV Communications, Inc.
local access	Many NH communities
name	Northwest Nexus Inc.
local access	WA: Seattle
name	RealTime Communications (wixer)
local access	TX: Austin

Table 1-3: *PDIAL* Service Provider Examples (Continued)

name	Systems Solutions
local access	DE: Wilmington
name	UUNET Canada, Inc.
local access	ON: Toronto, Ottawa, Kitchener/Waterloo, London, Hamilton, QC: Montreal, AB: Calgary, BC: Vancouver
name	Vnet Internet Access, Inc.
local access	NC: Charlotte, Research Triangle Park, Raleigh, Durham, Chapel Hill, Winston Salem/Greensboro
name	XNet Information Systems
local access	IL: Chicago, Naperville, Hoffman Estates

How to Get the Lists

If you already have E-mail or an Internet connection, you can get the latest versions of each of these lists. This will help you select a SLIP or PPP service provider. **Important:** If, however, you do not have either of these, you should use the lists in the Appendix to get started.

Heads Up!

You may be ready to select a SLIP or PPP provider from the lists in the Appendix. If that's the case, you should just jump ahead to the section Selecting Your SLIP/PPP Provider at the end of this session.

*HANDS-ON
Activity 1*

GETTING *PDIAL*

PDIAL may be retrieved in either of two ways. You can either send an E-mail request, or you can use File Transfer Protocol (FTP). We will show you how to do each.

Getting *PDIAL* Using E-mail

1.   Connect to your E-mail service and log in

2. Prepare an E-mail message to
`info-deli-server@netcom.com`

3. Leave the Subject blank

4. Go to the body of your message

5. Type the phrase
`Send PDIAL`

6. Send the E-mail message

You will receive the latest copy of *PDIAL* by return electronic mail.

Getting *PDIAL* Using FTP

1. Connect to your Internet account and log in

2. Type the command
`ftp ftp.netcom.com`

3. At the Name prompt, type the word
`anonymous`

4. At the Password prompt, type your own full E-mail address, such as
`dsachs@world.std.com`

5. At the ftp> prompt, type
`ASCII`

6. At the ftp> prompt, type
`cd /pub/info-deli/public-access/`

7. At the ftp> prompt, type
`dir pdial`

The screen should list the file *PDIAL* and information about it.

8. At the ftp> prompt, type
`get pdial`

9. At the ftp> prompt, type
`close`

10. At the ftp> prompt, type
`quit`

What you will see is illustrated below.

```
host% ftp ftp.netcom.com
Connected to netcom9.netcom.com.
220 netcom9 FTP server (Version 2.0WU(10)) ready.
Name (ftp.netcom.com:yourname): anonymous
331 Guest login ok, send your complete e-mail address as password.
Password: yourname@your_service.com
230-
230-          Welcome to NETCOM On-line Communications Services, Inc.
230-          -------------------------------------------------------
230-NETCOM provides business and personal connections to the Internet.
230-For more information about NETCOM, see the files in /pub/netcom or
230-call +1 (408) 554-8649.
230-
230-This archive is provided as a service to our customers.
230-
230- NETCOM makes no warranty of any kind, either expressed or implied,
230- regarding the quality, accuracy, or validity for the data and/or
230- information available from this archive. Use of information obtained
230- from or through NETCOM services is at the risk of the user.
230-
230-*** Please note that all transfers are logged with your host name and
230-***          e-mail address. If this bothers you, disconnect now!
230-
230 Guest login ok, access restrictions apply.
Remote system type is UNIX.
Using binary mode to transfer files.
ftp> ascii
200 Type set to A.
ftp> cd /pub/info-deli/public-access/
250 CWD command successful.
ftp> dir pdial
200 PORT command successful.
150 Opening ASCII mode data connection for /bin/ls.
-r--r--r-- 1 1758      50           68429 Dec 10 07:13 pdial
226 Transfer complete.
ftp> get pdial
200 PORT command successful.
150 Opening ASCII mode data connection for pdial (68429 bytes).
226 Transfer complete.
70180 bytes received in 3.6 seconds (19 Kbytes/s)
ftp> close
221 Goodbye.
ftp> quit
host%
```

You now have a copy of *PDIAL* on your host account. You may choose to read it there or download it to your PC.

GETTING *NIXPUB*

Getting *NIXPub* Using E-mail

1. Connect to your E-mail service and log in
2. Prepare an E-mail message to
   `mail-server@bts.com`
3. Leave the Subject blank
4. Go to the body of your message
5. Type the phrase
   `get PUB NIXPub long`
6. Send the E-mail message

You will receive the latest copy of *NIXPub* by return electronic mail.

GETTING THE PROVIDER'S LIST USING FTP

1. Connect to your Internet account and log in
2. Type the command
   `ftp is.internic.net`
3. At the Name prompt, type
   `anonymous`
4. At the Password prompt, type your full E-mail address, for example
   `dsachs@world.std.com`
5. At the ftp> prompt, type
   `ASCII`
6. At the ftp> prompt, type
   `cd /infoguide/getting-connected/us-dedicated`
7. At the ftp> prompt, type
   `dir internic*`
8. At the ftp> prompt, type
   `get internic-provider-list`
9. At the ftp> prompt, type
   `close`
10. At the ftp> prompt, type
    `quit`

What you will see is illustrated below

```
SCREEN host% ftp is.internic.net Connected to is.internic.net.
220-
220-*******************************************************
220-**                                                  **
220-**   Welcome to the Internic InfoGuide Archive      **
220-**                                                  **
220-*******************************************************
220-
220-
220-General Atomics makes no warranty or guarantee, express or
220-implied, concerning the content or accuracy of the information
220-stored and maintained by General Atomics for the InterNIC Information
220-Services and made available to INTERNET users, and General Atomics
220-expressly disclaims any implied warranties of merchantability and
220-fitness for a particular purpose.
220-
220-For REGISTRATION Services,           please ftp to rs.internic.net
220-For DIRECTORY AND DATABASE Services, please ftp to ds.internic.net
220-For INFORMATION Services,            please login as user "anonymous"
220-                                               and cd /infoguide
220-
220-
220-
220-Questions? Send e-mail to info@internic.net
220-
220-
220 is FTP server (Version wu-2.4(2) Thu Apr 14 13:25:36 PDT 1994) ready.
Name (is.internic.net:yourname): anonymous
331 Guest login ok, send your complete e-mail address as password.
Password:
230-
230-Logged Access from: your_service
230-
230-IMPORTANT NOTE:
230----------------
230-If you have problems accessing this archive:
230-Try using a dash (-) as the first character of your password
230-This will turn off the continuation messages that may
230-be confusing your ftp client.
230-
230 Guest login ok, access restrictions apply.
Remote system type is UNIX.
Using binary mode to transfer files.
```

```
ftp> ascii
200 Type set to A.
ftp> cd /infoguide/getting-connected/us-dedicated
250 CWD command successful.
ftp> dir internic* 200 PORT command successful.
150 Opening ASCII mode data connection for /bin/ls.
-rw-rw-r--   1 29221    refdesk    6406 May 13 00:24 internic-provider-list
226 Transfer complete.
ftp> get internic-provider-list
200 PORT command successful.
150 Opening ASCII mode data connection for internic-provider-list
226 Transfer complete.
6591 bytes received in 0.63 seconds (10 Kbytes/s)
ftp> close
221 Goodbye.
ftp> quit
host%
```

You now have a copy of the list of Internet services providers on your host account. You may choose to read it there or download it to your PC.

SELECTING YOUR SLIP/PPP PROVIDER_____

Now you should have enough information to enable you to select a provider. In fact, you may have too much information. Here, we will try to help you pick one. This is not a lifetime selection, by the way. If, after some months, you wish to change providers, you can. Here are some thoughts about how to make your first selection.

Suggestions for Selecting Providers

For SLIP and PPP services, most providers offer about the same service. There are not large differences in the service itself. Almost all providers offer the highest speed modems available. The largest difference may be in the total cost to you.

For most of us, cost is a key issue when selecting a service, Internet or any other. There are three cost elements to consider when using Internet service providers by dial-up telephone services:

1. Monthly service charges to have the service

2. Per hour service charges

3. Telephone call costs to reach the provider

Some providers charge an initial sign-up fee, but this is usually small compared to a year's worth of service and telephone costs.

Depending on where you live, the actual telephone costs may be the largest cost element. If you live near the provider's access telephone number, the per-minute cost of the call may be zero. That is, it's a local call. Many of us, however, must make toll or long distance calls.

Some service providers offer 800 number service, but that adds to their cost and they pass that along to you, the customer. You may want to calculate how many minutes a month you plan to use the Internet and then see if an 800 number is cheaper for you than a long distance call might be.

Other service providers offer lower rates on weekends and at night. If most of your use will be at times other than during the business day, this could save you money.

Some long distance telephone companies offer discounts to frequently called numbers. You might investigate making the service provider one of your frequently called numbers. (A modem is my best friend?)

Contacting the Service Provider

Service providers usually have voice telephone numbers for new account sales. Some, however, prefer E-mail. If you do not yet have any E-mail or Internet accounts, you will have to contact them by telephone. Almost all will take Mastercard or Visa charge cards to set up and bill your account.

Make sure you that you ask for the right services when you contact the provider. You should be sure to ask for a SLIP or PPP account. Ask them which they support on their service. Also, remember to ask them if they use SLIP or CSLIP. The account person you speak to may not know, but we can work that out later.

Heads Up!

You may decide to use one of the Internet service providers for which there is a preconfiguration file on your Chameleon Sampler disk. If so, you will find that there is a help file for each one of the Internet service providers on the Chameleon Sampler disk which will tell you what type of service (SLIP or PPP or CSLIP) they provide. For example, should you decide to use Panix as your Internet service provider, you would retrieve the file PANIX.TXT into your favorite word processor. You would find that Panix provides CSLIP access.

TIP

Be sure to tell the provider that you want a SLIP or PPP account. They may also include a traditional UNIX shell account; that's OK. You MUST have a SLIP or CSLIP or PPP account for Chameleon Sampler and NCSA Mosaic to work.

Generally, the provider will mail you one or more letters containing your account information a week or two after you sign up for the service. While you are waiting for the letters, we will help you install your Chameleon Sampler.

SESSION SUMMARY

This introductory session has been intended to provide you with the information required for you to have obtained an Internet service provider who can provide you with a SLIP or CSLIP or PPP connection to the Internet. You should have been able to obtain this information by using either E-mail or ftp, or by referring to the Appendix. Having a SLIP or CSLIP or PPP connection is the first step towards being able to use NCSA Mosaic.

SESSION 2

Activity 1:	Installing Chameleon Sampler
Activity 2:	Configuring Chameleon Sampler Using a Preconfigured File
Activity 3:	Completing the Configuration Using a Preconfigured File
Activity 4:	Configuring Chameleon Sampler by Defining Your Own Interface
Activity 5:	Completing the Configuration by Defining Your Own Interface
Activity 6:	Editing Your SLIP.INI File

The Chameleon
Sampler Diskette

SESSION OVERVIEW

This session focuses on installing the Chameleon Sampler. If you already have a TCP/IP stack installed, there is no need to complete any of the activities in this session. You may wish to rejoin us in Session Three when we begin to use Chameleon Sampler to connect to the Internet.

Heads Up!

In this session, we will install the Chameleon TCP/IP programs onto your PC. Before we start, we need to review your PC configuration and make sure that you have everything needed to make the programs work correctly. Here is the *must have* list:

1. You *must have* an IBM personal computer or compatible PC running Microsoft's Windows 3.1 in enhanced mode. That is, you will need what is known as an 80386 (or higher) processor and 640 kilobytes of conventional memory, plus at least 4 megabytes of extended memory.

2. In addition, you *must have* a $3\frac{1}{2}$" floppy disk drive and a minimum of 2 megabytes of free hard disk space for files from the Chameleon Sampler diskette.

3. You *must have* a modem and a telephone line connected to your computer.

In addition to these *must haves*, we strongly recommend that you consider the following. While these are not absolutely necessary, they will make your use of Chameleon and NCSA Mosaic a much happier experience.

4. We *recommend* that you have at least 6 megabytes of free disk space on your PC for the information you will be receiving from your travels with us about the Internet.

5. We also strongly *recommend* that your modem be high speed. A high-speed modem runs at 14,400 bits per second or higher. The faster your modem, the quicker the information will be transferred to your computer.

If you have the PC and Windows 3.1 ready to go, let's begin to install the Chameleon Sampler. First, we will take inventory.

What the Chameleon Sampler Disk Contains

Here's a list of the files on the Chameleon Sampler diskette. You may wish to check them yourself.

```
Volume in drive A is CHAMSAMPLE
Volume Serial Number is 1358-14D3
Directory of A:\

SETUP    EXE      81,792 07-13-94    6:14p
SETUP    INF       6,564 07-13-94    4:44p
ALTERNET CFG       1,027 07-10-94    9:32a
ANSREMOT CFG       1,063 07-10-94    9:24a
CERFNET  CFG       1,055 07-10-94    9:24a
CICNET   CFG       1,031 07-10-94    9:25a
CLARKNET CFG       1,037 07-10-94    9:24a
CRL      CFG       1,021 07-10-94    9:26a
CTS      CFG       1,022 07-10-94    9:26a
CYBRGATE CFG       1,034 07-10-94    9:26a
DIGEX    CFG       1,023 07-10-94    9:26a
HOOKUP   CFG       1,041 07-10-94    9:26a
IGLOU    CFG       1,034 07-10-94    9:27a
INTERACC CFG       1,055 07-10-94    9:57a
JVNCNET  CFG       1,043 07-10-94    9:28a
MRNET    CFG       1,042 07-10-94    9:28a
NWNEXUS  CFG       1,042 07-10-94    9:28a
OLYMPUS  CFG       1,030 07-10-94    9:49a
ONRAMP   CFG       1,043 07-10-94   10:18a
PANIX    CFG       1,029 07-10-94    9:29a
PICNET   CFG       1,055 07-10-94    9:30a
```

```
PINGNET   CFG       1,048 07-10-94    9:30a
PORTAL    CFG       1,661 07-10-94    9:30a
PSINET    CFG       1,037 07-10-94    9:31a
TIAC      CFG       1,025 07-10-94    9:31a
WLN       CFG       1,024 07-10-94    9:31a
TCPIP     CFG       1,069 07-10-94    9:10a
ALTERNET  TXT       1,155 07-12-94   10:24a
ANSREMOT  TXT       1,493 07-12-94   10:24a
CERFNET   TXT       1,807 07-12-94   10:24a
CICNET    TXT       1,440 07-12-94   10:24a
CLARKNET  TXT       2,086 07-12-94   10:24a
CRL       TXT       1,257 07-12-94   10:24a
CTS       TXT       1,383 07-12-94   10:24a
CYBRGATE  TXT       1,261 07-12-94   10:24a
DIGEX     TXT       1,308 07-12-94   10:24a
HOOKUP    TXT       1,946 07-12-94   10:24a
IGLOU     TXT       1,228 07-12-94   10:25a
INTERACC  TXT       1,309 07-12-94   10:25a
JVNCNET   TXT       1,309 07-12-94   10:25a
MRNET     TXT       1,030 07-12-94   10:25a
NWNEXUS   TXT       1,508 07-12-94   10:25a
OLYMPUS   TXT       1,234 07-12-94   10:25a
ONRAMP    TXT         923 07-12-94   10:25a
PANIX     TXT       1,457 07-12-94   10:26a
PICNET    TXT       1,680 07-12-94   10:26a
PINGNET   TXT       1,375 07-12-94   10:26a
PORTAL    TXT       2,863 07-12-94   10:27a
PSINET    TXT       1,425 07-12-94   10:27a
TIAC      TXT       1,464 07-12-94   10:27a
WLN       TXT       1,894 07-12-94   10:28a
PROVIDER  TXT       6,484 07-12-94    3:34p
CUSTOM    EX_      96,458 07-14-94   11:41a
CUSTOM    HL_      22,252 07-07-93    5:00p
FTP       EX_      75,456 09-15-93    2:45p
FTP       HL_      15,514 07-07-93    5:00p
FTPSRVR   DL_       9,536 07-07-93    5:00p
MAIL      EX_     126,225 10-04-93   11:50a
MAIL      HL_      24,022 07-07-93    5:00p
POP       DL_       9,281 07-07-93    5:00p
RFC822    DL_      20,597 07-07-93    5:00p
PING      EX_      13,705 07-07-93    5:00p
PING      HL_       8,977 07-07-93    5:00p
TELNET    EX_      62,196 07-07-93    5:00p
TELNET    HL_      14,432 07-07-93    5:00p
README    WRI      24,832 07-13-94    5:00p
FTP       DL_      12,758 07-07-93    5:00p
```

```
WSFTP      DL_          12,950  07-07-93    5:00p
SMTP       DL_           6,938  07-07-93    5:00p
NMLIB      DL_          20,640  09-14-93   12:30p
NMPCIP     DL_         100,547  11-18-93    1:37p
WINSOCK    DL_           9,466  08-03-93    8:39p
NEWT       EX_          16,095  09-15-93    6:24p
NEWT       HL_           7,231  07-07-93    5:00p
PROTOCOL                  441  07-07-93    5:00p
SERVICES                1,660  07-07-93    5:00p
SLIP       INI            544  04-14-94    6:30p
         77 file(s)        871,766 bytes
                           563,200 bytes free
```

We will need to understand only a few of these many files.

1. Clearly, the first, and at the moment most important file, is the one called SETUP.EXE. That's the one we are about to use.

2. Then, there is SLIP.INI. If the configuration file for your Internet service provider is not included in the list above, then we will be working quite a bit with the SLIP.INI file.

3. Finally, there are files that end in .CFG. These are files which are already prepared for specific Internet service providers. Let's make a separate list of these.

```
ALTERNET  CFG        1,027  07-10-94    9:32a
ANSREMOT  CFG        1,063  07-10-94    9:24a
CERFNET   CFG        1,055  07-10-94    9:24a
CICNET    CFG        1,031  07-10-94    9:25a
CLARKNET  CFG        1,037  07-10-94    9:24a
CRL       CFG        1,021  07-10-94    9:26a
CTS       CFG        1,022  07-10-94    9:26a
CYBRGATE  CFG        1,034  07-10-94    9:26a
DIGEX     CFG        1,023  07-10-94    9:26a
HOOKUP    CFG        1,041  07-10-94    9:26a
IGLOU     CFG        1,034  07-10-94    9:27a
INTERACC  CFG        1,055  07-10-94    9:57a
JVNCNET   CFG        1,043  07-10-94    9:28a
MRNET     CFG        1,042  07-10-94    9:28a
NWNEXUS   CFG        1,042  07-10-94    9:28a
OLYMPUS   CFG        1,030  07-10-94    9:49a
ONRAMP    CFG        1,043  07-10-94   10:18a
PANIX     CFG        1,029  07-10-94    9:29a
```

```
PICNET     CFG          1,055 07-10-94    9:30a
PINGNET    CFG          1,048 07-10-94    9:30a
PORTAL     CFG          1,661 07-10-94    9:30a
PSINET     CFG          1,037 07-10-94    9:31a
TIAC       CFG          1,025 07-10-94    9:31a
WLN        CFG          1,024 07-10-94    9:31a
```

If your service provider is on the list above, you should use the file that has already been created for it. If, as we suspect, many of you will have other providers, we will help you to build a new .CFG file for your provider. Don't worry; it's almost automatic.

Let's begin the installation. The installation takes only a few minutes. If you want to take a break after that, then you can do the configuration at another time.

INSTALLING CHAMELEON SAMPLER

HANDS-ON Activity 1

We are going to install Chameleon Sampler on your PC. Please follow the instructions below. Please do not simply copy the diskette to a directory on your hard disk. The setup program changes the files as they are installed.

1. Turn on your PC and start Microsoft Windows

2. Press the following keys in order (you don't need to hold them down):

    ALT (This selects the menu bar.)
    F   (This selects the File Menu.)
    R   (This brings up the Run box shown in Figure 2-1.)

Figure 2-1
The Run Box

3. Place the Chameleon Sampler in your diskette drive. (We will assume that it is Drive A; if you are using Drive B, then substitute that in the directions below.)

4. In the Run box, type the following: `a:\setup` as shown in Figure 2-2.

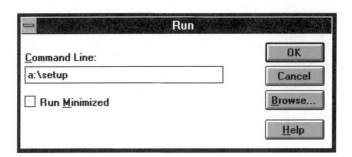

Figure 2-2
The Setup Command

5. Press **ENTER**

What you will see is a series of pop-up boxes. The first one is shown in Figure 2-3.

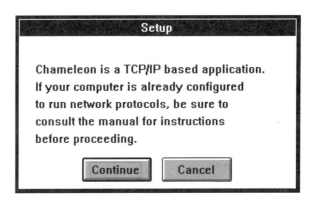

Figure 2-3
Setup Question Box

Most of you will not have your PCs on a Local Area Network or LAN and can safely press ENTER or click on the Continue bar.

Heads Up!

If you are on a LAN, or already have TCP/IP software running, you may wish to cancel this activity right now. Then you will need to contact your network administrator if you are on a LAN. If you are already running TCP/IP on the LAN, your administrator can help you.

6. Next, you will see the Directory Selection box. It looks like Figure 2-4.

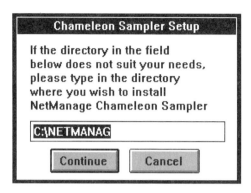

Figure 2-4
Install Directory

7. Unless there is a good reason to change this suggestion, press **ENTER** to accept the directory which is offered, C:\NETMANAG

Note: A good reason might be that you wish to put Chameleon Sampler on another disk drive, such as D:\. If this is true, then feel free to type in whatever drive and directory you would like.

Setup will now transfer the files to your PC. You will see the box in Figure 2-5 marking the progress of the installation.

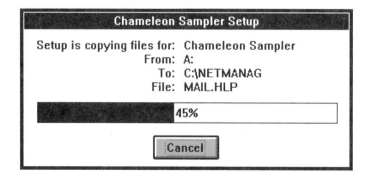

Figure 2-5
Installation Progress

When the installation is complete, two things will happen:

a. First, you will see the Installation Complete pop-up box, as shown in Figure 2-6.

Figure 2-6
Installation OK

When you press **ENTER**, or click on the **OK** button, everything will shrink to icons. This includes your Windows Program Manager. You will be left with your Windows background pattern. Not to worry; this is a normal part of the installation.

b. Next, move your mouse to the Program Manager Icon and double-click on it. You will be back to your normal Windows screen with an addition. The addition is the Chameleon Sampler Group on your screen. It looks like Figure 2-7.

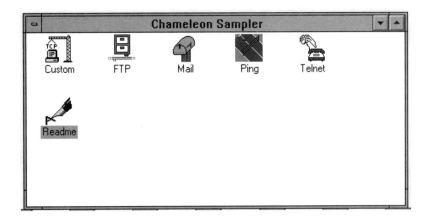

Figure 2-7
Chameleon Group

Heads Up!

This completes the first part of your installation of Chameleon Sampler. You may wish to take a break before our next activity. In Activity 2, we will configure or customize Chameleon Sampler for your PC setup. Then, we will configure Chameleon Sampler to match the specifications of your Internet service provider.

We are now going to help you configure your Chameleon Sampler. This will be done in three phases.

1. In the first phase, we will set up everything that we know about your PC.

2. In the second phase, we will enter the information you will have received from your Internet service provider.

3. Finally, if necessary, we will help you edit the SLIP.INI file.

Turn on your PC and start Windows. You should now see the Chameleon Sampler Group, either as an icon or as the expanded group from Figure 2-6. If it is an icon, double-click on it to show the whole group.

Now, double-click on the **Custom Icon.** This will start the customization process. It should look like Figure 2-8.

—	Custom - C:\NETMANAG\TCPIP.CFG	▼ ▲
File Interface Setup Services Connect Help		

Interface:	PPP0 - COM2, 19200 baud
Dial:	Listen for connections
IP Address:	1.1.1.1
Subnet Mask:	255.0.0.0
Host Name:	<Put the name of this PC here>
Domain Name:	<Put Domain here: example.com>

Name	Type	IP	Domain
*PPP0	PPP	1.1.1.1	<Put Domain here: example.co

Figure 2-8
The Custom Screen

Heads Up!

You have an important decision to make. Are you going to be using one of the 25 providers for which there are preconfigured access files (listed in the file PROVIDER.TXT on your disk), or are you going to be defining your own interface? If you are going to use a preconfigured access file, then follow the directions in Activity 2 and Activity 3. If you are going to have to define your own interface, then follow the directions in Activity 4 and Activity 5. We will all meet again in Activity 6.

HANDS-ON
Activity 2

CONFIGURING CHAMELEON SAMPLER USING A PRECONFIGURED FILE

Finding the Configuration File

Notice the menu bar across the top of the Custom box. We will be working with the File drop-down menu. Let's begin.

1. Click on the word **File**

2. Next, click on the word **Open...**

   You should see an Open Configuration File box resembling the one in Figure 2-9.

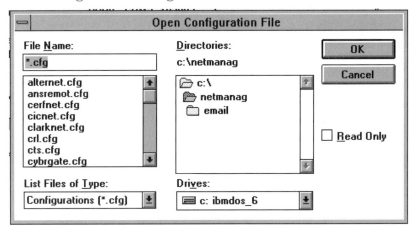

Figure 2-9
Open Configuration
File

3. Click on the file for your service provider, or else click on the down arrow in the File Name: scroll bar until your service provider's name appears.

4. When you find your service provider's name, click on it once so that it appears in the File Name: box. For illustration purposes, we have chosen to use panix.cfg, since we are going to use Panix as our service provider. Your screen should resemble the one in Figure 2-10.

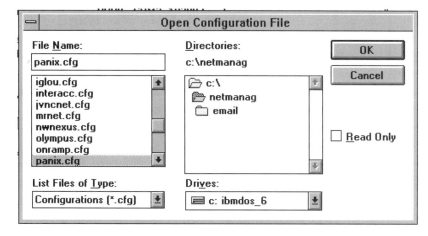

Figure 2-10
Open Configuration
File/Panix

5.   Click on **OK** and the Custom box should reappear with
     some of your service provider's information already
     entered. It should resemble the screen in Figure 2-11.

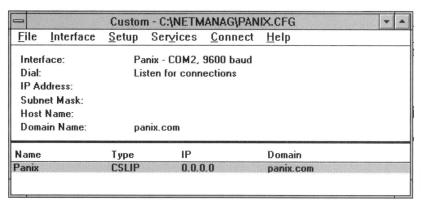

Figure 2-11
Custom Box

Modem Settings

Next, we will set up your modem. You will need to know the
make of your modem and whether it supports the Hayes modem
command set. This command set is also called the AT command
set. Check your modem's manual (unless, of course, you have a
Hayes).

1.   Click on **Setup** and then click on **Modem**. Your screen
     should resemble Figure 2-12.

Modem Settings

Commands	Prefix	Suffix	Modem Defaults

Commands

	Prefix	Suffix
Dial	ATDT	
Hangup:	+++	ATH
Binary **T**X:		
Binary **R**X:		
Answer:	ATS0=1	
Originate:	ATS0=0	
Initialize:	ATQ0V1E0M1L0	
E**x**it:		

Modem Defaults

○ None
◉ Hayes
○ Telebit
○ MultiTech

OK
Cancel

Figure 2-12
Modem Setup

2. Using the mouse, select your Modem Defaults from the upper-right box.

   Important: If your modem is not listed here, you are usually safe to specify Hayes as the default. Almost all PC modems support the Hayes modem command set.

   In fact, we would strongly urge you to try Hayes and the modem settings that appear before you try to change anything. If these default settings do not work, then consult your modem's manual for further information.

3. Now, click on **OK** and return to the Setup screen.

Port Settings

Next, we need to know how your modem connects to your computer. Specifically, you will need to know which communications port your modem uses. You will also need to know how fast your modem runs.

1. Click on **Setup** and click again on **Port...** Your screen will resemble Figure 2-13.

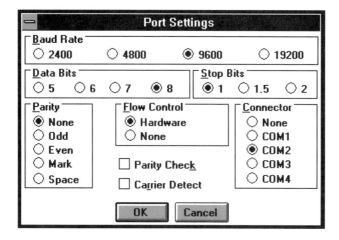

Figure 2-13
Port Setup

2. Using the mouse, select the Connector as **COM1**, **COM2**, **COM3**, or **COM4**.

3. Next, select the speed of your modem. Although your modem may run at a baud rate of 9,600 or 14,400, it may have compression features allowing it to run at 19,200. Select 19,200 if you have a 9,600 or a 14,400 modem. If necessary, you can come back to Setup later and change it.

    The default settings provided (Data Bits—8, Stop Bits— 1, Parity—None, Flow Control—Hardware) should agree with those being used by your service provider, since almost all providers now use the settings as shown in Figure 2-13. Leave them as they are if you are not sure.

4. Click on **OK** to return to the main Setup screen.

38

Choosing a Host Name

Heads Up!

Your computer is about to become a host on the Internet. As such, its name must be unique for the domain it is in. This means that for your particular service provider, there can be no other host with the name that will be used by your computer. Since the domain name of your service provider is unique as well, this means that your computer will have a unique name on the Internet.

Consequently, when you pick a name for your computer, you will need to confirm with your service provider that the name that you have selected is actually unique for their domain. Many providers will ask you what you want your PC's name to be, and they will then send you the complete domain name for your PC.

To give your PC an Internet name,

1. Click on **Setup** and then on **Host Name**

Figure 2-14
Host Name

2. Type in the name you have chosen that has been approved by your service provider. Your screen should resemble Figure 2-14. Should it be necessary to do so, it can be changed later. Again, it is important to realize that your host name must be unique for the domain that you are in and therefore must be cleared with your service provider. After you start using it as an E-mail address, you will want to keep a consistent name if you want to receive your E-mail.
3. Click on **OK** and return to the Setup screen
4. Now click on **File** and then on **Save**

All of your new information will be entered into the configuration file (such as PANIX.CFG) that you selected.

Heads Up!

At this point, you have done as much as possible to configure Chameleon Sampler before knowing your Internet service provider's information. If you are still waiting for this information, you will have to stop here. When the information comes in, you can start again right at this point. (This might also be a good chance to take a break!)

Configuring with the Internet Service Provider's Information

Assuming that you now have the information from your Internet service provider, we can complete the configuration process. Then, you will be ready to connect to the Internet as a full host!

Understanding What Your Internet Service Provider Tells You

There are really just five pieces of information that you need from the service provider for a dial-up only connection. They include:

1. A telephone number to dial

2. An Internet protocol (IP) address for your PC

3. The domain name for your PC given to you by your provider

4. The IP address(es) of a nameserver

5. Your login name and password

Telephone Number. The telephone number is pretty obvious, but you should be aware that some providers add extra digits to be dialed. We'll show you what to do when that happens. Most providers, however, just give you an ordinary phone number to dial.

Internet Protocol (IP) Address. We talked earlier about IP addresses. Most providers give you one of your own, but several give them out each time you connect. CERFnet, MRnet, and PSINet do this to conserve IP addresses. We'll show you how this works.

Domain Name. The domain name of the provider will let you send and receive E-mail by name.

Nameserver. We discussed nameservers earlier. Your PC has to know how to reach them for almost everything you would wish to do.

Login Name and Password. You will need to have this information so that you can correctly sign on to your Internet service
provider.

Now, let's complete your Chameleon Sampler configuration.

**HANDS-ON
Activity 3**

COMPLETING THE CONFIGURATION USING A PRECONFIGURED FILE

Adding Your IP (Internet) Address

1. Start Chameleon Sampler from Windows. Open the Custom Icon. Then, click on **Setup**

2. If you have been given an IP address by your service provider (some providers do not give them out), click on
   IP Address. Your screen will resemble Figure 2-15.

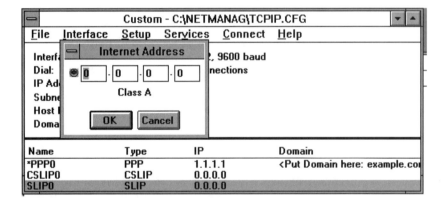

Figure 2-15
Internet Address

3. Now, enter your IP address carefully.

Heads Up!

You will be entering four sets of numbers, each of which will have
one, two, or three digits in it (for example, 192.1.1.1). It is important
to note that each set must be entered correctly. So, if one of your
sets has only one or two digits, be sure to enter the number(s) and
then a period, so that your cursor moves to the next box. For example, if you were to type the IP number we have used above, we
would type

192 . 1 . 1 . 1

Then, click on **OK**

We have entered this sample address in Figure 2-16 for illustration purposes only.

DO NOT USE THIS SAMPLE ADDRESS!

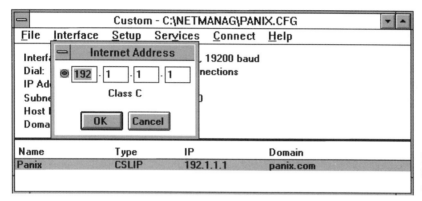

Figure 2-16
Sample Internet Address

Once you have entered your IP address, click on **OK** to return to the Setup screen.

Adding Your Domain Name

1. Click on **Setup** and again on **Domain Name:**

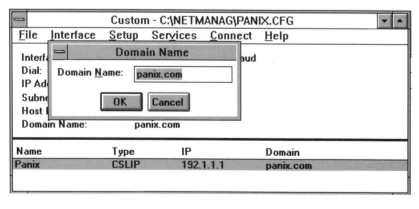

Figure 2-17
Domain Name

2. The domain name for the provider should already be in place, as it is in Figure 2-17.

3. Click on **OK**

Adding Your Telephone Number

Next, we will enter the telephone number your computer will
dial to connect to the service provider. Usually, this is just an
ordinary telephone number. Remember to add a 1 to the front of
it, if you would do that in regular dialing. A way to test the number is to just dial it from a regular telephone. If you have the
correct number, you will hear a modem or other tone.

1.   Click on **Setup** and then on **Dial:**. Your screen will
     resemble Figure 2-18.

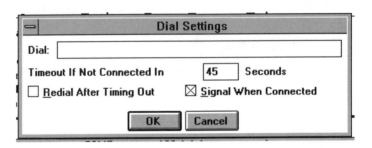

Figure 2-18
Dial Settings

2.   Enter the telephone number

3.   Consider making the Timeout longer than 30 seconds.
     Some providers' systems take a little longer to connect.
     A safer value is 60 seconds.

4.   Click on **OK** to return to the Setup screen.

If your provider uses extra digits in the number, you will enter them
here. ANSRemote does this by adding a seven-digit number after
the telephone number. For ANSRemote, you would enter the number as

1-800-555-1234,,,,,1234567

The commas are used to indicate a delay of about 2 seconds (for
each comma). For ANSRemote, the delay is needed so that your
computer waits for a connecting tone. After the tone is received,
the extra seven digits are sent (as telephone keypad tones) and
the call is then switched to a modem. If your provider uses this kind
of system, you may want to add or subtract some commas to allow
the right delay.

Entering Login Settings

Next, we will enter your login name, password, and startup command.

1. Click on **Setup** and then on **Login**. Your screen should resemble Figure 2-19.

Figure 2-19
Login Settings

2. Type in the user name that has been given to you by your Internet service provider.

    Note: User name and Login name are the same.

3. Type in the user password that has been given to you by your Internet service provider.

    Note: As you type in your password, only asterisks will show, so type the password very carefully.

4. The Startup Command (either SLIP or PPP) should have been already entered for you.

    Click on **OK**

5. Click on **File** and **Save** so that this information is saved properly with your configuration file.

Congratulations! If you have followed the directions above carefully, you should now be ready to connect to the Internet. We will begin to do this in Session Three.

Heads Up!

The following section is for those who need to create their own configuration files. If you have completed Activity Two and Activity Three, there is no need for you to work through Activities Four and Five. Feel free to meet us at the beginning of Session Three.

**HANDS-ON
Activity 4**

CONFIGURING CHAMELEON SAMPLER BY DEFINING YOUR OWN INTERFACE

Notice the menu bar across the top of Custom box. We will be working with the Interface, Setup, and Services drop-down menus. Let's start with the Interface menu.

Adding Additional Interfaces

1. Click on the word **Interface** on the menu bar and look at the drop-down menu, as shown in Figure 2-20.

```
┌──────────────────────────────────────────────────────────────────┐
│ ─              Custom - C:\NETMANAG\TCPIP.CFG            ▼  ▲       │
├──────────────────────────────────────────────────────────────────┤
│  File   Interface   Setup   Services   Help                        │
│       ┌──────────────┐                                             │
│  Inter│  Add...      │                                             │
│  Phys│  Duplicate... │                                             │
│  IP A│  Delete       │                                             │
│       └──────────────┘                                             │
│  Subnet Mask:                                                      │
│  Host Name:                                                        │
│  Domain Name:                                                      │
│                                                                    │
│  Name              Type        IP          Domain                 │
│  ................................................................  │
│                                                                    │
└──────────────────────────────────────────────────────────────────┘
```

Figure 2-20
The Add Interface Box

You will notice that a PPP interface is already set up. Although you will probably use only one or two interfaces, we will add two more interfaces. This will assure us that you can add whatever interfaces you may need for any service provider.

2. Click on the word **Add** on the menu bar. Now, you will see a box showing an interface with the name: SLIP0 This is a temporary name which can be changed to something else later. For now, we are going to add this interface to Chameleon Sampler.

3. Click on **OK** and you will be returned to the main Custom screen.

Notice that the Custom screen now lists two interfaces at the bottom. You will see the PPP Interface, plus the interface that you just added, as shown in Figure 2-21.

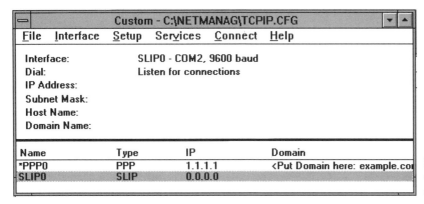

Figure 2-21
Custom with an
Added Interface

4. Click on **Interface** again, and then on the word **Add** to enable you to return to the Add Interface box.

5. Use the mouse to click the down arrow at the right end of the Type bar.

When you do this, you will see three interface types SLIP, PPP, and CSLIP, as shown in Figure 2-22.

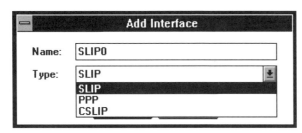

Figure 2-22
Add Interface Type

6. Click on the **CSLIP** line.

7. Click on **OK** to add this interface.

Your Custom screen should include the two interfaces that you have added at the bottom (as well as the original PPP interface), as shown in Figure 2-23.

```
┌─────────────────────────────────────────────────────────────────┐
│ ⊟        Custom - C:\NETMANAG\TCPIP.CFG              ▼ ▲          │
├─────────────────────────────────────────────────────────────────┤
│ File   Interface   Setup   Services   Connect   Help             │
├─────────────────────────────────────────────────────────────────┤
│ Interface:           CSLIP0 - COM2, 9600 baud                    │
│ Dial:                Listen for connections                      │
│ IP Address:                                                      │
│ Subnet Mask:                                                     │
│ Host Name:                                                       │
│ Domain Name:                                                     │
├─────────────────────────────────────────────────────────────────┤
│ Name          Type          IP            Domain                 │
│ *PPP0         PPP           1.1.1.1       <Put Domain here: example.co│
│ CSLIP0        CSLIP         0.0.0.0                               │
│ SLIP0         SLIP          0.0.0.0                               │
└─────────────────────────────────────────────────────────────────┘
```

Figure 2-23
Custom with Three
Interfaces

You now have three different interfaces in Chameleon Sampler. After you receive your account information from your Internet service provider, you will select one of them.

Some providers use CSLIP (compressed SLIP) but call it SLIP. That's one reason we had you set up all three. We may need to change the type in the next session if things don't seem to work right.

Setting Up an Interface

Whether or not you have already received your Internet service provider information, we will next set up your SLIP interface. You will most likely use this interface to get started in the next session.

Since you are about to set up your SLIP interface, it is necessary that the SLIP interface be highlighted. Move your cursor to the line where the Name is SLIP0 and the Type is SLIP and click on it once to make it active.

1. Click on the word **Setup** on the Custom Menu Bar. You will see the drop-down menu for Setup, as shown in Figure 2-24.

```
┌─────────────────────────────────────────────────────────┐
│ ─        Custom - C:\NETMANAG\TCPIP.CFG        ▼ ▲       │
│ File   Interface  Setup  Services  Connect  Help         │
│ ┌──────────────┬─────────────────────┬──────────────────┤
│ Interface:      IP Address...        00 baud            │
│ Dial:           Subnet Mask...       ions               │
│ IP Address:     Host Name...                            │
│ Subnet Mask:    Domain Name...                          │
│ Host Name:      ─────────────                           │
│ Domain Name:    Port...                                 │
│                 Modem...                                 │
│ Name            Dial...                 Domain          │
│ *PPP0           Login...                <Put Domain here: example.co│
│ CSLIP0          ─────────────                           │
│ SLIP0           Interface Name...                       │
│                 Primary Interface                       │
│                 Route Entries...                        │
│                 ─────────────                           │
│                 Log...                                  │
└─────────────────────────────────────────────────────────┘
```

Figure 2-24
Setup Menu

We'll begin with the Interface name as shown in Figure 2-25.

```
┌─────────────────────────────────────────────────────────┐
│ ─        Custom - C:\NETMANAG\TCPIP.CFG        ▼ ▲       │
│ File   Interface  Setup  Services  Connect  Help         │
│ Interf┌─────────────────────────────────────┐           │
│ Dial: │ ─          Interface Name           │           │
│ IP Ad │                                     │           │
│ Subne │  Name:   SLIP0                      │           │
│ Host  │                                     │           │
│ Domain│      ┌──────┐   ┌────────┐          │           │
│       │      │  OK  │   │ Cancel │          │           │
│       └──────┴──────┴───┴────────┴──────────┘           │
│                                                          │
│ Name          Type      IP         Domain               │
│ *PPP0         PPP       1.1.1.1    <Put Domain here: example.co│
│ CSLIP0        CSLIP     0.0.0.0                          │
│ SLIP0         SLIP      0.0.0.0                          │
└─────────────────────────────────────────────────────────┘
```

Figure 2-25
Interface Name

You will need to select the Interface name that will work with
your Internet service provider. Choosing PPP0, CSLIP0, or
SLIP0, will enable you to select the correct .CFG file and to use
the interface that has already been defined there. The choice
you make here will be used by a file called SLIP.INI to start your
connection with the Internet service provider, so it has to be the
same here as in the SLIP.INI file.

In other words, if you are being provided with a PPP connection, then select **PPP0**. If you are being provided with a SLIP connection, then select **SLIP0**. And, if you are being provided with a CSLIP connection, then select **CSLIP0**.

Setting Up Your Modem

Next, we will set up your modem. You will need to know the make of your modem and whether it supports the Hayes modem command set, also called the AT command set. Check your modem's manual (unless, of course, you have a Hayes).

1. Click on **Setup** again, and then click on **Modem**

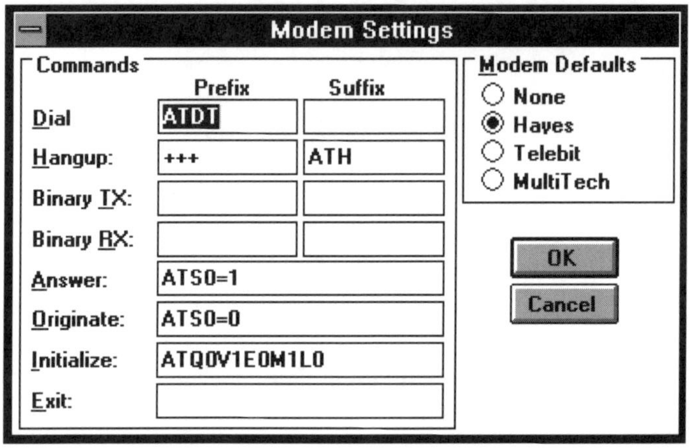

Figure 2-26
Modem Setup

2. Using the mouse, select your Modem Defaults from the upper-right box. Your screen will look like Figure 2-26.

    If your modem is not listed here, you are usually safe to specify Hayes as the default. Almost all PC modems support the Hayes modem command set.

    Important: For the most part, you should not change the modem information unless you are absolutely certain that it is necessary. We strongly recommend that you try using the default settings before changing anything.

3. Now, click on **OK** and return to the Setup screen.

Selecting Port Settings

Next, we need to know how your modem connects to your computer. Specifically, you will need to know which communications port your modem uses. You will also need to know how fast your modem runs.

1. Click on **Setup** and click again on **Port**

Port Settings			
Baud Rate			
○ 2400	○ 4800	⦿ 9600	○ 19200

Data Bits
○ 5 ○ 6 ○ 7 ⦿ 8

Stop Bits
⦿ 1 ○ 1.5 ○ 2

Parity
⦿ None
○ Odd
○ Even
○ Mark
○ Space

Flow Control
⦿ Hardware
○ None

☐ Parity Check
☐ Carrier Detect

Connector
○ None
○ COM1
⦿ COM2
○ COM3
○ COM4

[OK] [Cancel]

Figure 2-27
Port Setup

2. Using the mouse, select the connector as **COM1**, **COM2**, **COM3**, or **COM4**, as shown in Figure 2-27.

   Now, select the speed of your modem.

   The other settings should agree with those being used by your service provider. However, almost all providers now use the settings as shown in Figure 2-27. Leave them as they are if you are not sure.

3. Click on **OK** to return to the main Setup screen.

Giving Your PC a Name

In the last part of this activity, we will give your PC an Internet name.

Important: The name of your computer must be unique for the particular domain you are in. Therefore, it must be cleared with your service provider. For the most part, unless someone else has chosen the same name, it can be almost any name you wish, as it will be followed by the domain name your provider has told you to use when they sent you the information about your dial-up connection. Many providers will ask you what you want your PC name to be and will then send you the complete domain name for your PC. You should carefully type in here the exact name of your PC that your provider sent you.

1. Click on **Setup** and then on **Host Name**. Your screen will look like Figure 2-28.

```
┌─────────────────────────────────────────────────────────────┐
│ ─        Custom - C:\NETMANAG\PANIX.CFG          │▼│▲│        │
├─────────────────────────────────────────────────────────────┤
│ File   Interface   Setup   Services   Connect   Help          │
├─────────────────────────────────────────────────────────────┤
│ Interface:            Panix - COM2, 19200 baud                │
│ Dial:                 Listen for connections                  │
│ IP Address:                                                   │
│ Subnet Mask:                                                  │
│ Host Name:            daisy                                   │
│ Domain Name:          panix.com                               │
├─────────────────────────────────────────────────────────────┤
│ Name           Type        IP            Domain               │
│ Panix          CSLIP       0.0.0.0       panix.com            │
└─────────────────────────────────────────────────────────────┘
```

Figure 2-28
Host Name

2.   Type in the name that has been approved by your service provider. It may be changed later, should that be necessary. After you start using it as an E-mail address, you will want to keep a consistent name if you want to receive your E-mail.

3.   Click on **OK** and return to the Setup screen.

4.   Click on **File** and then on **Save**

     Your setup information for the SLIP interface will be saved in the file TCPIP.CFG.

Heads Up!

At this point, you have done as much as possible to configure Chameleon Sampler before knowing your Internet service provider's information. If you are still waiting for this information, you will have to stop here. When the information comes, you can start again right at this point. (Actually, this might be a good time for a break!)

Configuring with the Internet Service Provider's Information

Assuming that you now have the information from your Internet service provider, we can complete the configuration process. Then, if need be, we will edit the SLIP.INI file and you will be ready to connect to the Internet as a full host!

Understanding What Your Internet Service Provider Tells You

There are really just five pieces of information that you need from the service provider for a dial-up connection. They include:

1.   A telephone number to dial

2.   An Internet Protocol (IP) address for your PC

3. The domain name for your PC given to you by your provider

4. The IP address(es) of a nameserver

5. Your login name and password

Telephone Number. The telephone number is pretty obvious, but you should be aware that some providers add extra digits to be dialed. We'll show you what to do when that happens. Most providers, however, just give you an ordinary phone number to dial.

Internet Protocol (IP) Address. We talked earlier about the IP addresses. Most providers give you one of your own, but several give them out each time you connect. CERFnet, MRnet, and PSINet do this to conserve IP addresses. We'll show you how this works.

Domain Name. The domain name of the provider will let you send and receive E-mail by name.

Nameserver. We discussed nameservers earlier. Your PC has to know how to reach them for almost everything you would wish to do.

Login Name and Password. You will need to have your personal login name and password, so that you can sign on correctly.

Now, let's complete your Chameleon Sampler configuration.

COMPLETING THE CONFIGURATION BY DEFINING YOUR OWN INTERFACE

HANDS-ON Activity 5

Entering Your IP Address

1. Start Chameleon Sampler from Windows. Open the Custom Icon. Then click on **Setup**

2. If you have an Internet address, click on **IP Address** Your screen will resemble Figure 2-29.

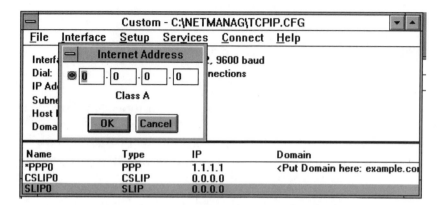

Figure 2-29
Internet Address

3. Now, enter your IP address carefully.

Heads Up!

You will be entering four sets of numbers, each of which will have one, two, or three digits in it (for example, 192.1.1.1). Each set must be entered correctly. So, if one of your sets has only one or two digits in it, be sure to type a period after the digit(s) so that your cursor moves to the next box. For example, if we were to enter the IP number we have used above, we would type

192 . 1 . 1 . 1

Then, click on **OK**

We have entered this sample address in Figure 2-30 for illustration purposes only.

DO NOT USE THIS SAMPLE ADDRESS!

Once you have entered your IP address, click on **OK** to return to the Setup screen.

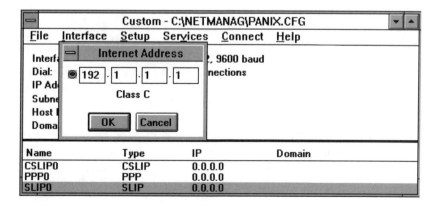

Figure 2-30
Sample Internet
Address

Entering Your Domain Name

1. Next, click on **Setup** and again on **Domain Name**. Your screen should resemble Figure 2-31.

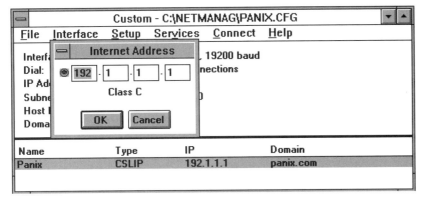

Figure 2-31
Domain Name

2. Now, type in the domain name given to you by the provider. This may take some looking in the provider's literature, but it's there and it's usually called domain name.

3. Click on **OK**.

Entering Your Telephone Number

Next, we will enter the telephone number your computer will dial to connect to the service provider. Usually, this is just an ordinary telephone number. Remember to add a 1 to the front of it, if you would do that in regular dialing. A way to test the number is to just dial it from a regular telephone. If you have the correct number, you will hear a modem or other tone.

1. Click on **Setup** and then on **Dial**. You will see the screen shown in Figure 2-32.

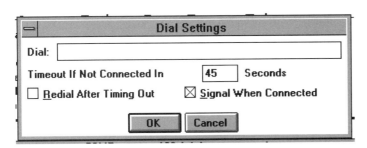

Figure 2-32
Dial Settings

2. Enter the telephone number

3.   Consider making the Timeout longer than 30 seconds. Some providers' systems take a little longer to connect. A safer value is 60 seconds.

4.   Select **Signal When Connected** by clicking on the box next to that phrase.

5.   Click on **OK** to return to the Setup screen

If your provider uses extra digits in the number, you will enter them here. ANSRemote does this by adding a seven-digit number after the telephone number. For ANSRemote, you would enter the number as

```
1-800-555-1234,,,,,1234567
```

The commas are used to indicate a delay of about 2 seconds (for each comma). For ANSRemote, the delay is needed so that your computer waits for a connecting tone. After the tone is received, the extra seven digits are sent (as telephone keypad tones) and the call is then switched to a modem. If your provider uses this kind of system, you may want to add or subtract some commas to allow the right delay.

Login Settings

Next, we will enter your login name, password, and startup command.

1.   Click on **Setup** and then on **Login**. You will see the screen shown in Figure 2-33.

Figure 2-33
Login Settings

2.   Type in the user name which you have arranged with your service provider.

     Note: Some providers call this a user name, but they mean login name.

3.   Type in the user password given by your provider.

Note: As you type in your password, only asterisks will show, so type the password very carefully.

4. Finally, on the line labeled Startup Command: type in the kind of connection being provided by your provider, SLIP or PPP, (Very few will put CSLIP here.)

5. Click on **OK**

We have now finished the Setup configuration, but we still have two things left to do. We need to tell your PC about the provider's Nameserver(s); and, we may have to edit your SLIP.INI file.

1. Click on **Services** to get the Services menu, as shown in Figure 2-34.

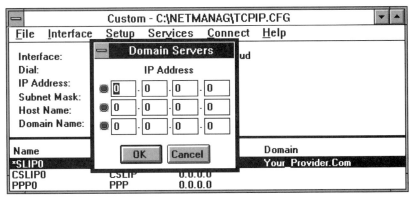

Figure 2-34
Services Menu

2. Click on **Services** and then on **Domain Servers**. Your screen will look like Figure 2-35.

Figure 2-35
Domain Servers

3. Type in the IP address(es) of the Domain Servers as given to you by your provider. They may also be called Nameservers. You may have been given two addresses or only one. Key in whatever you were given. Click on **OK**.

Again, as was true earlier when you entered your IP address, each of these addresses will consist of four sets of digits, such as 192.1.1.1 As you type in your particular addresses, it is important to remember that sets which have only one or two digits in them, MUST be followed by period, so that your cursor moves to the next appropriate box. Be sure to type, for example, 1 9 2 . 1 . 1 . 1 Then click on **OK**

4. Click on **File** and **Save** to store the information in the TCPIP.CFG file.

    Note: This file is encrypted so you (and others) cannot look at it. Should you wish to do so, you can use the Custom part of Chameleon Sampler to make any changes.

Congratulations! You have now completed the configuration process. The good news is that you won't have to go through all that again (unless you change Internet service providers). But, even if you do, only some of the items will need changing. The bad news is that we may not be finished.

Heads Up!

Most service providers can send you a listing of the SLIP.INI that they suggest for their service. You might wish to call them and ask if they will do this and then edit your SLIP.INI file (or check the standard SLIP0, PPP0, and CSLIP0 files) to be the same as their listing. If your provider cannot do this, the next section will show you how to discover what your .INI file should contain.

The SLIP.INI File

For each service provider that you use, there must be an entry in the SLIP.INI file that comes with Chameleon Sampler. This file tells your PC how to set up your session with the Internet service provider. Since this activity really consists of two computers trying to talk to each other, it has to be done correctly.

Here's a sample entry in SLIP.INI for NetCom.

```
[NetCom]
SCRIPT=login: $u$r word: $p$r
TYPE=SLIP
```

Here's what it says:

It tells the PC to follow the SCRIPT after the modems have connected with each other.

First, the PC is to wait for a phrase that ends in ... login: such as Please login:

Then, the PC is to answer with your login name and an Enter (ur)

Next, the PC waits for a phrase ending in ... word: such as Password:

The PC is to answer with your password and an Enter (pr)

This is a very simple and clear *script*. Depending on how your provider sets up the computers, it can get more complex. Notice that the Startup Command—SLIP—was not used.

Here's another, slightly more complex example from PSINet.

```
[PSINet]
SCRIPT=name: $u$r word: $p$r -n $6$c$r -i
TYPE=SLIP
```

Again, here's what it says:

It tells the PC to follow the SCRIPT after the modems have connected with each other.

First, the PC is to wait for a phrase that ends in ... name: such as Username:

Then, the PC is to answer with your login name and an Enter (ur)

Next, the PC waits for a phrase ending in ... word: such as Password:

The PC is to answer with your password and an Enter pr

Then, the PC is not to wait (-n)

The PC sends, after 6 seconds, the Startup Command and a return (6c$r) (The Startup Command here is SLIP)

Then the PC will receive an IP address to use for this session (-i)

This series of *handshakes* or interchanges is controlled by a set of commands. The commands come in two types: <sends> and <expects>.

The commands for Chameleon Sampler's <sends> are:

$n	send a new line
$r	send a carriage return
$s	send a space
$b	cause a short "break" on the line
$t	send a tab
$1–$9	pause the indicated number of seconds
$xXX	send the character with HEX code XX
$u	send the user id
$p	send the password
$c	send the SLIP Command
$d	send the phone number
$$	send a "$" character
$f	define a prompt

The commands for Chameleon Sampler's <expects> are similar to the <sends> mentioned above. In addition, within an <expect> string you can include the following escapes:

--	expect "-"
-n	skip an expect
-i	expect IP address (to replace your own)

EDITING YOUR SLIP.INI FILE

We will use Window's Notepad Editor to edit the SLIP.INI file. You should have obtained the SLIP.INI information from your Internet service provider. You should put that information in your SLIP.INI file.

The Notepad Editor can usually be found in Window's Accessories Group.

1.   Double-click on the **Accessories Group** and find the Notepad

2.   Double-click on the **Notepad**

3.   Click on **File** and then on **Open**

     You may then type in the location of the SLIP.INI file, for example C:\NETMANAG\SLIP.INI. Your screen should resemble Figure 2-36.

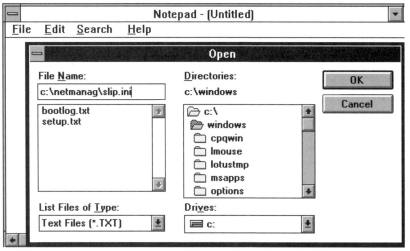

Figure 2-36
Notepad Editor

When you click on **OK** you will see the top of the SLIP.INI file displayed in the Notepad Editor as shown in Figure 2-37.

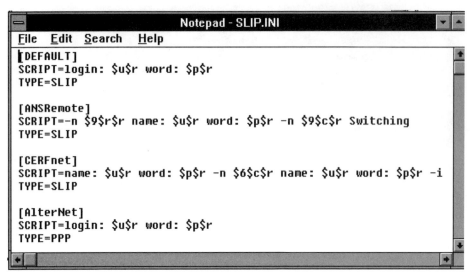

Figure 2-37
Notepad—SLIP.INI

4. Drag the right button down until you see the entries for PPPO, SLIPO, and CSLIPO. Your screen should resemble Figure 2-38.

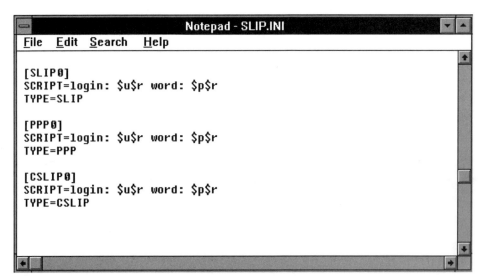

Figure 2-38
Notepad—SLIP.INI

5. Select the entry which is to be used for your Internet service provider, and edit it so that it matches the information which you have been given.

6.   Click on **File** and **Save**. Then close the Notepad to return to Windows.

SESSION SUMMARY

Well done! You have now edited your SLIP.INI file so that it can accommodate the commands required by your service provider. Your Chameleon Sampler software should be installed on your computer, and all necessary information has been provided to it.

In our next session, we will get you connected to the Internet using TCP/IP. Also, we will show you how to discover the login dialog of your provider if you are having difficulty.

SESSION 3

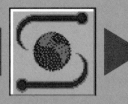

Connecting to the Internet

SESSION OVERVIEW_____

We are now going to connect to the Internet and begin exploring! As we start, we need to check that all is ready. We will do
that by reviewing hosts and accounts and doing a test connection. For our test connection, we will use the Microsoft Windows
communications program—Terminal. This will help us verify
that all of the little settings are correct.

Once all of the settings are correct, we will use the Chameleon
Sampler to make our first real Internet connection. Remember,
we need to have the TCP/IP software in place so that we can
run NCSA Mosaic on our computers.

In this session, we will use a tool called Ping to verify that we
really are on the Internet. Then, we will connect to a place
called the InterNIC or the Internet Network Information Center.
Finally, we will leave you to explore the InterNIC and all of its
treasures.

HOSTS AND ACCOUNTS _____

Remember that when we use the word *host*, we mean any computer that is connected to the Internet using TCP/IP software.
We are about to put your Windows PC right on the Internet as a

host. This means that your PC will be the equal (or peer) of every other Internet host. Before we do that, you will want to be sure what that means.

We will put your Windows PC on the Internet by connecting it to another larger computer that is also on the Internet. This computer is run by an Internet service provider. You must, by now, have received the information from your provider about your account.

Your account information is important, in the same way that your address and telephone number are important. If you give someone the wrong address or telephone number, they will not be able to reach you. Similarly, your account information must be correct if everything is to work well on the Internet.

You should have the written copy of that information before you, as we go through the tests which follow.

Your SLIP/PPP Account

Heads Up!

Your account is a little different from other types of Internet accounts that are available from the service providers. This account *must* be for a SLIP or PPP type connection to the provider. The Chameleon Sampler program which contains the TCP/IP stack of software, depends on this. It will be looking for a SLIP or PPP connection to get you fully connected. Remember, the Internet service provider is your gateway to the Internet.

Account Security

A quick reminder is also in order about security. Your account has a user name (or login name) and a password. Together these allow access to your account. You will want to be sure that you protect these, particularly the password. This is because your user name or login name is probably close to your real name or can be guessed. The only real protection that you have is your password. Treat it as you would treat your ATM Personal Identification Number or PIN.

If you believe that someone may have your password, contact your provider to have your password changed. Some providers allow you to change your password while you are online. Others require you to call them via voice telephone. The Chameleon Sampler encodes your password on your PC, but you should still carefully guard who has access to your PC. If you pay for your account by the hour, loss of a password could cost you a lot of money.

TESTING YOUR CONNECTION

Before we start connecting to the Internet with the Chameleon Sampler, we want to show you a way to verify that connection. We will do this with a tool you already have—*Microsoft Windows Terminal.* This general communications program comes with Windows 3.1 and can do all regular communications work. Here, we will use it to make sure that the handshaking is correct.

Handshaking means that the commands and responses from your provider and your PC are always in sync. This turns out to be the trickiest part of SLIP and PPP connections—getting the commands and responses right. Although the Chameleon Sampler can show these to you, Chameleon Sampler will not let you make changes as you go. With Windows Terminal, we will see that all is right. Also, if necessary, we can make changes and check them if we see that they are incorrect.

Once this pattern of command and response is correct, you should not have to change it again. If, however, you get a new service provider, you will need to redo it. And, if you have problems later on, you can use this technique to check things out. We hope it will be a big help to you.

**HANDS-ON
Activity 1**

USING WINDOWS TERMINAL

Terminal, illustrated in Figure 3-1, is usually found in Windows Accessories Group.

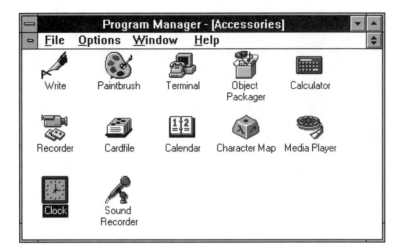

Figure 3-1
Windows Terminal

1. To find Terminal, first double-click on the **Accessories Group** and then double-click on **Terminal**. You will get a screen that looks like Figure 3-2.

   Note: If you have moved or deleted Terminal, you will need to use your Windows manual to find it. Most of us, however, have left it where Microsoft put it—in the Accessories Group. It looks like a telephone in front of a PC.

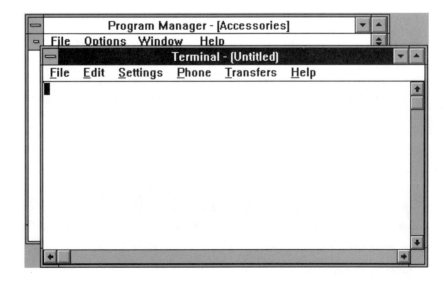

Figure 3-2
Terminal

Configuring Windows Terminal

We need to configure Terminal to "talk" to your Internet service provider. To do this, we will work with the Settings Menu in Terminal. The Settings Menu is shown in Figure 3-3.

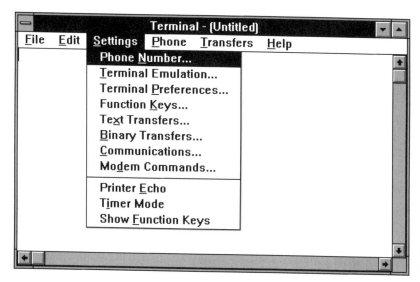

Figure 3-3
Settings Menu

1. Open the menu by clicking on **Settings** on the menu bar at the top. We will need to change only a few of the settings; most of them will use the defaults or Microsoft's factory settings.

If you use Terminal for other things, you may have changed some of the defaults. We will list all of the important ones so you can set them correctly for our test. This won't affect your other uses; we will save this set under a different name.

The Settings Menu

Phone Number

Although all of the settings are important, the phone number is critical for two reasons. First, you can't go any further unless you reach your provider. Second, you don't want to annoy some person with repeated modem calls.

1. Click on **Phone Number...**

2. First, type in the access number given to you by your provider. This is the *modem* access number, not the voice number for the provider. Remember to include a 1 or any other number that may be required by your local telephone company. Your screen should resemble Figure 3-4.

Figure 3-4
Phone Number

You may want to dial the number from your voice telephone to be sure you have it right. If it's OK, you will hear the familiar tones and hisses of the provider's modem.

3. Next, change **Timeout If Not Connected In**

The default is 30 seconds, but we have found that a value of 60 seconds may be needed for some providers. This is because SLIP and PPP connections have more handshaking to do!

4. Now, click on **OK**

Terminal Emulation

Next, we will just check on Terminal Emulation. Almost all Internet service providers use Digital Equipment's DEC VT-100 as a default.

1. Click on **Settings** again and then on **Terminal Emulation...** You will see the box shown in Figure 3-5.

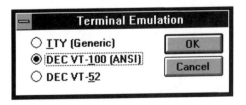

Figure 3-5
Terminal Emulation

Unless you have used Terminal for other services, it should already be set to DEC VT-100 (ANSI). If not, change it by clicking on that line and then click on **OK**

2. Click on **Settings** again and pass over the next four items:

> Terminal Preferences...
>
> Function Keys...
>
> Text Transfers...
>
> Binary Transfers...

While these settings can be changed, they will not affect our test of your provider. The next setting, Communications, is very important.

Communications

The Communications settings determine how the bits move across the telephone lines between your PC and the Internet service provider. We need to be sure that the settings on your PC agree with the settings supported by your provider. First let's set your Baud Rate or modem speed.

This will depend more on what modem you have than on what your provider can offer. Most providers support a full range of standard speeds from 1200 to 19200. If you don't know the speed of your modem, check the modem manual. If your modem is outside your computer, the name or number on the modem will give a clue. If it has a 24 or 2400 in the name or number, it will probably run at 2400. Similarly, a 96 or 9600 will go at 9600. If there's a 14 or 14400 in the name or number, select **19200** from **Baud Rate**.

While it's not critical to get exactly the right speed, it will affect your speed of use later. If you set the speed too slow, it will usually work, but things will take longer. If you set it too fast, it will usually simply fail to work.

Try setting the modem at 2400 and getting everything to work. Then go back and try it again at 9600 and yet again at 19200. The last one to work properly will be your useful speed.

---

1. Click on **Settings** and then on **Communications**. Your screen should look like Figure 3-6.

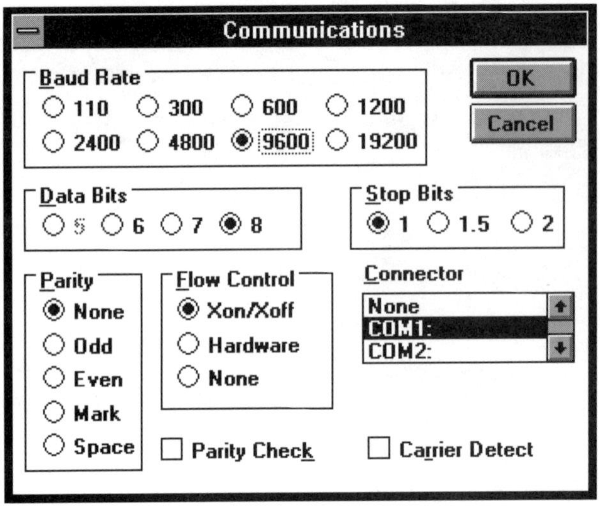

Communications

Baud Rate
○ 110 ○ 300 ○ 600 ○ 1200
○ 2400 ○ 4800 ◉ 9600 ○ 19200

OK
Cancel

Data Bits
○ 5 ○ 6 ○ 7 ◉ 8

Stop Bits
◉ 1 ○ 1.5 ○ 2

Parity
◉ None
○ Odd
○ Even
○ Mark
○ Space

Flow Control
◉ Xon/Xoff
○ Hardware
○ None

Connector
None
COM1:
COM2:

☐ **Parity Check**   ☐ **Carrier Detect**

Figure 3-6
Communications

2. Set the Baud Rate by clicking on the speed you believe your modem supports.

3. Next, check the Data Bits, Stop Bits, Parity, and Flow Control. Almost all providers support the following:

    8 Data Bits

    1 Stop Bit

    Parity—None

    Flow Control—Xon/Xoff

    Of course, if your provider's information differs, use the settings recommended by the provider.

4. Finally, you need to determine the Connector for your modem. Move your cursor to the Connector box. If you don't know what port to use, click on **COM1:** When we start the connection, we will discover if this is right or wrong. If necessary, it is simple to change it.

5. Now, click on **OK** and on **Settings** again

6. This time, click on **Modem Commands...**

    If you see your modem listed in the lower right of the box, select it. Otherwise, be sure that Hayes is selected. Almost all modems support what is called the Hayes (AT) command set. Your screen should resemble Figure 3-7.

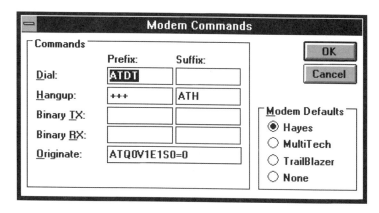

Figure 3-7
Modem Settings

7. Click on **OK** and now click on **File** on the menu bar. From the drop-down menu, click on **Save As...**

8. In the File Name: box, type a name you can remember for this provider. You may want to use these settings again to verify your connection.

Now, you are ready to test your provider connection.

Activity 2:

TESTING YOUR PROVIDER CONNECTION WITH TERMINAL

HANDS-ON
Activity 2

Now we will use Windows Terminal to check the provider connection, as well as to be sure that all of the items we have set will work. Then, we can move to the Chameleon Sampler and be off on the Internet!

We are going to go through the series of handshakes between your PC and your provider's computer. By doing this, we will understand how the handshake process works, so we can fix it if it breaks (or if it's not working). As we go, Terminal will capture the commands and expected responses (what it expects in return) from both computers.

You may be asking: Why do I need to know all these things and why can't it be simpler?

One answer is that soon all of this will be simpler, no more complex than dialing a telephone. The other answer is that it is not yet that simple, and we have to know how it works if we are going to make it work for us.

Here's what will happen during the test connection:

First, Terminal will dial your provider and the modems will negotiate speeds and compression protocols (remember protocols?).

Next (usually), the provider's computer will ask for a command.

You will then type in the command that will simulate your PC's response as the Chameleon Sampler will give it.

At some point, the provider's computer will ask for your login name or user name and a password. Again, you can type this in to be sure that all will work well. If all goes according to plan, the SLIP or PPP connection will complete and be active.

Terminal will record all this information on the screen. Using Windows Clipboard, we will then record it for later use.

At this point we will hang up and look at the results. If they agree with what we expect, we can go on to the Chameleon Sampler. If not, we will need to revise your SLIP.INI file and/or Chameleon Sampler's configuration before we proceed.

1.   Let's start Terminal, open the file we just saved, and click on **Phone** from the menu bar.

2.   Click on **Dial:** and listen for sounds from your PC. You should see a screen which resembles Figure 3-8. You should hear the dial tone and dialing.

Figure 3-8
Terminal Dial

3.   If you hear no sounds, the Connector setting may be wrong. Click on **Cancel** and go back to the Settings and open the Communications Menu.

Move your cursor to the Connector box. Change the COM setting to the next higher number.

Click on **OK**, **File**, and **Save** to keep the new setting. Now go back to **Phone** and try **Dial:** again.

Repeat the process until you hear the modem dialing.

Some computers hang or freeze when a modem command is given to a wrong Connector setting. Don't worry if this happens; just press **CTL-ALT-DEL** or **power off** and **power on** again. Then go to Terminal Settings, move your cursor to the Connector box, and try the next COM port.

---

4. Now, watch for the series of commands and responses. Unlike the Chameleon Sampler, you may type in commands and responses with Terminal. This means that you can simulate the Chameleon Sampler start-up session.

    If you have a PPP connection and the screen asks you to enter SLIP or PPP, type in PPP

    If you are then asked for a user name and password, enter yours

    When this is complete (or if you have trouble), click on **Phone** and again on **Hangup**

Every provider asks for information in a different way. Some want SLIP or PPP entered first (as in our example). Some want user names and passwords entered first. Others have yet different schemes. This is the hardest part of a SLIP or PPP connection. But, once you have mastered it, you won't have to do it again!

We have captured a sample screen in Figure 3-9 to show you what this may look like. Since there are not yet standards among providers, each provider's session will look different.

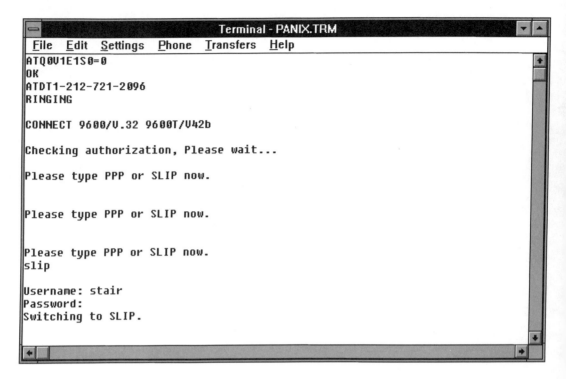

```
Terminal - PANIX.TRM
File  Edit  Settings  Phone  Transfers  Help
ATQ0V1E1S0=0
OK
ATDT1-212-721-2096
RINGING

CONNECT 9600/V.32 9600T/V42b

Checking authorization, Please wait...

Please type PPP or SLIP now.


Please type PPP or SLIP now.


Please type PPP or SLIP now.
slip

Username: stair
Password:
Switching to SLIP.
```

Figure 3-9
Sample Terminal
Connection

5. Now, click on **Edit** from the menu bar and click on **Select All**

   The window will change color and you can click on **Edit** again

   Now, click on **Copy** to copy the selected screen to Windows Clipboard

6. Click on **File** and **Exit**

7. Now, find Windows Clipboard. (It's probably in Windows Main Group.)

   Double click on **Clipboard Viewer** and you should find the Terminal session. We have captured our sample session in Clipboard Viewer in Figure 3-10 as an example.

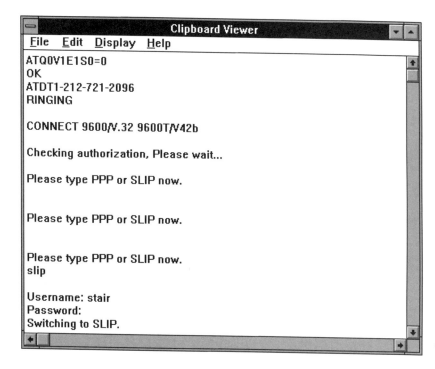

```
Clipboard Viewer
File   Edit   Display   Help

ATQ0V1E1S0=0
OK
ATDT1-212-721-2096
RINGING

CONNECT 9600/V.32 9600T/V42b

Checking authorization, Please wait...

Please type PPP or SLIP now.


Please type PPP or SLIP now.


Please type PPP or SLIP now.
slip

Username: stair
Password:
Switching to SLIP.
```

Figure 3-10
Windows Clipboard

8. You should now click on **File** and **Save As...** Give the file
    a name and save it as a Clipboard file for later review.

This Terminal session has shown, hopefully, what the sequence
of commands and responses will be for your provider.

If you have trouble connecting when you are using the Chameleon Sampler, you will want to review the sequence. Then, you can
return to Session Two and edit your SLIP.INI file to follow the right sequence. You may have to use Terminal several times if the provider's sequence is very different.

Heads Up!

Here is the SLIP.INI entry for the example Terminal session shown above:

```
[Panix]
SCRIPT=now. $4$c$r name: $u$r word: $p$r switching $4$r
TYPE=CSLIP
```

It says: Expect a phrase ending in "now." (Notice the period; it's important.)

Pause for 4 seconds ($4). Then, send the command that we set up in Chameleon Sampler (that was SLIP), followed by a carriage return (cr).

Now wait for a phrase ending in "name:" (Notice the colon.)

Then, send the user name ($u) followed by a carriage return ($r).

Then, look for a phrase ending in "word:" and send the password followed by a carriage return (pr).

Then, look for the command switching.

Finally, there is a wait of four seconds, and a carriage return (4r).

As a reminder, here are the <expects> and <sends> that Chameleon Sampler uses:

```
<expect1><send1><expect2>...
```

Words are separated by white space, that is, spaces or tabs. Within a <send> string you can include the following escapes:

$n	send a new line
$r	send a carriage return
$s	send a space
$b	cause a short "break" on the line
$t	send a tab
$1–$9	pause the indicated number of seconds
$xXX	send the character with HEX code XX
$u	send the user id
$p	send the password
$c	send the SLIP Command

`$d`	send the phone number
`$$`	send a "$" character
`$f`	define a prompt

Within an <expect> string you can include the following escapes:

`--`	expect "-"
`-n`	skip an expect
`-i`	expect IP address (to replace your own)

CONNECTING USING CHAMELEON SAMPLER_____

Now we will start a Chameleon Sampler connection and do some early exploring of the Internet. If all does not go right the first time, be patient and use Terminal again to discover the correct sequence of <expects> and <sends>.

CONNECTING WITH CHAMELEON SAMPLER

HANDS-ON Activity 3

We now begin our connection to, and exploration of, the Internet.

1. Double-click on the **Chameleon Sampler Group**

2. Double-click on **Custom** and then on **Setup**

   Watch the lower left of your screen. A little green *NEWT* will appear as part of this process. (A NEWT is a measuring tool that can help you when you are having trouble with the provider's host or the telephone line. For now, you can ignore it.)

3. Click on **Log...** (It's at the bottom of the Settings Menu.)

   The Log window appears. At this stage, we will use the Log window to check on our connection's progress. After you are making regular connections, you may want to bypass this step. Now, however, we need to see what's happening.

4. Put the mouse cursor on the top bar of Log and hold down the left mouse button to move the Log window down on your screen. This will let you see the Custom screen and the Log screen at the same time. It should look something like Figure 3-11.

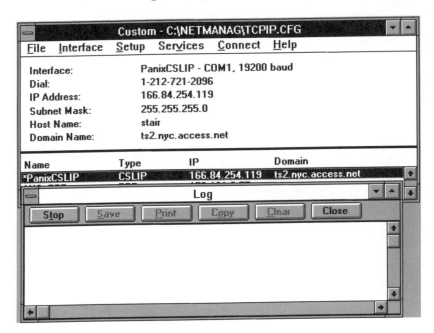

Figure 3-11
Chameleon and the Log

5. Be sure that the name of your provider is highlighted in the lower part of the Custom window. (In Figure 3-11, we have highlighted `PanixCSLIP`.)

6. Click on **Connect**

The first thing that you will see will be the Chameleon Sampler - Connect screen. If you wish to learn more about the support provided by NetManage, Inc., or how to upgrade your copy of Chameleon Sampler, just click on the appropriate button. If you would like to continue, just click on **OK**.

You will see a pop-up Connect window and you should hear your modem beginning to dial.

> **Note:** The Log window will display what is happening. Log will scroll down as the connection progresses. The Connect pop-up window will continue to appear until the connection with your provider has been completed.

Once the connection has been completed, your Connect pop-up window will disappear, and the word Connect on the menu bar will change to Disconnect. This may take a number of seconds following the last action in the Log window.

Figures 3-12, 3-13, and 3-14 show sample connection logs for ANSRemote, Netcom, and Panix. These are examples of what the log may look like. If you are using another provider, your log may look quite different. These will just give you an idea of what to look for. Following each figure, we show the SLIP.INI entry for that provider.

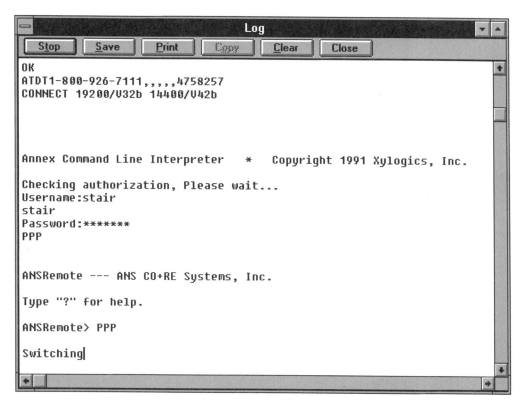

The SLIP.INI file entry for ANSRemote is

Figure 3-12
ANSRemote Log Screen

```
[ANSRemote]
SCRIPT=-n $9$r$r name: $u$r word: $p$r -n $9$c$r Switching
TYPE=SLIP
```

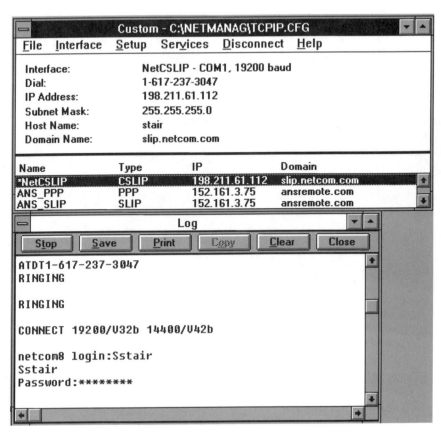

Figure 3-13
Netcom Log Screen

The SLIP.INI file entry for Netcom is

```
[NetCom]
SCRIPT=login: $u$r word: $p$r beginning.... $2$r
TYPE=CSLIP
```

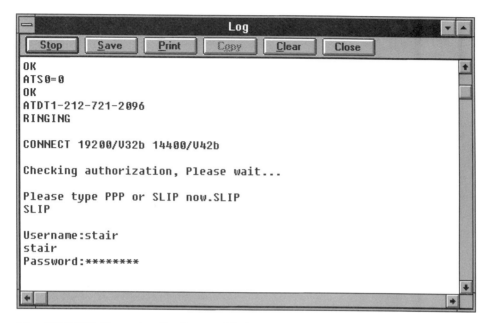

The SLIP.INI file entry for Panix CSLIP is:

```
[PanixCSLIP]
SCRIPT=now. $4$c$r name: $u$r word: $p$r switching $4$r
TYPE=CSLIP
```

Figure 3-14
Panix Log Screen

Important: Look at the Custom screen and watch the top menu bar. You should see that the Connect menu item has changed to Disconnect. This is all that you will see to tell you that the connection has been successful. When Disconnect appears, you are connected to your provider.

To complete our connection to the Internet,

1. Click on the **Save** button of Log and save it for later review.

2. Then click on the **Minimize** button to the right of Custom. (It's the little button with the arrow pointing down.) This will shrink Custom down to the bottom of your screen and reveal the Chameleon Sampler's main window.

Pinging around the World

Now we will check to see if you really are on the Internet. We will do this with a well-known tool called *Ping*. Notice the Ping-Pong Table Icon in the Chameleon Sampler window. Ping is a way of sending a short "are you alive?" message across the Internet. It verifies that another host is up and running and can be reached from your host (your PC).

PINGING AROUND THE WORLD

1. Double-click on **Ping** and the Ping window will appear. Figure 3-15 shows the Ping window. Next, we will set up Ping.

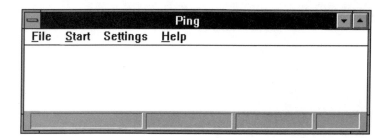

Figure 3-15
Ping

2. Click on the **Settings** menu item on the menu bar.

3. In the Settings box, click on **Preferences...**

    The Preferences box is shown in Figure 3-16.

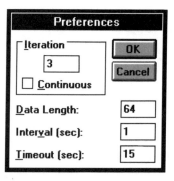

Figure 3-16
Preferences

4. In Preferences, we will make three changes:

    a. Change **Iteration** to 3

        This will let us see three responses, rather than just one.

    b. Change **Timeout[sec]:** to 15 (seconds)

        We will be doing some long-distance Pings and may need the extra time.

Note: Timeout just declares that the test packets are lost if they don't come back within the timeout value.

c.   Change **Data Length:** to 64

This will permit you to receive some longer amounts of data.

5.   Click on **OK** and you will be back at the Ping main window.

6.   Now, click on **Start** and you will be presented with the Host box which is shown in Figure 3-17. We're going to type the first destination here.

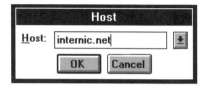

Figure 3-17
Ping Host Box

Type `internic.net` in the box and click on **OK**

If you really *are* connected to the Internet, you will immediately see the responses. We captured a similar response for you in Figure 3-18.

```
                          Ping                      ▼ ▲
 File   Start   Settings   Help
    64 bytes received, icmp_seq=1, time=385 ms
    64 bytes received, icmp_seq=2, time=330 ms
    64 bytes received, icmp_seq=3, time=275 ms
--- Round-trip (ms)  min/avg/max = 275/330/385 ---

Host: internic.net [198.41.0.  3 transmitted    3 received    0% loss
```

Figure 3-18
InterNIC Pings

Notice several things in the Ping window:

a.   Each message of 64 bytes has been received; that is, it has gone to the InterNIC and returned. (InterNIC is short for Internet Network Information Center; we'll actually go there in a moment.)

b.   At the end of the line is the time (in ms or milliseconds or thousandths of a second) that it took to go round trip.

c. At the bottom of the Ping window, look for the Host: name and part of the actual IP address of the Inter-NIC. This tells you that your Internet service provider's nameserver was able to find an IP address for the host name you typed.

d. Finally, the number of packets transmitted (meaning sent by your computer), received, and lost is shown. This gives you an idea of how well the network is working to that host destination.

You can see that Ping is a very handy tool to use. Should you ever have problems trying to reach another host on the Internet, you can use Ping to see if your destination host is reachable.

Now, let's go a little further.

1. Click on **Start** again. If the Host: box is highlighted, it will clear as soon as you begin to type new information. Now, type gopher.itu.ch and click on **OK**

This is a host in Geneva, Switzerland, at the International Telecommunications Union. Figure 3-19 shows the response you should see.

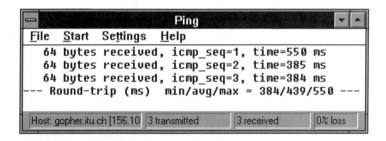

Figure 3-19
Pinging Switzerland

Lastly, we'll go to the South Pole.

1. Click on **Start** again

Type mcmvax.mcmurdo.gov and click on **OK**

Our final destination is McMurdo Sound on the continent of Antarctica. The host is a DEC VAX machine at the U.S. Government's McMurdo Sound outpost. Figure 3-20 is what you should see (although the times may differ).

```
 ─                        Ping                    ▼ ▲
 File   Start   Settings   Help
      64 bytes received, icmp_seq=1, time=988 ms
      64 bytes received, icmp_seq=2, time=934 ms
      64 bytes received, icmp_seq=3, time=933 ms
 --- Round-trip (ms)   min/avg/max = 933/951/988 ---

  Host: mcmvax.mcmurdo.go│ 3 transmitted  │ 3 received  │ 0% loss
```

Figure 3-20
Pinging Antarctica

You will notice that the round-trip times differ widely on these three destinations. Some of this is network delay, perhaps due to congestion. The last Ping also involves a satellite hop in order for us to go to and from Antarctica and that adds at least another 600 milliseconds.

If one (or more) of these Pings was successful, you can be assured that you are fully connected to the Internet.

Close Ping by double-clicking on the **file drawer handle** in the upper-left corner. You will be asked if you want to save the changes to your PING.CFG file. Click on **Yes** to keep your preferences changes.

A VISIT TO THE INTERNIC

For our final activity in this session, we are going to explore the Telnet feature of Chameleon Sampler.

TELNET TO THE INTERNIC

*HANDS-ON
Activity 5*

1. Double-click on **Telnet** and the Telnet window will open.

2. Click on the **Connect** menu item and you will see the Connect To box.

3. In the Host Name: box, type `ds.internic.net` and then click on **OK**

   Note: You should see a screen similar to Figure 3-21. Notice that Connect on the menu bar has changed to Disconnect. If you get hung up or stalled while using Telnet, just click on **Disconnect** to break the remote host session.

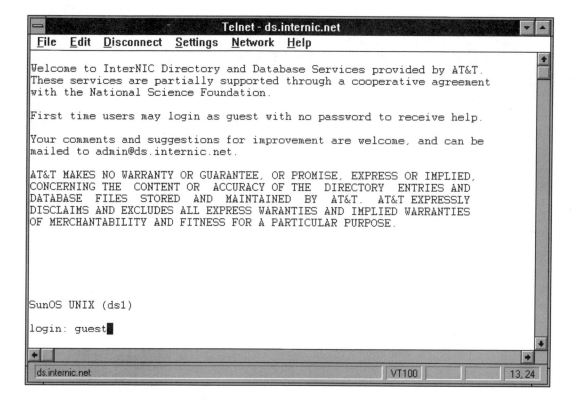

```
─                         Telnet - ds.internic.net                    ▼ ▲
 File  Edit  Disconnect  Settings  Network  Help

Welcome to InterNIC Directory and Database Services provided by AT&T.
These services are partially supported through a cooperative agreement
with the National Science Foundation.

First time users may login as guest with no password to receive help.

Your comments and suggestions for improvement are welcome, and can be
mailed to admin@ds.internic.net.

AT&T MAKES NO WARRANTY OR GUARANTEE, OR PROMISE, EXPRESS OR IMPLIED,
CONCERNING THE  CONTENT OR  ACCURACY OF THE  DIRECTORY  ENTRIES AND
DATABASE  FILES  STORED  AND  MAINTAINED  BY  AT&T.  AT&T EXPRESSLY
DISCLAIMS AND EXCLUDES ALL EXPRESS WARANTIES AND IMPLIED WARRANTIES
OF MERCHANTABILITY AND FITNESS FOR A PARTICULAR PURPOSE.




SunOS UNIX (ds1)

login: guest█

─────────────────────────────────────────────────────────────────────
 ds.internic.net                                   VT100          13, 24
```

Figure 3-21
The InterNIC Welcome

4. At the `login:` prompt, type `guest` and press **Enter**

5. At the `password:` prompt, just press **Enter** again. This will bring you to the InterNIC's Main Menu screen. It may look similar to Figure 3-22.

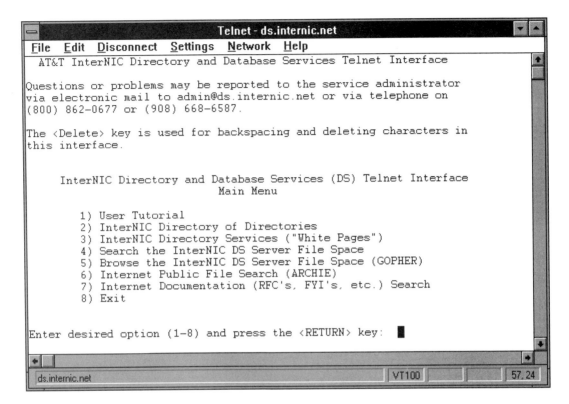

You may make a number of choices. We recommend that you begin with the choice that says Browse the InterNIC DS Server File Space (GOPHER) which leads to a menu of information.

Since these menus change frequently, it may or may not look like Figure 3-23. But, there will be helpful choices for you on the menu.

Figure 3-22
The InterNIC Main Menu

```
─                    Telnet - gopher.internic.net                    ▼ ▲
 File   Edit   Disconnect   Settings   Network   Help
            ┌─────────Internet Gopher Information Client v1.11─────────┐   ▲
                      InterNIC Information Services (General Atomics)

   -->   1.   NOTICE TO GOPHER USERS.
         2.   README.
         3.   About the InfoGuide/
         4.   About InterNIC Information Services/
         5.   About the Internet/
         6.   Getting Connected to the Internet/
         7.   Beginners: Start Here/
         8.   Using the Internet/
         9.   Internet Resources/
        10.   Advanced Users: NIC Staff, System Administrators, Programmers/
        11.   Frequently Asked Questions at InterNIC IS/
        12.   Scout Report/
        13.   WAIS search InfoGuide (and elsewhere) by keyword/
        14.   InfoGuide INDEX.



 Press ▓ for Help, ▓ to Quit, ▓ to go up a menu              Page: 1
                                                                     ▼
 ◄                                                                ►
 gopher.internic.net                          │ VT100 │      │  5, 5 │
```

Figure 3-23
The InterNIC Gopher

The menus will offer you a number of choices and ways of moving around. Many of the screens will offer help screens or tutorials. When you have finished your visit to the InterNIC, return to their Main menu and select **Exit**.

6. Now, click on **Disconnect** from Telnet's menu bar to close the Telnet connection.

   Double-click on the **down arrow** in the upper right-hand corner of the Telnet screen. This should reduce Telnet to an icon and return you to the Program Manager - [Chameleon Sampler] screen.

Important: Remember, you are still connected to your service provider.

Our last activity will disconnect your PC from the service provider.

HANDS-ON Activity 6

CLOSING THE CONNECTION

1. Double-click on the **Custom Icon** on your screen. You should see the Custom window again looking like Figure 3-24.

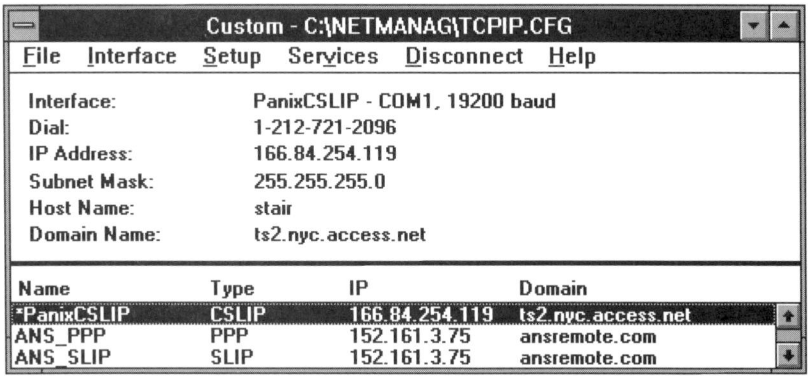

```
┌──────────────────────────────────────────────────────────┐
│ ─            Custom - C:\NETMANAG\TCPIP.CFG         ▼ │ ▲ │
├──────────────────────────────────────────────────────────┤
│ File  Interface  Setup  Services  Disconnect  Help        │
│                                                            │
│ Interface:        PanixCSLIP - COM1, 19200 baud            │
│ Dial:             1-212-721-2096                           │
│ IP Address:       166.84.254.119                           │
│ Subnet Mask:      255.255.255.0                            │
│ Host Name:        stair                                    │
│ Domain Name:      ts2.nyc.access.net                       │
├──────────────────────────────────────────────────────────┤
│ Name          Type        IP              Domain           │
│ *PanixCSLIP   CSLIP       166.84.254.119  ts2.nyc.access.net ▲│
│ ANS_PPP       PPP         152.161.3.75    ansremote.com      │
│ ANS_SLIP      SLIP        152.161.3.75    ansremote.com    ▼ │
└──────────────────────────────────────────────────────────┘
```

Figure 3-24
Custom

2.   Click on **Disconnect** and click on **Yes** when you are asked `Are you sure you want to disconnect...?`

If the Log is still open, you will see the commands issued to the modem to hang up the line (+++ATH). Disconnect will change back to Connect.

Your connection and session are now closed and you may close Chameleon Sampler.

You are now NCSA Mosaic Ready!

In the next part, "Mosaic Set," we will use Chameleon Sampler's tools so that we may download the software that we need to get started with NCSA Mosaic.

EMERGENCY EXITS

There will be times when things seem to get hung up and you can't get out or make anything work. Don't worry; we all have this happen more frequently than we would like. When this happens to you, there is a series of things you can do. Listed in order, they are

Return to **Custom** and **Disconnect**

Close Chameleon Sampler (**ALT—Spacebar—C**)

Reboot Windows (**CTL—ALT—DEL**)

Reboot the PC (**CTL—ALT—DEL** again)

Power off the PC and **power on** again

IN CASE OF TROUBLE

We hope that all has gone well in starting the connection to your Internet provider. We also recognize that things sometimes go awry. If you are having difficulty getting the connection to work, there are several things you can do. We will go over them here to help you get connected.

1. Go back over the information given you by your provider. Some providers use carbon forms for security, and they may be very hard to read. Check them carefully to see if a number 1 looks like a letter l or a number 0 looks like a capital letter O.

2. Check to see that you have Microsoft Version 3.1 Windows. When you start Windows, the big blue box should say Version 3.1 just below Windows.

3. Go back to Session Two and redo the configuration of Chameleon Sampler. Check each entry in Interface, Settings, and Services to make sure it agrees with both your provider's information and your PC's configuration. If you are in doubt about what your provider calls Default Gateway or Domainserver, contact the provider and ask them. Tell them you are using Chameleon Sampler.

4. If your modem is not dialing any numbers or you don't hear any tones from the modem, you may have the wrong Connector. Check the port settings in Custom or experiment with Windows Terminal.

5. Check the SLIP.INI file to make sure that the name in the square brackets agrees exactly with the Interface name in Custom's settings—including any special characters such as underlines. The sequence of <expects> and <sends> must be exact and in the correct order.

6. If you are using SLIP, you may need to try using CSLIP as the connection type in the Custom Interface section. Some providers use compressed SLIP (CSLIP) but call it SLIP.

7. Return to Windows Terminal and see if you can get a connection with your provider. Then check Terminal's settings to see if they differ from Custom's settings in Chameleon Sampler.

8. Finally, contact your provider and give them all the information you have developed about the problem. The more information you can give them, the faster they may be able to help you resolve the problem.

SESSION SUMMARY

If you have successfully completed the activities in this session, then your computer is Mosaic Ready. Your computer is a host on the Internet that is capable of sending and receiving information to and from all other Internet hosts. In the next part, "Mosaic Set," you will download all the software you will need to have on hand so you can download and install NCSA Mosaic. Once you have downloaded the necessary software, we will download NCSA Mosaic and begin to explore all the power that NCSA Mosaic has to offer.

Mosaic Set will prepare you for downloading and installing NCSA Mosaic for MS Windows on your personal computer.

In **Session Four**, you will learn about the E-mail capabilities of Chameleon Sampler.

In **Session Five**, you will use the FTP capabilities of Chameleon Sampler to learn about file compression and virus protection. You will download copies of PKZIP and PKUNZIP, as well as a copy of SCAN. You will learn how to prepare all of this software for use, so that you will be ready to download NCSA Mosaic.

In **Session Six,** you will learn about the World Wide Web and the various browsers which are available. Next, you will download a copy of NCSA Mosaic for MS Windows, and install it. Finally, you will test Mosaic by doing several activities.

How To Use Mosaic Set

It is useful to have E-mail capabilities while using Mosaic, so we recommend that you spend a short time working through the activities in **Session Four**. However, if you are eager to download Mosaic, you may skip Session Four and return to it later.

You must have the ftp capabilities of Chameleon Sampler (or another TCP/IP stack of software) to complete many activities in *Hands-On Mosaic*. Therefore, we would recommend that you work through the activities in **Session Five**. You will learn how to use Chameleon Sampler's ftp program. More importantly, you will download copies of PKZIP, PKUNZIP, and SCAN, and prepare them for use. Note that you need fully functioning copies of PKZIP and PKUNZIP to install NCSA Mosaic for MS Windows.

However, if you already have PKZIP and PKUNZIP, and a current copy of SCAN (or comparable virus protection software) and you are eager to download NCSA Mosaic, you can skip ahead to **Session Six**.

Session Six provides a first look at the World Wide Web. Most importantly, it is where NCSA Mosaic 1.0 is downloaded and installed. If you do not presently have NCSA Mosaic for MS Windows installed on your personal computer, you must work through the activities in this session.

PART 2

SESSION 4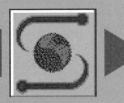

First Steps on the Internet

Our primary goal in this part of *Hands-On Mosaic* is to get you set for NCSA Mosaic. This particular session is intended to provide you with a very brief introduction to the Chameleon Sampler Mail program. Therefore, we will spend a minimum amount of time helping you to get the Chameleon Sampler Mail program up and running. Should you wish to learn more about all of the features that Mail contains, feel free to explore on your own or read the documentation that is provided with the full version of Chameleon.

OVERVIEW OF CHAMELEON SAMPLER MAIL

Chameleon Sampler contains an extremely powerful program to facilitate your use of electronic mail. This program, which is called *Mail*, will permit you to do the usual E-mail activities such as sending and receiving E-mail. In addition, quite a few advanced choices and features permit you to customize the way that your E-mail is received by others, as well as how your E-mail is handled by your computer.

When the Chameleon Sampler Program Group initially appears on your screen, one of the seven icons you will see is the mailbox which is used to indicate Mail. Before you will be able to use

Mail, you will have to set up a mail account for yourself and for any others who might be using your computer.

**HANDS-ON
Activity 1**

There are really two parts to the process:

1. In the first part, you have to log in as *Postmaster*. This will enable you (as Postmaster) to define a user's name, password, real name, and mail directory.

2. In the second part, you have to log in as the *user* so that you can define a mail gateway and mail server.

   If some of this does not make sense to you right now, just keep on going; it will soon!

To Log In as Postmaster

1. Double-click on the **Mail Icon**. You should see the User Login box that is pictured in Figure 4-1.

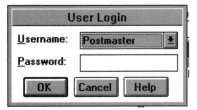

Figure 4-1
User Login

2. Accept the word `Postmaster` that appears in the User-name: box. Click on the **OK** button. Once you have done that, the Mail-Postmaster window appears. It should resemble Figure 4-2.

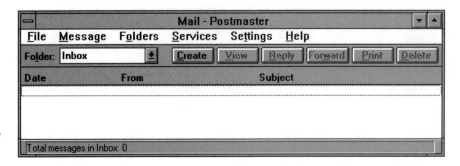

Figure 4-2
Mail-Postmaster

3. Click on **Services** Then, click on **Mailboxes...** The Mailboxes window should resemble the one shown in Figure 4-3.

Note: The Mailboxes option appears only when you are logged in as Postmaster. Should you wish to add additional users at a later time, you must remember to log in as Postmaster.

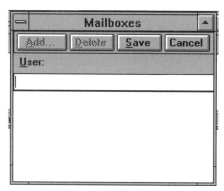

Figure 4-3
Mailboxes

4. Add your user name to the User: field. For example, I have always used dsachs as my user name, so that is what I will enter here.

Note: As soon as you do this, the Add... button becomes active.

Click on the **Add...** button. Once you have done so, a dialog box resembling Figure 4-4 should appear.

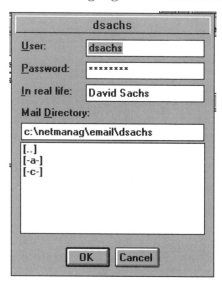

Figure 4-4
Entering Information

stop

Figure 4-6
Mail Gateway

Your Internet service provider should have given you information about what is called the *mail (POP) server*. Sometimes, this information will be just a domain name (i.e., panix.com). Other times, it may require that a host name be specified as well (i.e., dialup.oar.net).

Carefully examine the information sent to you by your service provider. It is **very** important that you enter this information correctly into the Host: box.

Once you have done that, click on **OK**

---

6. One more step!

   a. First, click on **Settings**

   b. Next, click on **Network**

   c. Finally, click on **Mail Server...**

The Mail Server window should appear. It should resemble the one shown in Figure 4-7.

Figure 4-7
Mail Server

7. You will have to enter the required information:

   a. Enter the name of the mail (POP) server on the Host: line.

   b. Enter your **user name** on the User: line.

   c. Enter your **password** on the Password: line.

d.   Leave an X next to Delete retrieved mail from server (or add one, if necessary)

       e.   Finally, click on the **OK** button.

8.   One final step!

       a.   Click on **Settings**

       b.   Click on **Preferences...**

       c.   Click on the **Advanced** button

       d.   In the From field be sure to enter your correct return E-mail address (i.e., dsachs@panix.com).

       e.   Click on **OK** twice to return to your Mail Inbox.

Congratulations! If you have followed all of the directions in this first activity, you should have successfully configured Chameleon Sampler Mail.

**HANDS-ON
Activity 2**

CREATING AND SENDING MAIL

1.   From the main Chameleon Sampler window, double-click on **Custom**. Then, click on **Connect** to connect to your Internet service provider.

       Then, minimize the Custom application by clicking on the **down arrow** in the upper-right-hand corner.

2.   From the main Chameleon Sampler window, double-click on **Mail**

3.   When the User Login window appears, type in your password

       Then double-click on **OK**

You should see the Main Mail window, which is shown in Figure 4-8.

Figure 4-8
Inbox Folder

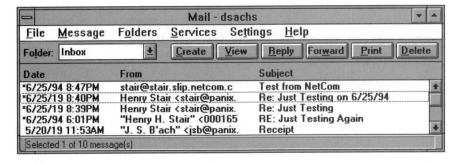

4. Click on **Message** and then click once on **Create**

A New Mail #1 window should appear. It should resemble the screen in Figure 4-9.

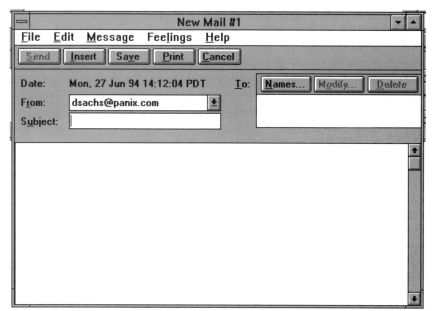

As you can see, some information has been already added for you. Here are some steps to follow for the rest of the message:

Figure 4-9
New Mail #1

a. Fill in the Subject: of your message. Since this is your first message, let's call it Just Practicing #1

b. Pressing **Tab** once will move your cursor to the **Names...** button.

Click once on **Names...**.

You will have to enter an address, if you wish to have your message sent. Since you are just practicing, enter your own Internet address. That way, you will not bother anyone else, and you can see if the message gets through all right.

c. Enter a practice message in the message area. If you would like to add some Feelings to your message, just click on **Feelings** and make your selection.

d. When you have finished adding your text, just click on **Send** and your message will be sent.

Heads Up!

So that you will be ready for the activities which follow, it might be a good idea to have three or four practice messages awaiting you in your Inbox. Follow the steps above and create a few more.

HANDS-ON Activity 3

RECEIVING MAIL WITH CHAMELEON SAMPLER

1. Open your Main Mail window. It should have a number of practice files in it by now and should resemble the one in Figure 4-10 (although you may not have 13 messages awaiting you).

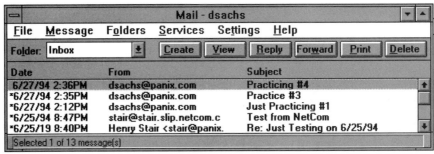

Figure 4-10
Inbox Folder

2. To read one of your messages, do the following:

   a. Click on the message you wish to view

   b. Click on **View**

Quite a few choices are available to you. Let's begin with the simplest.

3. Click on **Reply** and enter your response

   Important: You still have to tell Mail where you would like to send the reply. Be sure to enter an appropriate Internet address.

4. Once you have entered your text, click on **Message** and then on **Send** to send your message.

When you are viewing messages, two new buttons appear which should make your life much easier. You will be able to see the Next or Previous messages by clicking on the **Next** or **Prev** buttons.

Since they are context sensitive, you will not see a Next button if you are at the end of your messages (or if you have only one message), nor will you see a Prev button if you are just beginning to look at your messages (or if there is only one message).

SESSION SUMMARY

The Mail program that is included with Chameleon Sampler is quite powerful. We have spent time in this session exploring the concepts that you will need once you begin to use Mosaic. Obviously, there are quite a few other features of Mail which we have left for you to explore. Should you be interested in reading more about them, feel free to use the "Help" which is included in the program, or to purchase the complete Chameleon program from NetManage, Inc.

SESSION 5

Anonymous ftp

SESSION OVERVIEW

This session is extremely important. You will use Chameleon
Sampler's file transfer protocol (ftp) to obtain copies of compression and virus protection software. In order to install NCSA
Mosaic, you will have to have compression software. If you are
going to download binary files, you should have good virus protection software and use it regularly. By the end of this session,
you will be completely ready to download and install NCSA
Mosaic.

REVIEW OF ANONYMOUS FILE TRANSFER PROTOCOL
(FTP)

As you may be aware, one of the most exciting aspects of using
the Internet has to do with the process of transferring files from
around the world to your own computer using the *file transfer
protocol (ftp)*. File transfer protocol enables us to transfer ascii
and binary files from remote host computers to our own host
computer.

We will use Chameleon Sampler's ftp in the following activities
as we continue to get set to use NCSA Mosaic in the sessions to
come. Using Chameleon Sampler's ftp is a pleasurable and powerful way to experience anonymous ftp. It is a one-step process

to move files from the remote host to your own and the interface is a very friendly point-and-click Windows one.

BINARY VERSUS ASCII FILES

As you are probably aware, *ASCII files* are the plain *raw text* that can be generated by many word processors (or spreadsheets). The files are stripped of all of the code that might be particular to a given word processor, such as Word Perfect® or Microsoft Word®, and are, instead, just the text that forms those files. In addition, since you are retrieving "just text," you do not usually need to be concerned about introducing viruses to your computer or network.

Binary files, or *graphics files* as they are also known, are all of the other files that are out there. Typically, binary files are software programs, pictures, sounds, images, or video clips.

Downloading binary files may enable you to have a new software program, or a new set of graphics files. Potentially problematic, however, is the fact that you also run the risk of bringing an unintended virus to your own computer or computer network. We will return to that point later in this session.

*HANDS-ON
Activity 1*

USING FTP TO GET AN ASCII FILE

This first activity will provide you with an opportunity to become familiar with the file transfer protocol capabilities of Chameleon Sampler as we download a text file. In addition, during this activity you will obtain a current copy of Scott Yanoff's *Internet Services List*. This wonderful Internet resource should be on your must have list; it is updated every two weeks (on the first and the fifteenth of each month) and is one of the best ways of keeping current about Internet resources. It is also a perfect illustration of how to use the Chameleon Sampler to enable us to get, save, and print a text file using anonymous ftp.

The ftp application provided by Chameleon Sampler is used to provide file transfer services across a wide variety of systems through the use of file transfer protocol (ftp). You will be pleased to see that the directory structure of the remote host (the one to which you are going for files) will be displayed just as local files and directories are displayed in Windows. You can use your usual point and click techniques to browse through directories, as well as to transfer files. Let's get started!

Before we actually use ftp, let's take a few moments to configure it to our liking, as well as become more familiar with its various options.

1. Open the Chameleon Sampler window

2. Double-click on **FTP**

You will see the Chameleon Sampler FTP window shown in Figure 5-1.

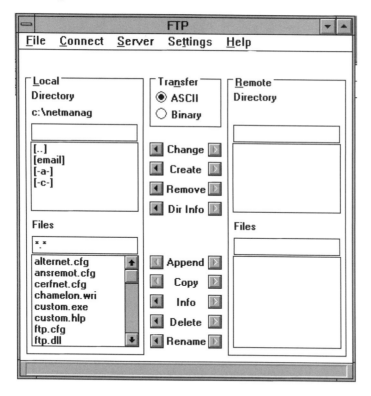

Figure 5-1
FTP Window

You will be transferring quite a few files from other computers to your own. It is probably wise to have a special directory into which these files will be transferred. We would advise that you create one now called INCOMING. If you do this, you will always know where to look for the files that you download, and you will protect other files from being overwritten. Here is how to do so:

a. Move your cursor to the Local Directory box. Notice that the default directory is **c:netmanag**

Just below that, type `c:\incoming`

b. Click once on the **left arrow** next to **Create**

c. Click once on the **left arrow** next to **Change**

d. Your local directory should be **c:\incoming**

e. Click on **File** and then **Save**

---

3. Click on **Settings** and then choose **Connection Profile...**

Your screen should look like the one in Figure 5-2.

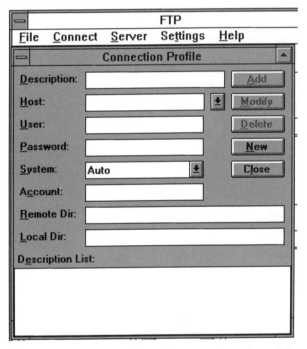

Figure 5-2
Connection Profile

4. We will enter some information that will enable us to retrieve Scott Yanoff's Internet Services file—and preserve our ability to do so easily and quickly whenever we again wish to have a current copy. Here is how to do it:

a. In the Description box, enter something which will remind you about this ftp archive and this particular set of files; for example,
`Yanoff/U. of Wisconsin`

b. Tab to the Host box and enter the correct, fully qualified domain name for the remote host computer. For the Yanoff List, we will need to enter `csd4.csd.uwm.edu`

c. Tab to the User box and enter the name that is to be entered when the remote host prompts for a user name. Since we are using anonymous ftp as the protocol, we must enter the word `anonymous`

d. Tab to the Password box and enter the correct password. Assuming that you do not have a password on the University of Wisconsin host, you should follow Internet protocol and enter your fully qualified E-mail address. For example, I would enter `dsachs@panix.com`

Note: When you do this, your password will *not* appear in the Password box, so be sure to type it correctly.

e. Tab to the System box and select **Auto**

f. Move your cursor to the Local Dir: box, and type in the drive and pathname for where you would like to have your ftp files saved, for example, `c:\incoming`

g. Finally, you should click on the **Add button**, which will cause the Description to be added to the Description List, and the configuration information to be added to your Chameleon Sampler program.

If you have other favorite ftp locations, you should feel free to add them at this time. Otherwise, you can return to this set of operations at any time to add additional ftp locations.

5. When you are done adding information about ftp hosts, click on **Close**

6. Then, click on **File** and then **Save**

7. Finally, click on **File** and then **Exit** which should return you to the main Chameleon Sampler window.

Now, using the information that was just added, we can use the Chameleon Sampler to download the Yanoff Internet Services file.

Hands-on Mosaic

Important: If you are not already online with your service provider, double-click on the **Custom Icon**, and then click on **Connect**

Minimize the Custom window into an icon, by clicking on the **down arrow** in the upper-right-hand corner of your screen.

Then, double-click on the **FTP Icon**

8. Click on **Connect**

    The Connect window should appear and should resemble the one in Figure 5-3.

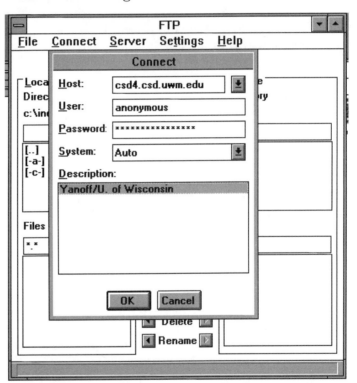

Figure 5-3
Connect University of Wisconsin

9. Slide your cursor down to the Description: box and click on **Yanoff/U of Wisconsin**. Instantly, all of the necessary information appears in the upper boxes on your screen.

    Since that is the remote host to which we wish to connect, click on **OK**

    Notice how quickly and efficiently you are connected to the host computer at University of Wisconsin.

10. The first thing you will see, in the Remote Directory box, is a slash (/) which indicates that you are at the root directory. Since we wish to change to the pub subdirectory, double-click on **/pub**

11. Move your cursor down to the Remote Files box in the lower-right-hand corner of your screen. By clicking on the **down arrow** in the scroll bar, you will be able to see a listing of the files in the pub directory.

Stop when you come to one called inet.services.txt and click once on it. Your screen should resemble the one in Figure 5-4.

Figure 5-4
Downloading
inet.services.txt

We would, in effect, like to copy this file, from the *remote* host computer (with the file in the right-hand Files box) to our own local host computer (with the list of files in the left-hand Files box).

12. Double-click on the **left-hand copy** button and watch the magic!

Note: Chameleon Sampler automatically converts the name into one which is more usable by your computer. In our case, the file was automatically named !inet.txt

If you would like to give this file another name, do the following:
  a. Highlight the name of the file
  b. Click on the **left-hand Rename button**
  c. Type in the new name on the To: line in the Rename box, and then click on **Yes** when you have finished.

13. If you wish to download any other files from the University of Wisconsin, you may do so now.

Otherwise, click on **Disconnect** to end this ftp session now.

Note: To read this file, just use your favorite word processor. It is a text file and should be immediately accessible. You may have to change the margins to one-half inch on each side.

COMPRESSED FILES

Binary files tend to be large. For example, it is not uncommon to find binary files that are 600,000 bytes or larger. It does not take very long to transfer files of this size from one host computer to another. However, as you might imagine, there are costs affiliated with files of this size.

All of the resources being used in this process cost time and money. There is a cost affiliated with your use of the remote host computer, as well as the cost affiliated with using your local host computer. Finally, there is a cost affiliated with using your own time. Consequently, people have developed methods that are intended to minimize these costs. This work has focused on compressing files, so that they will be much smaller than they originally were.

The advantages are many. First of all, the file may be stored in a much smaller space on its resident host computer. Second, the file may be transferred from one host computer to another in much less time. Finally, the file may be saved in much less space than would normally be required. All of these, when added together, represent sizable savings of time and money for all concerned.

WHERE DOES COMPRESSION TAKE PLACE? _____

One location where compression may take place is on a remote computer. The person who has developed the program may wish to reduce its size before uploading it to a host computer, or before putting it on disks for distribution, and uses a file compression program to do so. Once you have retrieved such a file, you will need to have in your possession the compression program that can be used to uncompress the file. For example, if the program was *zipped* after it was created, it will need to be *unzipped* once it has been retrieved.

It is also possible that you may wish to compress files on your own computer in an attempt to conserve storage space. Once you begin to download large graphics and audio files using Mosaic, you will quickly discover the value of being able to do this!

USING FTP TO LEARN ABOUT COMPRESSION

**HANDS-ON
Activity 2**

If the topic of compression is new to you, it is possible to become somewhat overwhelmed by it all. So, before we learn about all of the possible methods of compression that can be used, let's just focus on a few of them. There are two parts to the conversation:

1. The first part has to do with the file extensions that are commonly used by those who have compressed files.

2. The second part has to do with the programs that are used to compress and uncompress software programs.

Typical File Extensions

In the DOS environment, you have probably seen file extensions such as the ones in Table 5-1.

Table 5-1

File Extension	ASCII or binary	File Type
com	binary	executable file
doc	ASCII	text file
exe	binary	executable file
ps	ASCII	to be printed on a PostScript printer
txt	ASCII	text file
wp	binary	WordPerfect file

In this context, we are going to focus on files with some new file extensions. Some (of the many) are presented in Table 5-2.

Table 5-2

File Extension	ASCII or binary	Compression Program Required
gif	binary	graphics file
tif	binary	graphics file
zip	binary	PKZIP/PKUNZIP

Notice, first of all, that these new files are all binary files. This means that when we are using ftp, we must be sure to indicate that we are getting and transferring binary, not ASCII files. In addition, you should notice that some of these programs require compression programs to be used before you will be able to have a fully functional program on your personal computer.

Not only do you need to know about file extensions and the compression program that might be required, but you will also need to know where such files are located should you require them. Fortunately, David Lemson has done a particularly good job of providing such information. While the Lemson file can be, at least initially, a bit intimidating, our second activity of this session will be to retrieve this text file. Then, we will begin to walk you through it, so that you will have a better sense of what you need, where to find it, and how to get it.

In this second activity, we will go to the source about compression. The file we are seeking is, cleverly enough, called *compression*. Here is how to get it:

1. Open your **Chameleon Sampler Icon**. Double-click on **Custom** and click on **Connect** so that you are connected to your service provider.

2. Minimize the Custom window to an icon by clicking on the **down arrow** in the upper-right-hand corner.

3. Double-click on **FTP**

During this session, we are going to log in to several host computers. You can either enter the specific information for each host computer when it is necessary to do so, or you can do so all at once. We have chosen to do so all at once, in the information provided below.

Heads Up!

---

4. Before getting the actual compression file, we should add several host computers to our list of ftp resources. To do this, first click on **Settings** and then click on **Connection Profile...**

5. Click on **New**. Next, type the following:

    Description: Washington University

    Host: wuarchive.wustl.edu

    User: anonymous

    Password: This should be your actual fully qualified domain name, such as dsachs@panix.com

    System: Auto

    Local Dir: c:\incoming

    When you have finished typing this information, review it, and, if it is correct, click on **Add**. If it is not correct, just retype it.

6. Now, let's add another host. First, click on **New**. Then, type the following:

    Description: University of Illinois

    Host: ftp.cso.uiuc.edu

    User: anonymous

    Password: This should be your fully qualified domain name, such as dsachs@panix.com

System: `Auto`

Local Dir: `c:\incoming`

When you have finished typing, review the information. If it is correct, click on **Add**. If it is not correct, just retype it.

7. Finally, let's add one more host. First, click on **New**. Then, type the following:

Description: `Oakland`

Host: `oak.oakland.edu`

User: `anonymous`

Password: This should be your fully qualified domain name, such as `dsachs@panix.com`

System: `Auto`

Local Dir: `c:\incoming`

Review the information you have entered. If it is correct, click on **Add**

8. Now, we are ready to get the compression file. First, **close** your Connection Profile window.

Then, click on **Connect**

Once the Connect window is open, highlight `University of Illinois`

Then, click on **OK**

9. Slide your cursor to the **down arrow** in the scroll bar in the Remote Directory (upper-right-hand) part of your screen.

Click on the **down arrow** until the doc (document) sub-directory appears.

Double-click on the **doc** subdirectory to make it active.

10. Once the doc subdirectory is active, click on the **down arrow** in the Remote Directory part of your screen, until you see a listing for the sub-subdirectory called pcnet

Double-click on **pcnet** so that the listing of files in this sub-subdirectory may be seen. Your screen should resemble the one in Figure 5-5.

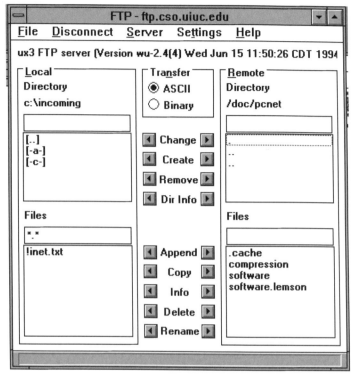

Figure 5-5
Downloading
Compression

11. You should see the file called compression which is maintained by David Lemson.

Click once on **compression** to make it active.

Then click once on the **left-hand Copy arrow** to copy the file from the remote host computer to your local host computer.

The file will be copied into your subdirectory, c:\incoming. Chameleon Sampler automatically renamed the file !compres

Once the file has been transferred to your computer, click on **Disconnect** to end the ftp connection.

Note: You can pull this file into your favorite word processor to see what it looks like. Be sure to set the margins so that 80 columns can be printed by your printer.

As you can tell from David Lemson's complete list, the number of file compression techniques is enormous. For the most part, you will not need to know about all of the compression techniques that exist, nor will you need to use them all.

However, there is one file compression technique known as PKZIP® that appears frequently when you are looking for software. You should certainly have the software on hand to let you utilize programs that have been compressed by this technique. And, you should certainly know where to go to find additional compression software should you ever need to have it.

Heads Up!

There is quite a bit of software available on the Internet. Some of it is known as *freeware*. This means that the people who developed it are purposely providing you with the software for free.

There is other software that is more properly thought of as shareware. The first instance of that is the Chameleon Sampler software that has been provided with *Hands-On Mosaic*. As you might imagine, the people at NetManage, Inc. are hopeful that you will try their software, like their software, and then decide to upgrade your program to the full version, for which there will be a fee paid to them. Several of the programs that we are about to acquire fall into this latter category.

In each case, we will make you aware of where it is possible to purchase the full version of the software, with the complete documentation and files that may be missing from the shareware version. We would urge you to purchase the full version, should the software have value to you.

A much used file compression technique is known as *PKZIP*, and the files that are compressed this way typically have an extension of .ZIP. This program was developed by a company called PKWARE, Inc. To purchase the latest complete version of the software with all of the documentation, you may contact:

PKWARE, Inc.
The Data Compression Experts
9025 N. Deerwood Drive
Brown Deer, WI 53223

For us to use the shareware version of PKZIP, we will have to first have a copy of pkz204g.exe. This file can be found (using Lemson's compression list) at location B, that is identified in the "Where to Get Them" section of Lemson's compression list as wuarchive.wustl.edu.

Note: Although we have been told to look elsewhere, you should be aware that this program (and many more) may be found at the same host computer (ftp.cso.uiuc.edu) where we retrieved David Lemson's compression file. In fact, while writing about this, when we first tried to get a copy of pkz204g.exe, we were told that wuarchive.wustl.edu was "busy"—so, we went, instead, to ftp.cso.uiuc.edu!

USING FTP TO GET A COPY OF PKZ204G.EXE

HANDS-ON
Activity 3

Many files on the Internet have been compressed using PKZIP, and you would be unable to use them if you were not able to *unzip* them once you had retrieved them. We will learn how to unzip files shortly. In this following activity we will download a copy of pkz204g.exe.

Interestingly, at the time that we were writing this, two things occurred. First, as mentioned above, we were unable to log in to wuarchive.wustl.edu—all 255 of the anonymous ftp slots were taken! So, we decided to return to ftp.cso.uiuc.edu—which was fine, except that the response time was amazingly slow.

This is where David Lemson's compression list again proves to be a wonderful resource. In the "Where to Get Them" section of the compression list, resource H indicates that "oak.oakland.edu" is what is known as a *primary mirror* and "wuarchive" is a *secondary mirror.* This means that software that is posted in one location is also automatically posted in other locations—known as *mirror* sites. Some of them, such as oak.oakland.edu, are here within the United States; others are located around the world. In this activity, we will use the resources at oak.oakland.edu so that we can locate the file pkz204g.exe. Here is how to do that:

1. With Chameleon Sampler active, use the **Custom Icon** to log in to your service provider. Then, minimize the Custom window to an icon by clicking on the **down arrow** in the upper-right-hand part of the window.

2. Double-click on the **FTP Icon**

    Important: Since we are about to transfer a software program (a binary file), it is imperative that you change the Transfer mode from ASCII to Binary. Click once on the **Binary button** to do this.

3. Click on **Connect** and highlight the name **Oakland** which is found in the Description box. Your screen should resemble the one in Figure 5-6.

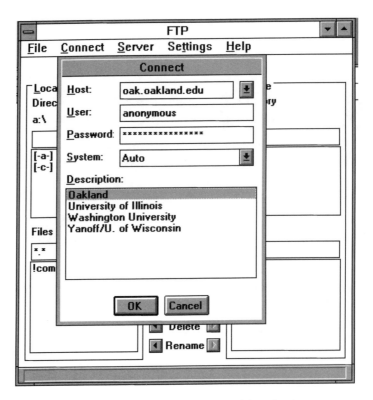

Figure 5-6
Connect Oakland

4. Click on **OK** to connect to oak.oakland.edu

5. Click on the **down-arrow** in the Remote Directory box to move the names of the files until you come to the one called pub

6. Double-click on **pub** so that you can see the subdirectories that it contains. Since we are looking for a file that can be used in an MS-DOS environment, it seems logical to change to that subdirectory. Double-click on **msdos**

7. Click on the **down-arrow** in the Remote Directory box, until you come to the sub-subdirectory called zip

8. Double-click on **zip** so that you can change to that sub-subdirectory.

    Once you have done so, click on the **down-arrow** in the Remote Files box until the file called pkz204g.exe is visible. Your screen should resemble the one in Figure 5-7.

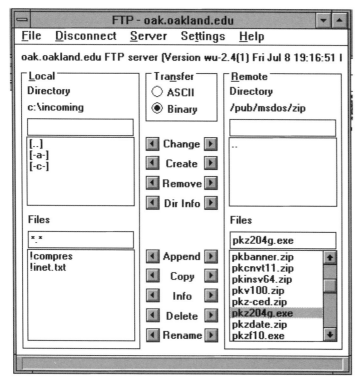

Figure 5-7
Locatiing pkz204g.exe

Important: Be sure that you are prepared to transfer a binary file.

9.   Once you are ready to download the pkz204g.exe file, just click on the **left-hand arrow** for **Copy** and watch the magic!

If you have done this correctly, you should see a screen that resembles the one in Figure 5-8.

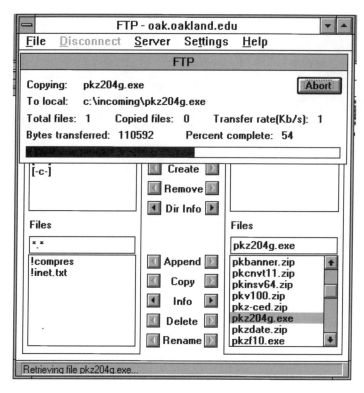

Figure 5-8
Downloadiing
pkz204g.exe

10. Once the file has been successfully transferred to your computer, be sure to disconnect from oak.oakland.edu, as well as from your Internet service provider.

HANDS-ON
Activity 4

GETTING PKZ204G.EXE READY TO USE

First, you should be aware that pkz204g.exe is what is known as an *executable* file. That is, it may be **executed** (run) by just typing the name of the file. For example, if you wish to run pkz204g.exe, you just have to type `pkz204g`—*But please wait a minute before doing that!*

In addition to being an executable file, pkz204g.exe is also, in effect, a compressed version of the actual files which you will be using. That is, this one file contains quite a few additional files, which will be (according to the folks who developed pkz204g.exe) *inflated* as soon as we issue the magic command.

With that in mind, it would probably be good if you were to copy this file to its own subdirectory on your hard disk, so that there is lots of space for these new files once they have been inflated. We would suggest that you copy the pkz204g.exe file in a new subdirectory called c:\pkware

Here is how to do this:

    a.   Make a new subdirectory on your hard drive. At the c: prompt, type `md pkware`

    b.   Copy the file from incoming to the new subdirectory. Type
        `copy c:\incoming\pkz204g.exe c:\pkware`

Once you have copied pkz204g.exe into this subdirectory, it is quite simple to activate it. Assuming that you have pkz204g.exe in its own subdirectory called c:\pkware, then do the following:

    1.   Change to the subdirectory cd pkware

    2.   Type `pkz204g`

Notice that pkz204g has inflated 16 files, which will occupy 370,000 bytes of additional space (!) in addition to the 202,000 bytes that were occupied by the original pkz204g program.

Also, notice that one of your files (manual.doc) is a complete manual. However, you should be warned that at 202,252 bytes, this file will print out approximately 100 pages of text.

Heads Up!

Should this be too overwhelming for you, the company that sells PKZIP will be delighted to sell you a complete manual and the latest version of the software. Information about that option is included in the file ORDER.DOC—you may look at that file on your screen by typing `type order.doc|more`

This will enable you to read the information one screen at a time. Should you wish to print out the information, just type `print c:\pkware\order.doc` and the file will be sent to your printer.

We will not do any more with this set of files at this time (although we will use them shortly). However, while you have them in front of you, you should notice that two of the files that have been inflated are called PKZIP.EXE and PKUNZIP.EXE. For our purposes, these are the two important files we were seeking. In addition, since they are both executable files, they are both ready to run by just typing their names. We will return to this momentarily.

**HANDS-ON
Activity 5**

USING FTP TO GET VIRUS PROTECTION SOFTWARE

If you have been using anonymous ftp for the transfer of ASCII files, then you should not have had to worry too much about the transfer of viruses to your personal computer or to your network. However, as soon as you begin to transfer new binary programs to your computer, you should begin to think carefully about protecting your computer and its software from harmful viruses that might harm some or all of your programs. To do that, you would be well advised to have a virus protection program installed on your computer and to use it regularly.

There are quite a few commercial programs available. In addition, there is a well-known shareware program, called *SCAN®*, developed by McAfee Associates, which is available to us on the Internet.

If you wish to order the latest commercial version of the software, you can order it from

> McAfee Associates
> 2710 Walsh Avenue
> Santa Clara, CA 95051
> (408) 988-3832

Here is how to get the shareware version of SCAN and how to use it.

1. Double-click on the **Custom Icon** and then click on **Connect** so that you are connected to your service provider.

2. Minimize the Custom window into an icon by clicking on the **down arrow** in the top-right-hand side of your Custom window.

3. Double-click on the **FTP Icon**

4. Review the FTP screen and be sure that Transfer is set to **Binary**

5. Click on **Connect** and select **oak.oakland.edu** as the host

6. Click on the **down-arrow button** in the Remote Directory box, until you find the subdirectory pub

Next, double-click on **pub** so that you can see which directories it contains.

7.   Double-click on the sub-subdirectory **msdos** to make it active

8.   Click on the **down-arrow button** in the Remote Directory box, until you find the sub-sub-subdirectory named virus

Double-click on **virus** to make it active

9.   Click on the **down-arrow button** in the Remote Files box to see the files that are contained in the virus sub-sub-subdirectory.

10.   You will notice that one of the files is named scn-xxx.zip (when we did this, it was called scn-202.zip). This is the SCAN file that you would like to retrieve.

Note: This file is a binary file, that has (most likely) been compressed using the PKZIP/PKUNZIP compression program that we referred to and retrieved earlier. First, we will retrieve scn-202.zip; then we will use PKUNZIP to convert it into a usable program.

11.   You will need to copy this program from the remote host (oak.oakland.edu) to your computer.

We will copy this file into the subdirectory on drive c: called incoming.

Click once on **scn-202.zip** to make it active. Once you have done so, just click on the **left-hand Copy button** and the file will be copied.

12.   Once the file has been transferred, be sure to leave the oak.oakland.edu host by clicking on **Disconnect**. Then click on **Disconnect** again when it appears in the Disconnect window.

13.   Next, you should close the FTP window.

14.   Once the file has been successfully transferred to your personal computer, you may disconnect from your service provider and exit from the Chameleon Sampler. Now we just need to get the SCAN program ready for use!

USING PKUNZIP TO GET SCN-202.ZIP READY TO USE

1. We will assume that you have followed all of the directions in Activity Four and that all of your PKZIP and PKUNZIP files are on your hard drive, in a subdirectory called pkware.

2. Next, you should put the SCAN program into its own directory. At the `c:` prompt, type `md scan`

3. Assuming that the scn-202.zip file is on drive C in the subdirectory incoming, type
   `copy c:\incoming\scn-202.zip c:\scan` and press **ENTER**

4. In addition to the scn-202.zip file, we would like to also have a copy of PKUNZIP.EXE in that same directory. To copy PKUNZIP.EXE from the pkware subdirectory to the SCAN subdirectory type
   `copy c:\pkware\pkunzip.exe c:\scan`
   Once you press **ENTER**, the file will be copied.

5. Change to the SCAN directory by typing `cd scan`

6. Once you are in the SCAN directory, just type
   `pkunzip scn-202.zip` and press **ENTER**

   Watch the magic! All of the files that have been compressed will be uncompressed, and you should wind up with approximately 20 files in your SCAN directory (the exact number will depend upon the version of the program that you are unzipping).

   To use the SCAN program to check your computer for viruses is remarkably simple.

7. At the `c:` prompt, change to the SCAN directory (`cd scan`) and then type the word `scan` followed by the name of the drive you wish to check.

   For example, type `scan c:` and the program will do the rest.

SESSION SUMMARY

In this session, we have advanced our knowledge of anonymous ftp techniques and have added some new software to our Internet Toolbox in the process.

If you have been following along, you have

1. Used anonymous ftp to retrieve two text files: Yanoff's Internet Services List and David Lemson's compression file

2. Learned about three well-known sites for ftp files:

    wuarchive.wustl.edu

    ftp.cso.uiuc.edu

    oak.oakland.edu

3. Used anonymous ftp to retrieve two binary files:

    pkz204g.exe and scn-202.zip

4. Inflated both software programs so that we now have fully functioning copies of both PKUNZIP and SCAN

5. Used PKUNZIP to unzip scn-202.zip into its actual program files

6. Used SCAN to check your hard disk for viruses

We are now extremely close to being able to use NCSA Mosaic. As will become obvious in the next session, without the skills you have just learned in this session (and the software you have just acquired), you would not be able to proceed. Let's take a short break, and then we will return to Session Six, in which you will get a copy of NCSA Mosaic and install it on your personal computer.

SESSION 6

Mosaic on Your PC

SESSION OVERVIEW

In this session, we will introduce the *World-Wide Web*, also called *WWW*, and show you how to access this web of information. WWW is a set of conventions or protocols (remember them?) for anyone on the global Internet wishing to offer information. Most of these information methods, including the Web, have been around for quite a while but were a bit difficult for beginners to use.

The ease-of-use problem has kept many away from Internet information because of the complexity of access. Recently, however, some people have put their energies into making access easier. These access tools don't change the information; they just make it easier for the rest of us to find and retrieve it. As such, these tools are referred to as *information browsers*. One browser that has caught everyone's fancy is called Mosaic. The original Mosaic was developed at the National Center for Supercomputer Applications (NCSA) at the University of Illinois at Urbana-Champaign.

Mosaic is the information browser we will introduce here. As you will see in the next several sessions, Mosaic is not limited to the Web. The Web, however, is its starting point.

Background Information:
World-Wide Web (WWW) and Mosaic_____

According to Kevin Hughes (more about him in a moment),

> The World-Wide Web has been officially described as a "wide-area hypermedia information initiative aiming to give access to a large universe of documents." What the World-Wide Web (WWW, W3) project has done, is to provide users on computer networks with a consistent means to access a variety of media in a simplified fashion. Using a popular software interface to the Web called Mosaic, the Web project has changed the way people view and create information—it has created the first true global hypermedia network.

> The operation of the Web relies mainly on hypertext as its means of interacting with users. Hypertext is basically the same as regular text—it can be stored, read, searched, or edited—with an important exception: hypertext contains connections within the text to other documents.[1]

In other words, if you were reading a hypertext document about Mosaic and you came across the name **Kevin Hughes**, you might be able to point and click on the name Kevin Hughes, and you would be connected instantly to a document that would tell you more about him. If you were interested in knowing more about Mosaic, if a *hyperlink* were in place, you would be able to click on the word Mosaic and be connected to additional hypertext that would tell you more about Mosaic.

In addition to hypertext, there is also *hypermedia*. Again, according to Kevin Hughes:

> Hypermedia is hypertext with a difference—hypermedia documents contain links not only to other pieces of text, but also to other forms of media—sounds, images, and movies. Images themselves can be selected to link to sounds or documents. Hypermedia simply combines hypertext and multimedia.

Here are some simple examples of hypermedia:

1. *Entering the World-Wide Web: A Guide to Cyberspace Version 6.1*; Kevin Hughes/eit/Webguide, from ftp.eit.com; 1994

1. You are reading a book which contains some French passages. You select the French passage, and then are able to hear it spoken by a native French person.

2. You are planning a trip to Palo Alto. You browse through the information they have compiled, and then click on the hotels which are of interest to you. Instantly, you can see a picture of the hotel, and you are able to make a reservation.

Credit for the creation of the World-Wide Web is given to Tim Berners-Lee of the European Particle Physics Laboratory (which is also known as CERN, a collective of European high-energy physics researchers). The project's original intent was to facilitate research and ideas throughout the organization. The Web's popularity has been enormous, and its use has been explosive since its initial availability at the end of 1990.

TRYING OUT THE WORLD-WIDE WEB

*HANDS-ON
Activity 1*

Hypertext and hypermedia are wonderfully appealing concepts. In order to use them, it is necessary to have what is known as a browser, which is a program for reading hypertext. There are line-oriented browsers and window-oriented browsers. We will begin with the simplest one, which is the line-oriented, text-only browser. To do this, try the following:

1. First, use Custom to log in to your Internet service provider.

2. Double-click on **Telnet**

3. At the main Telnet window, click on **Connect**

4. When the Connect To window appears, enter the following information:

   a. Host Name: `info.cern.ch`

b. Port: 23

c. Emulate: VT100

Click on **OK**

The screen that appears should resemble the one in Figure 6-1.

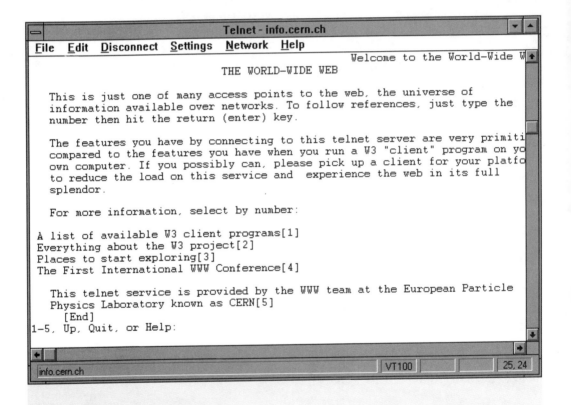

Figure 6-1
Telnet-info.cern.ch

5. On the screen that is visible, there are five choices, each one of which has a number inside a set of brackets. Typing one of those numbers and then pressing **Enter** will take you to the next screen. We have chosen to enter the number 1

6. After pressing **<RETURN>** twice (this may differ for you), we come to the screen in Figure 6-2.

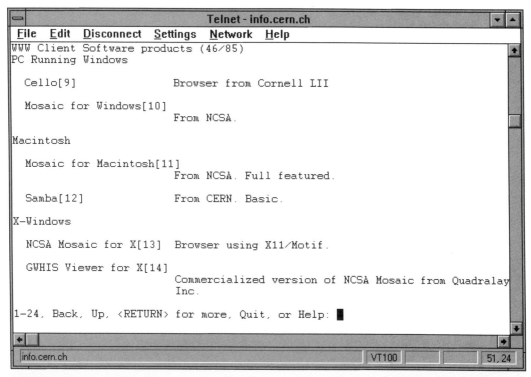

```
═                         Telnet - info.cern.ch                    ▼ ▲
 File   Edit   Disconnect   Settings   Network   Help
WWW Client Software products (46/85)                                    ▲
PC Running Windows

  Cello[9]                   Browser from Cornell LII

  Mosaic for Windows[10]
                             From NCSA.

Macintosh

  Mosaic for Macintosh[11]
                             From NCSA. Full featured.

  Samba[12]                  From CERN. Basic.

X-Windows

  NCSA Mosaic for X[13]   Browser using X11/Motif.

  GWHIS Viewer for X[14]
                           Commercialized version of NCSA Mosaic from Quadralay
                           Inc.

1-24, Back, Up, <RETURN> for more, Quit, or Help: █
                                                                         ▼
 ◄                                                                    ►
 info.cern.ch                                     VT100            51, 24
```

Figure 6-2
WWW Client Software
Products

7. Since we are particularly interested in the information
which is labeled: Mosaic for Windows[10] From NCSA,
we will enter the number 10 and then press **Enter**

When we do so, we see the screen in Figure 6-3.

```
─                    Telnet - info.cern.ch                    ▼  ▲
 File   Edit   Disconnect   Settings   Network   Help
                                        Status -- MosaicForWindo ▲
                  NCSA MOSAIC FOR WINDOWS

   This is a full-function WWW browser for Microsoft windows.

  Authors:              Jon Mittelhauser Chris Wilson, NCSA[1] , UIUC, USA.

  Platforms:            IBM/PC  (386 up) with MS-DOS and Microsoft Windows.
                        (See also: version for X[2] )

  Status:               Beta release.  See developer's documentation.

  Availability          Anonymous FTP from ftp.NCSA.uiuc.edu in PC/Mosaic[3]

  More details:         Developer's documentation[4]

                                                          Tim BL[


     [End]


1-5, Back, Up, Quit, or Help: █                                      ↓
 ←                                                                →
 info.cern.ch                                 VT100            31, 24
```

Figure 6-3
NCSA Mosaic from
CERN

8. Typing 3 and then pressing **Enter** provides us with the information in Figure 6-4.

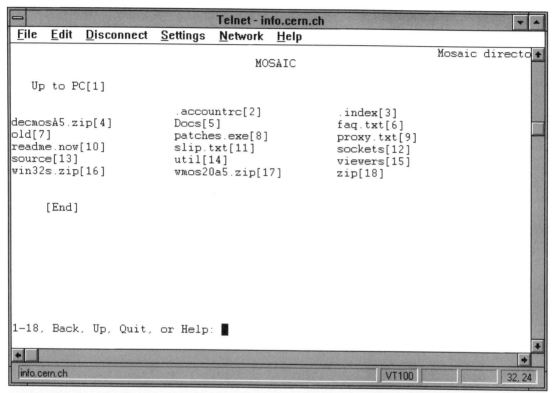

```
┌─────────────────────────────────────────────────────────────────────┐
│  ─                      Telnet - info.cern.ch                    ▼  ▲ │
├─────────────────────────────────────────────────────────────────────┤
│  File   Edit   Disconnect   Settings   Network   Help                 │
├─────────────────────────────────────────────────────────────────────┤
│                                                      Mosaic directo ▲ │
│                              MOSAIC                                    │
│                                                                        │
│     Up to PC[1]                                                        │
│                                                                        │
│                          .accountrc[2]            .index[3]           │
│  decmosA5.zip[4]         Docs[5]                   faq.txt[6]          │
│  old[7]                  patches.exe[8]            proxy.txt[9]        │
│  readme.now[10]          slip.txt[11]              sockets[12]         │
│  source[13]              util[14]                  viewers[15]         │
│  win32s.zip[16]          wmos20a5.zip[17]          zip[18]             │
│                                                                        │
│                                                                        │
│       [End]                                                            │
│                                                                        │
│                                                                        │
│                                                                        │
│                                                                        │
│                                                                        │
│                                                                        │
│  1-18, Back, Up, Quit, or Help: █                                   ▼  │
│  ◄ │                                                              │  ► │
├─────────────────────────────────────────────────────────────────────┤
│  info.cern.ch                                 VT100          32, 24    │
└─────────────────────────────────────────────────────────────────────┘
```

We will end our first activity here. The goal was to give you a brief feel for the way that hypertext functions. Should you be interested in pursuing your hypertext connections, feel free to do so. Otherwise, disconnect from info.cern.ch and return to your Chameleon Sampler main window.

Figure 6-4
Mosaic directory

GETTING A COPY OF "ENTERING THE WORLD-WIDE WEB: A GUIDE TO CYBERSPACE" BY KEVIN HUGHES

There is lots of good information about Mosaic available. Perhaps the best (and most accessible) article is one written by Kevin Hughes of Enterprise Integration Technologies. The 35-page article (as of this writing) is available in both PostScript and text (ASCII) formats. Here is how to get either or both of them:

1. Double-click on **FTP**

2. Click once on **Settings**

3. Then click on **Connection Profile...**

4. Once the Connect Profile window is open, click on the **New button**

5. Then, enter the following information:

   a. Description: `Kevin Hughes/eit/Webguide`

   b. Host: `ftp.eit.com`

   c. User: `anonymous`

   d. System: `Auto`

   e. Local Dir: `c:\incoming`

6. Once you have entered all of the above information, click on **Add** so that this information is added to your list of ftp sites.

7. Then, click on **Close**

8. Now, click once on **Connect** so that the Connect window appears

9. Click once on **Kevin Hughes**, and so forth, and then click on **OK**

10. In the Remote Directory box, double-click on the subdirectory called **pub**

11. Click on the **down arrow** in the Remote Directory box, until you come to the following listing of sub-subdirectories:

    web.guide

    web.icons

web.primer

web.software

We are interested in the web.guide subdirectory, but you may wish to return here later for some other interesting information.

12. Double-click on **web.guide**

At the time that we did this, the screen looked like the one in Figure 6-5 and the most current version was called guide.61

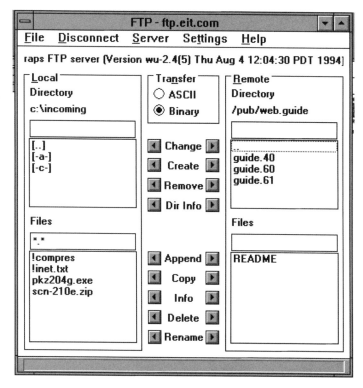

Figure 6-5
web.guide Window

13. Double-click on **guide.61** (or whichever seems to be the latest version)

In the Remote Files box, you should see a listing of several different versions of guide.61—including the Post-Script version (guide.61.ps) and the text version (guide.61.txt).

Click on the version you would like to have. If you have the ability to print or view PostScript files, choose the .ps version. If you do not, or are not sure, choose the .txt version.

14. Then, click on the **left Copy** button to have the file copied onto your local directory.

Note: When we transferred the file, it was renamed !guide.txt. Use your favorite word processor to read and print this file. It is filled with an enormous amount of very interesting information.

15. Once your files have been copied, click once on **Disconnect** and again on **Disconnect** in the Disconnect window.

WHY IS EVERYONE SO EXCITED?

The activity you just used to retrieve Kevin Hughes' document, was a bit complex. Not only did you need to know how to follow quite a few steps, but, in addition, you needed to look up the ftp address and directory names. Wouldn't it be lovely if all you had to do was look at a name and point and click? This is what Mosaic is all about, and this is why everyone who sees it is so excited.

The excitement is spreading too fast to measure, but here are several indications:

1. In 1993, few commercial companies were interested in the Internet. In 1994, largely due to Mosaic, many companies, ranging from the large ones such as Apple, DEC, HP and IBM, to small ones such as the local hardware store or florist, all wanted to have home pages on the World-Wide Web. (We'll get to home pages shortly.)

2. Commercial Internet organizations such as CommerceNet and MecklerWeb are now online using Mosaic.

3. On August 12, 1994, a *New York Times* article entitled "Attention Shoppers: The Internet Is Open" discussed the success of a company called the Net Market Company. Using X-Mosaic and a data encryption program called PGP, they are able to permit shopping to occur securely on the Internet.

In particular, Mosaic's ability to display both attractive text and graphics as well as sound has generated lively interest. Also, companies have begun to compete over the appearance of their company's home page. Every company CEO wants his or her picture and voice to be included on their company's home page as a welcome. So what's a home page?

When you use Mosaic to go somewhere, the first thing you usually see is what is known as the *home page*. This home page is much like the cover of a university's or company's marketing brochure. Here is where an organization wants to catch your attention. A home page is also a very low-cost form of advertising. All a company has to do is to keep a computer running in case someone comes along via the Internet.

After we get Mosaic up and running with you, we will investigate many of these home pages and show you how to find more.

WHERE TO FIND MOSAIC

The National Center for Supercomputing Applications (NCSA) has been in the forefront of offering Mosaic by ftp. However, they are often swamped with requests and you may have trouble getting in. For this reason, we have listed a number of alternate places where Mosaic is kept. In a moment, we will list them.

In the following activity, we will download version wmos1_0.zip of Mosaic (we will call this Mosaic 1.0). Mosaic 1.0 is a relatively stable version and requires only the software that you presently have on hand and the techniques that we have taught you so far.

In later sessions, we will download more current (and somewhat less stable) versions of Mosaic. For the most recent 32-bit version of NCSA Mosaic, you will need some additional software. We will show you how to download that, also.

Heads Up!

We are going to download a file called wmos1_0.zip from NCSA. If you would like to try to retrieve the Mosaic program from NCSA, that is certainly a good place to look. However, due to NCSA's popularity, you might have to be quite persistent before you are successful. Therefore, we will suggest alternate ftp locations first.

Alternate Mosaic Sources

Below is a list of alternate ftp sites where you might try to download Mosaic. Notice that several are located outside of North America.

The list below is the result of an Archie search for the file called wmos1_0.zip, which is an abbreviation for Windows-Mosaic-Version 1.0-Zipped

---

As you may be aware, Archie is an Internet searching tool. Archie frequently searches ftp sites around the world and keeps lists. To do this Archie search, you can:

1. telnet to an Archie server
2. log in as archie
3. search using the command **prog** (i.e., you would type `prog wmos1_0.zip`)

Here's a list of known Archie server sites:

> archie.ans.net (USA [NY])
>
> archie.rutgers.edu (USA [NJ])
>
> archie.sura.net (USA [MD])
>
> archie.unl.edu (USA [NE])
>
> archie.mcgill.ca (Canada)
>
> archie.funet.fi (Finland/Mainland Europe)
>
> archie.au (Australia)
>
> archie.doc.ic.ac.uk (Great Britain/Ireland)
>
> archie.wide.ad.jp (Japan)
>
> archie.ncu.edu.tw (Taiwan)

Here's the result of an Archie search on wmos1_0.zip

```
Welcome to Archie.AU (aka plaza.AARNet.EDU.AU)
Public access services provided on this machine are
archie      The Archie System
de          Directory Service netfind
Network     Search Utility
Unauthorized access to any other account is prohibited.
```

```
login: archie
Last login: Fri Jul 1 02:11:54 from 129.228.120.127
SunOS Release 4.1.3 (PLAZA) #12:
Wed Oct 20 18:12:43 EST 1993
# Bunyip Information Systems, 1993, 1994
# Terminal type set to `vt100 24 80'.
# `erase' character is `^?'.
# `search' (type string) has the value `sub'.
Archie.AU> prog wmos1_0.zip
# Search type: sub.
# Your queue position: 7
# Estimated time for completion: 1 minute, 44 seconds.
working...
Host ftp.une.edu.au (129.180.4.7)
Last updated 05:29 22 Jun 1994

Location: /pub/NCSA/PC/Mosaic/old
FILE -r--r--r-- 240175 bytes 09:00 11 Nov 1993 wmos1_0.zip
List of Alternate FTP Sites
Host: ftp.une.edu.au (129.180.4.7)
Last updated 05:29 22 Jun 1994

Location: /pub/NCSA/PC/Mosaic/old
FILE -r--r--r-- 240175 bytes 09:00 11 Nov 1993 wmos1_0.zip
Host: ftp.uws.edu.au (137.154.16.20)
Last updated 03:37 22 Jun 1994

Location: /pub/pc/winsock/mosaic/old
FILE -r--r--r-- 240175 bytes 09:00 11 Nov 1993 wmos1_0.zip
Host: uniwa.uwa.edu.au (130.95.128.1)
Last updated 21:09 21 Jun 1994

Location: /pub/pc/networks/mosaic
FILE -rw-r--r-- 240175 bytes 09:00 15 Nov 1993 wmos1_0.zip
Host: han.hana.nm.kr (128.134.1.1)
Last updated 16:52 20 Jun 1994

Location: /pub/pc/win3/winsock
FILE -r--r--r-- 240175 bytes 10:00 12 Nov 1993 wmos1_0.zip
Host: bitsy.mit.edu (18.72.0.3)
Last updated 02:43 10 Jun 1994

Location: /pub/dos/mosaic
FILE ----r--r-- 240175 bytes 00:41 4 Mar 1994 wmos1_0.zip
Host: princeton.edu (128.112.124.1)
Last updated 10:50 5 Jun 1994

Location: /pub/mosaic
FILE -r--r--r-- 240175 bytes 02:34 10 Dec 1993 wmos1_0.zip
```

```
Host: hubcap.clemson.edu (130.127.8.1)
Last updated 02:52 5 Jun 1994
Location: /pub/Mosaic/Mosaic_for_PCs
FILE -rw-r--r-- 240175 bytes 04:00 14 Jan 1994 wmos1_0.zip
Host: ftp.ncsa.uiuc.edu (141.142.20.50)
Last updated 02:39 5 Jun 1994
Location: /PC/Mosaic/old
FILE -rw-r--r-- 240175 bytes 11:00 11 Nov 1993 wmos1_0.zip
Host: mcsun.eu.net (192.16.202.2)
Last updated 22:09 4 Jun 1994
Location: /network/Web/mosaic/Windows
FILE -rw-rw-r-- 240175 bytes 11:00 18 Nov 1993 wmos1_0.zip
Host: ftp.mr.net (137.192.240.5)
Last updated 19:30 4 Jun 1994
Location: /pub/dialip/pc/windows
FILE -r--r--r-- 240175 bytes 08:55 6 Jan 1994 wmos1_0.zip
```

If you do an Archie search, you may get a different results. You will only need to do the search if you cannot find wmos1_0.zip using the ftp hosts listed in the above list.

**HANDS-ON
Activity 3**

GETTING MOSAIC USING FTP

Heads Up!

As we have already noted, NCSA can be very busy much of the time. If, for any reason, you have a problem logging in, then feel free to use one of the many other sites listed above. All of them have exactly the same version of the Mosaic software known as wmos1_0.zip.

Getting Mosaic from NCSA

1. Be sure that you have used Custom to connect to your Internet service provider.

2. Double-click on **FTP**

3. Click on **Settings** and then on **Connection Profile...** and then on the **New button**

4. Add the following information:

   a. Description: NCSA

   b. Host: `ftp.ncsa.uiuc.edu`

   c. User: `anonymous`

   d. Password: your correct info here (i.e., `dsachs@panix.com`)

   e. Local Dir: `c:\incoming`

   Then, click on the **Add button** and then the **Close button**

5. Click on **Connect**

6. With the Connect window open, click once to highlight **NCSA**

7. Click on **OK**

8. Double-click on the **Web** subdirectory

9. Next, double-click on the **Mosaic** sub-subdirectory

10. Next, double-click on the **Windows** sub-sub- subdirectory

11. Next, double-click on the **old** sub-sub-sub- subdirectory

12. Highlight wmos1_0.zip Your screen should resemble the one in Figure 6-6.

Figure 6-6
Locating wmos1_0.zip

13. Be sure that

    a. You are prepared to transfer a binary file.

    b. You have selected **c:\incoming** as the directory to which you will be transferring the program.

14. Once you are ready, just click on the **left Copy button**, and the file will be transferred.

    You should now have a copy of NCSA Mosaic for MS Windows (wmos1_0.zip) in your c:\incoming directory.

15. Once the file has been transferred, click on **Disconnect** twice, so that you are disconnected from the NCSA ftp server. You can also close the FTP window at this time.

UNZIPPING AND INSTALLING MOSAIC

We will use PKUNZIP to unzip wmos1_0.zip and then we will install Mosaic 1.0 on your PC.

1. With Program Manager open, double-click on the **Main Icon** to open it.

2. Once the Main window is open, double-click on the **IBM DOS** Icon to open DOS

3. Change to the c:\incoming directory.
    (Type `cd incoming`)

4. Type `DIR wmos1_0.zip` to see that Mosaic 1.0 is there

5. Let's set up a special subdirectory for your Mosaic 1.0 files. Here is how to do that:

    a. At the `c:` prompt, type `md mosaic10`

    b. Copy two files into that subdirectory:

        (1) Type
            `copy c:\incoming\wmos1_0.zip c:\mosaic10`

        (2) Type
            `copy c:\pkware\pkunzip.exe c:\mosaic10`

    c. Check to see that you have done this correctly:

        (1) At your c: prompt, type `cd\mosaic10`

        (2) Type `dir`

            You should see two files in this subdirectory.

6. Now unzip the wmos1_0.zip file. Type the following command `pkunzip wmos1_0.zip`

    You should see what appears in Figure 6-7.

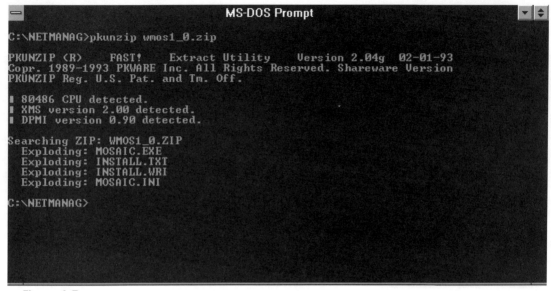

```
                        MS-DOS Prompt

C:\NETMANAG>pkunzip wmos1_0.zip

PKUNZIP (R)     FAST!     Extract Utility     Version 2.04g   02-01-93
Copr. 1989-1993 PKWARE Inc. All Rights Reserved. Shareware Version
PKUNZIP Reg. U.S. Pat. and Tm. Off.

■ 80486 CPU detected.
■ XMS version 2.00 detected.
■ DPMI version 0.90 detected.

Searching ZIP: WMOS1_0.ZIP
  Exploding: MOSAIC.EXE
  Exploding: INSTALL.TXT
  Exploding: INSTALL.WRI
  Exploding: MOSAIC.INI

C:\NETMANAG>
```

Figure 6-7
Exploding
wmos1_0.zip

Four files have been extracted:

MOSAIC.EXE

INSTALL.TXT

INSTALL.WRI

MOSAIC.INI

The two install files are nearly identical, but INSTALL.WRI is read with Windows Write and INSTALL.TXT is a plain text file. You can read the plain text file with Windows Notepad.

MOSAIC.EXE is the executable Mosaic file. We will get to MOSAIC.INI in a moment

We will try to simplify the installation by taking small steps, so we would suggest that you postpone reading the INSTALL files for now.

While you are still in DOS, we will copy two of the files:

a. Copy the file MOSAIC.INI to your Windows directory. Type
COPY C:\MOSAIC10\MOSAIC.INI C:\WINDOWS (or wherever you have your Windows directory).

Note: This is *very* important, as Mosaic will look in the Windows directory for this .INI file as it runs.

b. Copy the file MOSAIC.EXE to the Netmanag directory. Type

```
COPY C:\MOSAIC10\MOSAIC.EXE C:\NETMANAG
```

INSTALLING MOSAIC

HANDS-ON
Activity 5

1. Return to Windows and open the Chameleon Sampler Group.

2. Click on **Windows File** at the Program Manager's menu bar. From the drop-down menu, click on **New**

3. Click on **OK** from the New Program Object box (it should already have selected **New Program Item**)

4. You will now see the Program Item Properties screen. Fill out the screen with the following information:

a. Description: Mosaic

b. Command Line: C:\mosaic\mosaic.exe

c. Working Directory: c:\netmanag

d. Shortcut Key: None

Your screen should resemble Figure 6-8.

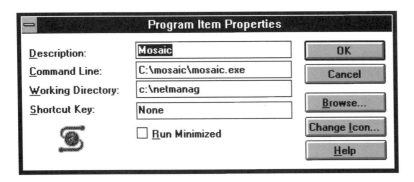

Figure 6-8
Program Item
Properties

5. 6. Click on **OK** and Mosaic's Icon should appear with the Chameleon Group. (You may have to maximize the Chameleon Group to see it.)

You have installed NCSA Mosaic for MS Windows and are ready for a test drive! Congratulations!

WHAT'S HAPPENING AS YOU RUN MOSAIC

Mosaic is really just a very nice information collector and displayer—a browser. What Mosaic does (quite well) is to hide a lot of the details of information collection from you. It then displays what it has found.

We will run through several examples to show you how it works. In Session Seven, we will show you how to tailor Mosaic for your own interests.

Heads Up!

The Internet is a constantly changing place. We have listed a number of possible places for you to try. Due to the constant flux, some of these may no longer be available or may have changed their addresses. Try each of them so that you can get a sense of what these locations are all about. Don't be discouraged if some of them don't work as shown in the figures. You may also get error messages and an occasional Windows General Protection Fault. It's not your fault, but you may have to shut down Mosaic and start it up again.

MODEM SPEEDS AND MOSAIC RESPONSE TIME

One of NCSA Mosaic's most appealing features is its ability to display fetching graphics. However, you should be aware that when you begin to deal with graphics which are quite large, the transfer time may take a few minutes. This is particularly true when you are transferring files with NCSA Mosaic, since the graphics images affiliated with a given file must all be transferred before you are able to work with the file. Consequently, you will find that some of the files that you transfer may take many seconds to come in.

Be patient and you will be rewarded with the pictures. You should also note that there are many places on the Web that also offer text-only versions. These will display much more quickly on your modem-connected PC.

TESTING MOSAIC

1. Connect to your Internet service provider using Custom.

2. After the connection is established, double-click on the **Mosaic Icon**.

Make sure that you can see the bottom of the Mosaic screen; lots will be happening there. If need be, maximize the Mosaic screen by clicking on the up-arrow in the upper-right-hand corner of your screen.

3. Click on **File** from Mosaic's Menu Bar, and then click on **Open URL...** (We'll explain what a URL is shortly.)

4. Move the cursor so that you can type in the URL: window and type `http://www.internic.net`

    Your screen should resemble Figure 6-9.

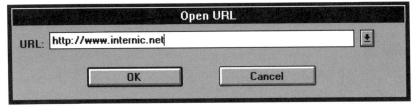

Figure 6-9
Open URL

5. Then, click on the **OK** button

6. At the bottom of the screen, you should see commands flashing by, such as

    Connecting to HTTP Server

    Sending Command

    Getting Response

    Receiving...

The InterNIC Home Page should appear, looking somewhat like Figure 6-10.

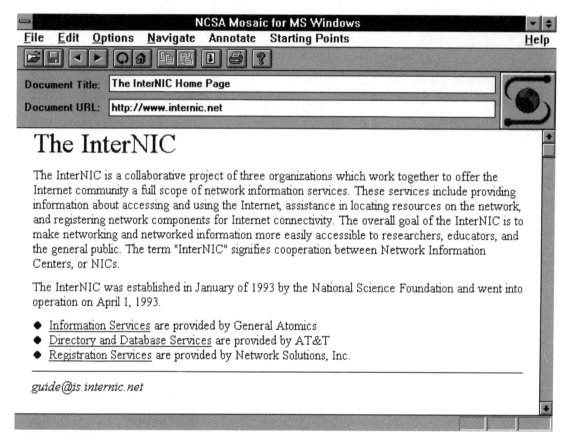

Figure 6-10
The InterNIC Home Page

Notice the **blue** text. These are the **hyperlinks** we talked about earlier. If you click on them with your mouse, you will be taken immediately to those references.

In NCSA Mosaic, text that is blue, or text that is in blue boxes or that has blue underlines is a hyperlink and can be used to go on to another place or for more information. Now, you can begin to understand the claim that "there is no top to the Web."

Next, we will go to Switzerland, the home of the Web.

1. Click on **Starting Points** on NCSA Mosaic's Menu Bar

   Look for World Wide Web Info and notice the small pointer to its right. This means that another menu lies below.

Click on this line to see the next menu as shown in Figure 6-11.

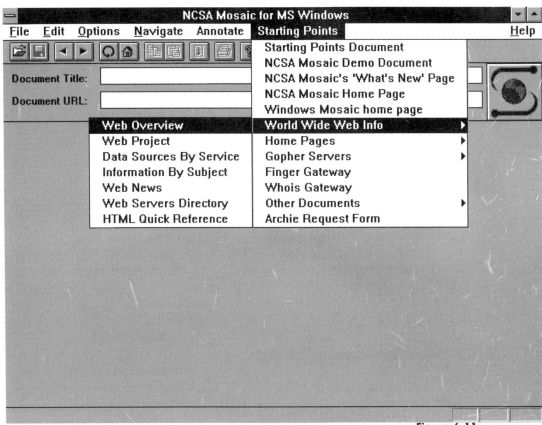

Figure 6-11
Web Overview

2. Click on **Web Overview** (on the top line) and watch the bottom of the Mosaic screen for the commands. Shortly, you should see the screen resembling Figure 6-12.

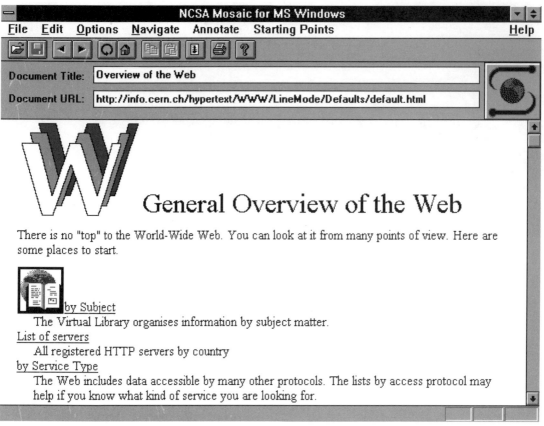

Figure 6-12
Overview of the Web

Next, we will go back to the Open URL box from Mosaic's File Menu.

1. Click once on File and then click once on **Open URL...**

2. Move your cursor to the URL: box and type
`http://shop.internet.net`

3. Then, click on **OK**

Your screen will resemble Figure 6-13.

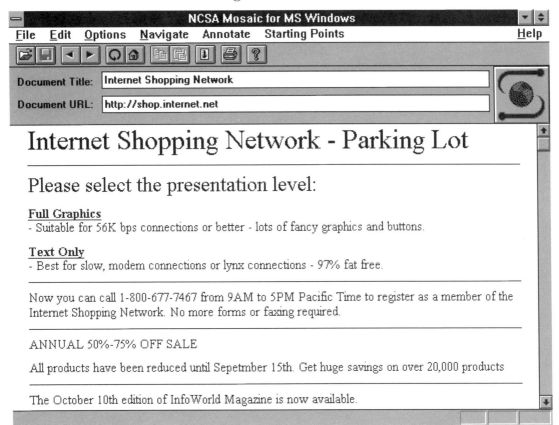

Figure 6-13
Internet Shopping
Network

Here, in the Internet Shopping Network™ - Parking Lot, you are offered a choice of *Full Graphics* or *Text Only*. If you choose to look at the full graphics, you will see something like Figure 6-14.

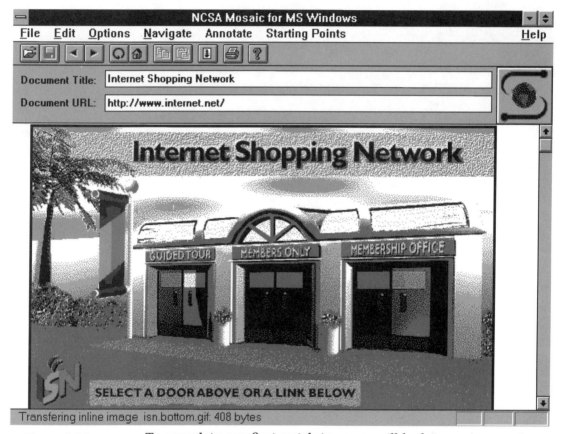

Figure 6-14
Internet Shopping
Network (continued)

To complete our first quick tour, we will look in on two magazines.

1. Click on **File** and then on **Open URL...**

2. Move your cursor to the URL: box and type
   `http://www.wired.com`

3. Then, click on **OK**

You should see a screen resembling Figure 6-15.

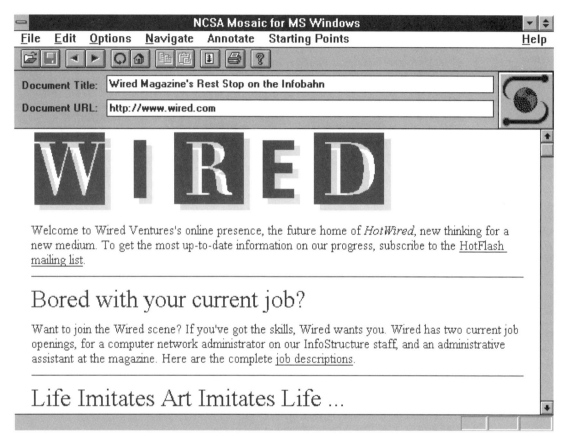

Figure 6-15
Wired Magazine

This is the home page of *Wired* magazine. You may read about the current issue and look up things from back issues. Of course, they would like you to subscribe, which is why they put this home page here.

Another magazine publisher we can reach is Ziff-Davis, publisher of *PC Week*, among others.

1. As you have done before, click on **File** and then on **Open URL...**

2. Move your cursor to the URL: box, and type
```
http://www.ziff.com
```

3.   Then, click on **OK**

Figure 6-16 shows a recent home page from Ziff-Davis Publishing.

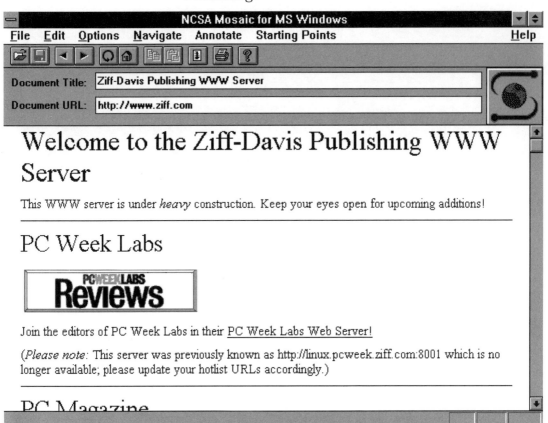

Figure 6-16
Ziff-Davis Publishing
WWW Server

We hope that several of these URLs worked for you and gave you a good first taste of NCSA Mosaic.

A TOUR OF THE NCSA MOSAIC SCREEN

Now that you have seen a few example screens from NCSA Mosaic, we will pause for a moment to take a tour of the screen. This brief tour will explain all parts of the screen and what you can do with each feature. Let's start with an overview of the screen that's shown in Figure 6-17.

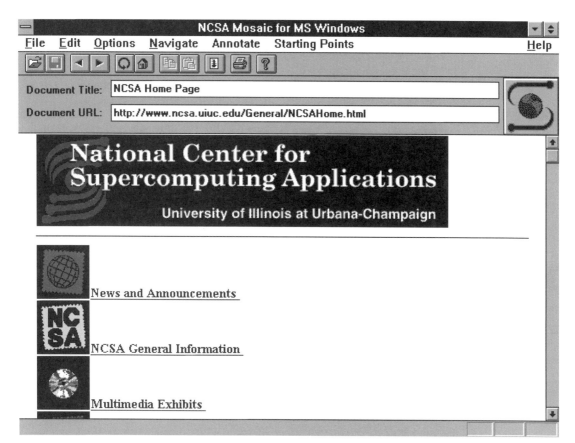

Mosaic was developed by the National Center for Supercomputing Applications (NCSA). We have chosen to use their home page to explain their Mosaic screen. Either take a look now at Figure 6-17 or log in to your service provider, go to the Open URL... box, and type

Figure 6-17
NCSA Home Page

```
http://www.ncsa.uiuc.edu/General/NCSAHome.html
```

You can then follow along either on the figures in the text or on your own screen.

We will start at the top of the screen. Notice that NCSA Mosaic has many of the features we are used to from Microsoft Windows. The top *title bar* of Figure 6-18 tells us what program we are using. In this case it is NCSA Mosaic for MS Windows.

Figure 6-18
The Title Bar

NCSA Mosaic for MS Windows

At the left end of the title bar is the usual *Control Menu box*, often called the *File Drawer*. A single click on this box will produce the Windows-type drop-down menu. A double-click on this box will close the window. At the right end of the title bar are the minimize and maximize buttons, shown in Figure 6-19.

Figure 6-19
Maximize/Minimize
Buttons

The *minimize button* will shrink NCSA Mosaic to a small icon at bottom of your screen. It does not stop the program, it merely minimizes it. Double-clicking on the minimized icon will bring it back as an open window. The *maximize button* will allow NCSA Mosaic to occupy your entire screen and will then change to a double-arrow button to allow you to return the program to a smaller window.

Going down the screen, we see a familiar *Windows-type menu bar*. This is illustrated in Figure 6-20.

Figure 6-20
The Menu Bar

Here we see individual words, each with a single letter underlined. We can either single-click on the word or type ALT and the underlined letter to activate a drop-down menu. You may be aware that these underlined letters are sometimes referred to as accelerators. (Annotate, Starting Points and Personal are missing their underlines, but ALT A, ALT S and ALT P work anyway).

You may want to look at each drop-down box to see what it contains. You will notice that some items in the drop-down menu are dimmed or not as dark as others. This means the item is not available either at all (not implemented yet) or not now (nothing to apply it to).

Continuing down the screen, we come to the tool bar that is shown in Figure 6-21.

Figure 6-21
The Tool Bar

The *tool bar* contains icons as a fast path to many NCSA Mosaic commands. Not all are active, but let's look at a few that are. Clicking on the far-left *Opening File Icon* takes us directly to the Open URL box. The left- and right-arrow boxes allow us to navigate back and forth to URLs we have already visited in a session. This is the same as using the Navigate drop-down menu Back and Forward commands.

The *circle arrow* means reload the current document and the little house means load our defined home page. (We have seen a few home pages already and we'll talk about pointing to specific home pages in the next session.)

The next four, *Copy, Paste, Search* and, *Print,* are not implemented in this version of NCSA Mosaic. In Session Nine, we will show you how to get the latest version of NCSA Mosaic where at least Search and Print are active. Finally, the *Question Mark Icon* will tell you much about the version of the program you are running. If you click on it, it will tell you which version of NCSA Mosaic you are running, when it was copyrighted and by whom, who developed it, and how to reach the development team by E-mail.

Next down the screen is the *Document box* containing two items—the Document Title and the Document URL. (Think of them as a command and an address for now; we'll explain URLs in the next session.) This box (shown in Figure 6-22) tells you what you are looking at and how you got it.

Figure 6-22
The Document Box

At the right end of this box is the NCSA Mosaic Globe, shown in Figure 6-23.

Figure 6-23
The NCSA Mosaic Globe

The *globe* serves several purposes. First, it is the NCSA Mosaic logo. Second, the globe also tells you when NCSA Mosaic is communicating with the Internet. You may have already noticed that the globe spins (or turns) and the little yellow highlights move toward the globe when data is flowing. Finally, the globe is a tool. Clicking on the globe's box will cancel a request while you are sending a command. It won't stop an incoming data flow but it will stop a request. In a moment we'll tell you how you can tell what's happening with the data flows.

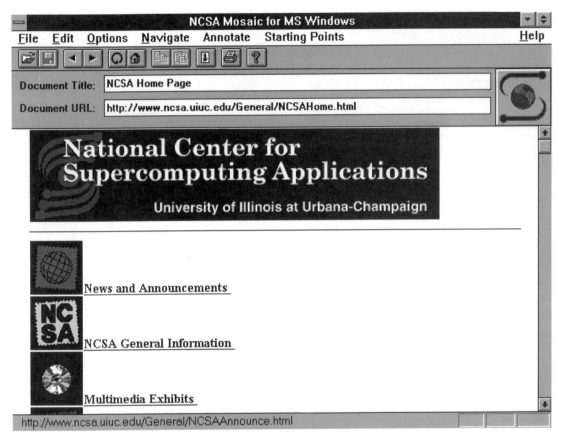

Figure 6-24
The Working
Document Area

The entire center of your screen is the *working document area* (Figure 6-24) that displays documents and images from Internet sources. Here you will find the blue underlines and blue boxes that indicate hyperlinks to other information.

At the right side of the screen, you will sometimes find a Windows-type *scroll bar* (Figure 6-25). This will tell you that there is more information above or below the screen you are viewing. You may click on the up or down arrows to move slowly up or down or put your cursor on the button and hold down the left mouse button to drag the button. You may also click on the scroll bar above or below the button to move in bigger jumps. If a wide screen of data arrives, you may also get a scroll bar at the bottom of your screen. It works the same way but moves right or left.

Most of the time the *cursor* on your screen will look like a typical Windows arrow-type pointer cursor, as shown in Figure 6- 26.

Figure 6-25
The Scroll Bar

Figure 6-26
The Pointer Cursor

In NCSA Mosaic, there is another cursor—the pointing hand, which is shown in Figure 6-27.

Figure 6-27
NCSA Mosaic's
Pointing Hand

When the normal arrow cursor changes to a *pointing hand*, the cursor has landed on a hyperlink and the status line at the bottom of the screen will show the command and address (URL) of that link. Notice the pointing hand in Figure 6-24. It is pointing at News and Announcements. Now look at Figure 6-28, which shows the Status Line. It shows the URL for News and Announcements from the NCSA.

http://www.ncsa.uiuc.edu/General/NCSAAnnounce.html

Figure 6-28
The Status Line

The *status line* is worth a glance whenever you are requesting a new hyperlink, waiting for something to come in, or just to see what is happening. At the right end of the status line are three small boxes (not shown in Figure 6-28). These are there to tell you if you have your PC's Caps Lock, Num Lock, or Scroll Lock keys turned on.

As NCSA continues the development of Mosaic, there will be changes to the screen. We hope this first tour has given you a start on using the screen and its tools. Now let's use NCSA Mosaic to visit a few more places. We won't give you detailed instructions here but will just show you screens. See if you can find the URLs on the screens in Figures 6-29 through 6-33, and then go to these places.

Pointer

The first one, Starting Points for Internet Exploration, doesn't show its full URL in Figure 6-29. However, it is hiding as the first item (Starting Points Document) in the Starting Points drop-down menu from the menu bar.

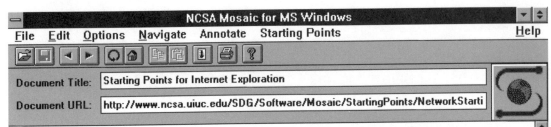

Starting Points for Internet Exploration

This document contains hyperlinks to many common Internet-based information resources.

If you are new to NCSA Mosaic, the Mosaic demo document will allow you to explore Mosaic's hypermedia capabilities; this document focuses on Internet resources in general, including several different types of information systems that do not have intrinsic hypermedia capabilities.

Disclaimer: NCSA has no control over any of the resources referenced by this document. Some or all of these resources may be unavailable at any time. This is a random sampling of Internet resources and makes no claim to be general or comprehensive.

- Web Overview: An overview of the World Wide Web, a distributed hypermedia system developed at CERN in Switzerland. NCSA Mosaic is a World Wide Web *client* with additional features.
- Web Project: An overview of the World Wide Web project, headed by Tim Berners-Lee at CERN.
- Other Web Documents
  - Data Sources By Service: A listing of data sources within the World Wide Web, organized by information service (Gopher, WAIS, etc.).

Figure 6-29
Starting Points for
Internet Exploration

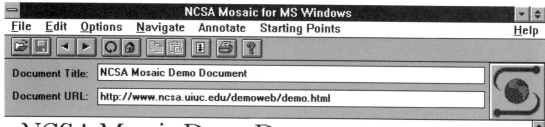

NCSA Mosaic Demo Document

In revision - July 20, 1994

Welcome to NCSA Mosaic, an information browser developed at the National Center for Supercomputing Applications at the University of Illinois, Urbana-Champaign. This document is an interactive hypermedia tour of Mosaic's capabilities.

Disclaimer: *This tour assumes that you have good network connectivity, that you have properly installed Mosaic and appropriate external viewers, and that the various information servers (at NCSA and elsewhere) the document references are alive and functioning well.*

Every time you see this icon: you can click on it to hear an audio clip narrating the current topic (if you have a workstation with appropriately configured audio hardware and software).

Introduction

Figure 6-30
NCSA Mosaic Demo
Document

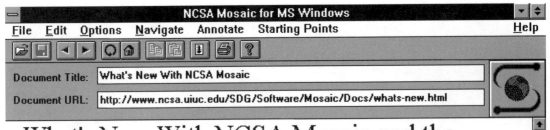

| NCSA Mosaic for MS Windows | | | | | | |

File   Edit   Options   Navigate   Annotate   Starting Points   **Help**

Document Title: What's New With NCSA Mosaic

Document URL: http://www.ncsa.uiuc.edu/SDG/Software/Mosaic/Docs/whats-new.html

What's New With NCSA Mosaic and the WWW

This document covers recent changes and additions to the universe of information available to Mosaic and the World Wide Web. Please follow these guidelines when sending announcements to whats-new@ncsa.uiuc.edu.

The entire archive of NCSA What's New pages is searchable via CUI's W3 Catalog.

For NCSA Mosaic news, see the new **NCSA Mosaic Announcements** document.

Details on the Second International WWW Conference '94: Mosaic and the Web

---

September 27, 1994

The Ceolas celtic music archive is now on the web. It carries information on many aspects of celtic music, including artist notes, schedules, festival info, instrument guides, celtic media, tunes and much more. Impediment Incorporated, distributor and integrator of workstation memory and peripherals announces that its Web server is now available. The Web server contains technical

http://www.ncsa.uiuc.edu/SDG/Software/Mosaic/Docs/archive-whats-new.html

Figure 6-31
What's New with
NCSA Mosaic

Pointer

For the next two, you will have to type in the URL. Remember the tool bar?

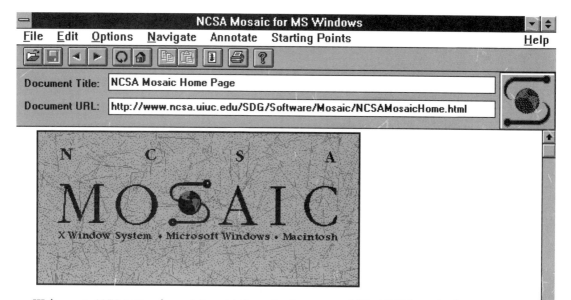

Welcome to NCSA Mosaic, an Internet information browser and World Wide Web client. NCSA Mosaic was developed at the National Center for Supercomputing Applications at the University of Illinois in Urbana-Champaign.

Each highlighted phrase (in color or underlined) is a hyperlink to another document or information resource somewhere on the Internet. *Single click* on any highlighted phrase to follow the link.

NCSA Mosaic Flavors

Figure 6-32
NCSA Mosaic Home
Page

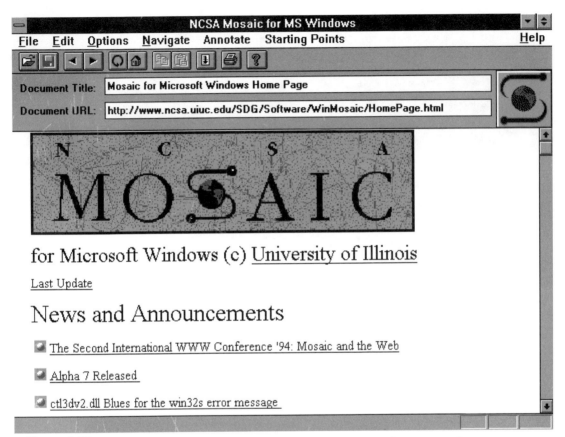

Figure 6-33
NCSA Mosaic for
Microsoft Windows
Home Page

We hope that these examples worked for you and gave you a taste of Mosaic. The tour of the screen should help you recognize what is happening and what can be done with NCSA Mosaic. As newer versions of NCSA Mosaic are released, some parts of the screen will change. The basics, however, should remain pretty much the same.

In our next session, we will explain URLs and http and all of this other new vocabulary. We'll also show you how to customize Mosaic.

If you have had some trouble, you may wish to use Ping to see if you can reach the addresses that we have given. Tell Ping just the part after http:// as that is the actual Internet name of the host you are trying to reach.

It is also possible that Internet congestion may have prevented you from getting through. You may wish to try again later, if you believe that that is the problem.

In the next session, we will begin to tune up your Mosaic.

SESSION SUMMARY

Congratulations! You have downloaded NCSA Mosaic, installed it on your computer, and begun to experience some of the power that this software can provide. You have seen some of the wonderful home pages which are available on the World-Wide Web. In addition, you have learned about the various components of the NCSA Mosaic screen. NCSA Mosaic is an extremely powerful software program; in the next three sessions, we are going to help you to more fully explore all that NCSA Mosaic has to offer you.

Overview

In **Mosaic Go!** you will learn a great deal about Mosaic. You will learn most of the common Mosaic terminology, as well as how to upgrade your version of Mosaic. In addition, you will learn how to add audio and graphics capabilities to Mosaic.

In **Session Seven**, you will learn about Hyper Text Transport Protocol, Uniform Resource Locators, and Hotlists. You will also learn about some of the many Home Pages which are available on the World Wide Web. In addition, you will download wmos20a2.zip (often referred to as Mosaic 2.2), which is the last 16-bit version of NCSA Mosaic for MS Windows. Finally, you will use Mosaic for ftp and gopher activities.

In **Session Eight**, you will focus on the multimedia capabilities of NCSA Mosaic for MS Windows. You will download and install software that allows you to view PostScript files and other photos and to hear sounds. Then, you will use Mosaic to download sound and photo files.

In **Session Nine**, you will learn about the World Wide Web Worm and the World Wide Web Wanderer. In addition, you will learn about the expanding role of business on the Internet, particularly as Mosaic is being used. As examples, we will focus on CommerceNet and MecklerWeb. Finally, you will learn how to keep Mosaic up to date. The most recent version (wmos20a7.zip) is now a 32-bit version. Therefore, you will learn how to download both the required Windows software (Win32s) and the newest version of Mosaic.

How To Use Mosaic Go!

It is our assumption that you purchased *Hands-On Mosaic* because you were/are interested in learning about the capabilities of NCSA Mosaic for MS Windows. All of the sessions in **Mosaic Go!** are intended to provide you with this information.

PART 3

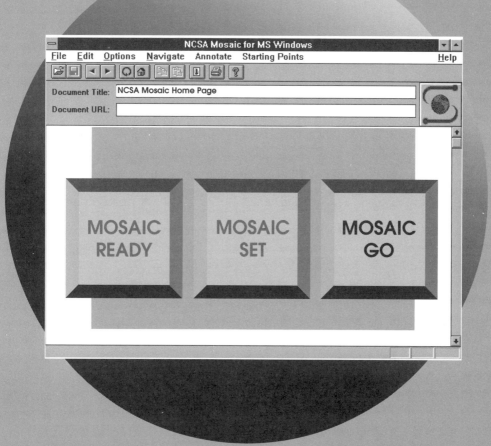

SESSION 7

Using NCSA Mosaic from Your PC

SESSION OVERVIEW

In this session you will have an opportunity to broaden your understanding of the World-Wide Web and NCSA Mosaic. We will look at some of the many resources which are available. Then we will download a wide array of home pages. Later in this session we will upgrade your copy of NCSA Mosaic. Let's get started!

WHAT'S OUT THERE ON THE WORLD-WIDE WEB?

The short answer is *everything*! The longer, and probably more useful, answer would provide you with some sense of the wide array of resources that can be found on the World-Wide Web. They include:

General Information about the World-Wide Web
> Information about WWW
> A List of World-Wide Web Clients

Mailing Lists
> Hypertext Discussion Lists
> Hypertext Archives

Courseware
> World-Wide Web Courseware
> World-Wide Web Literature

Lists of Tools and Convertors

Commercial Sites
   Wired Magazine
   MTV
   CommerceNet
   Global Network Navigator
   Silicon Graphics

Country Sites
   Guide to Australia
   Spain Web Sites
   Austria
   Chile
   Costa Rica
   Czechoslovakia
   Germany

Educational Sites
   Honolulu Community College
   The University of Notre Dame
   The Chinese University of Hong Kong

Interactive Sites
   Michigan State University Weather Movies
   Interactive World Map Interface

Legal Information and Government Sites
   Legal Information at Cornell
   U.S. Bureau of the Census
   U.S. Department of Commerce
   NASA
   The City of Palo Alto, CA

Literature
   English Server at Carnegie-Mellon
   Internet Book Information Center

Museums and Art
   San Francisco's Exploratorium
   University of California Museum of Paleontology

Music and Audio
   Internet Music Resources
   Internet Talk Radio

Organizations
   Electronic Frontier Foundation
   Association for Computing Machinery
   World Health Organization

This short list is intended to provide you with an awareness of some of the many resources that may be found on the World-Wide Web. As we will show you shortly, you can use NCSA Mosaic to help you find all of these resources from among the many that exist.

HOW DO WE ADDRESS THESE PLACES? _____

As you learned earlier, it is the Transmission Control Protocol and the Internet Protocol (TCP/IP) which permit us to have so many host computers effectively communicating with each other. As you might imagine, there are other similar protocols and conventions in place which make it possible for NCSA Mosaic to exist and to function.

The first protocol that we encounter goes by the acronym *URL* which means *Uniform Resource Locators*. According to Kevin Hughes:

> The World-Wide Web uses what are called Uniform Resource Locators (URLs) to represent hypermedia links and links to network services within HTML documents. (More about HTML in a moment.) It is possible to represent nearly any file or service on the Internet with a URL.

The first part of the URL (before the two slashes) specifies the method of access.

The second part is typically the address of the computer on which the data or service is located.

Further parts may specify the names of files, the port to connect to, or the text to search for in a database.

Important: A URL is always a single, unbroken line with no spaces.

Here are some examples of URLs:

- `http://www.hcc.hawaii.edu`
  Connects to Honolulu Community College WWW Service
- `http://www.eff.org`
  Connects to the Electronic Frontier Foundation
- `http://www.xerox.com`
  Opens a connection to Xerox, the document company
- `gopher://gopher.uiuc.edu:70/1`
  Connects to the gopher server at the University of Illinois at Urbana-Champaign

As you can see, all of these URLs have the same general format, and, in fact, look remarkably similar to the fully qualified Internet addresses which you may have seen before. In all likelihood, it is the first part of the URL (http: or gopher:) that might be new for you.

HYPERTEXT TRANSFER PROTOCOL: HTTP

You will notice that several of these URLs begin with the initials http.

You will see this term frequently being used at the beginning of URLs. *http* is an abbreviation for *Hypertext Transfer Protocol,* which refers to the language that is used by all of the World-Wide Web clients and servers to communicate with each other. All Web clients and servers must be able to use http if they are going to "speak" to each other.

HYPERTEXT MARKUP LANGUAGE: HTML

One of the examples above contains the extension html. You will see this extension used frequently; *html* is the abbreviation for what is known as *Hypertext Markup Language.* This is the programming language that is used by the World-Wide Web for creating and recognizing hypermedia documents. html permits those who are interested in doing so to take standard ASCII files and to *mark them up* with all of the formatting codes that are necessary to describe their layout and any hyperlinks they might have.

Now, let's look at several URL addresses again:

1.   Main CERN World-Wide Web Home Page

    `http://info.cern.ch/hypertext/WWW/TheProject.html`

    `http:` on the far left, tells us that this document
           adheres to the Hypertext Transfer Protocol

    `//info.cern.ch` is the host address that was used in
           an earlier telnet session to take us to Switzerland
           so that we could try out the World-Wide Web in
           text mode

`hypertext/WWW/TheProject.html` provides us with the names of the directories and the file name of this home page and indicates that it was created using html, the hypertext markup language

2. CommerceNet

`http://www.commerce.net`

`http:` on the far left, tells us that this document adheres to the Hypertext Transfer Protocol

`//www.commerce.net` tells us that this is a World-Wide Web server, provided by commerce.net—in all likelihood, this will be their home page (More about home pages in a minute.)

3. U.S. Bureau of the Census

`http://www.census.gov`

`http:` on the far left, tells us that this document adheres to the Hypertext Transfer Protocol

`//www.census.gov` tells us that this is a World-Wide Web server provided by the governmental organization known as the Bureau of the Census

WHAT'S OUT THERE ON THE INTERNET?

HANDS-ON Activity 1

This activity will actually be comprised of many short exercises. We will take a few minutes to sample some of the many World-Wide Web servers that exist. As noted above, all of them communicate with each other using the Hypertext Transfer Protocol (http)—which is why you will notice that many of the places we will visit during this session (although not all) begin with http.

Before seeing what our first exercise looks like, let's take a minute to dissect the address we are given. This is for the NCSA Demonstration Page. The address is:

`http://www.ncsa.uiuc.edu/demoweb/demo.html`

Reading from left to right:

`http:` refers to the Hypertext Transfer Protocol used to address this server `www.ncsa.uiuc.edu` tells us that this is a World-Wide Web server (WWW) at the National Center for Supercomputing Applications (NCSA) at University of Illinois, Urbana-Champaign (uiuc), and that it is an educational institution (edu)

`demoweb` is the name of the directory containing the file demo.html

`demo.html` is the name of the file we will retrieve; the extension html indicates that the file is in Hypertext Markup Language, the language used by the Web for creating and recognizing hypermedia documents

Now, let's go look at it.

Exercise A: NCSA's Demonstration Page
`http://www.ncsa.uiuc.edu/demoweb/demo.html`

1. Double-click on **Custom** and sign on to your Internet service provider

    Then, click once on the **upper-right-hand down arrow** to minimize the Custom window into an icon.

2. Double-click on **NCSA Mosaic**

3. Once the NCSA Mosaic for MS Windows main window is open, be sure to maximize it by clicking on the **up arrow** in the upper-right-hand corner.

4. Click once on **File** and then once on **Open URL...**

5. Click once in the **URL box** and then type

    `http://www.ncsa.uiuc.edu/demoweb/demo.html`

6. Then click on **OK**

You should see a screen that resembles Figure 7-1.

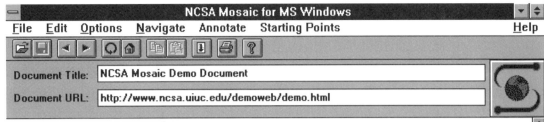

───

Figure 7-1
NCSA Mosaic Demo

Note: For the rest of the examples, we will *not* repeat steps 1 through 4; we will just assume that the Open URL window is open.

Take some time to wander through this first example. Click on the **down arrow** in the scroll bar on the right-hand side of your screen to scroll down through the NCSA Mosaic Demo Document. As you might imagine, clicking on the up arrow in the scroll bar will take you back to the beginning.

Navigation Hints

a.   When you move your cursor across one of the items that is in **blue**, your cursor becomes a **hand** with the forefinger pointing. Clicking once will take you to the item printed in blue.

b.   If you have chosen one of the words or boxes or names which is printed in blue and then decide that you would like to return to the home page where you began, just click on the left-pointing arrow on NCSA Mosaic's Toolbar at the top.

c.   If you decide that you would like to save this URL in what is known as your Hotlist (more about that shortly), just click once on **Navigate** and then once on **Add Current To Hotlist**

Exercise B: *Wired Magazine*
`http://www.wired.com`

1.   Open URL...

2.   Click once in the **URL box**

3.   Type `http://www.wired.com`

4.   Click on **OK**

Navigation Hints

a.   Use your up and down arrow keys (on the right-hand scroll bar) to navigate through this magazine.

b.   Use your left arrow button (located at the top on the tool bar) to jump back to the last document(s). Once you have done that, use your right arrow button to jump forward to this one.

Exercise C: Global Network Navigator
http://gnn.com/gnn/

1. Open URL...

2. Click once in the **URL box**

3. Type http://gnn.com/gnn/

4. Click on **OK**

Navigation Hints

    a. Use your up and down arrow keys (on the right-hand scroll bar) to navigate through the Global Network Navigator.

    b. Use your left arrow button (at the top) to jump back through the last few documents. Use your right arrow button to jump forward to this one.

Exercise D: Guide To Australia
http://life.anu.edu.au/education/australia.html

1. Open URL...

2. Click once in the **URL box**

3. Type
http://life.anu.edu.au/education/australia.html

4. Click on **OK**

Navigation Hints

    a. Use your up and down arrow keys (on the right-hand scroll bar) to navigate through the Guide To Australia.

    b. Use your left arrow button (at the top) to jump back through the last few documents. Use your right arrow button to jump forward to this one.

You should see the home page in Figure 7-2.

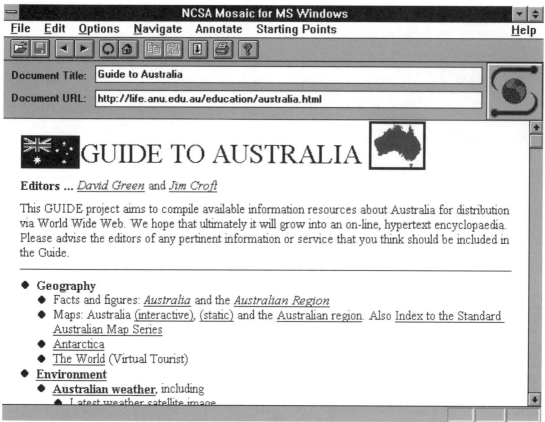

Figure 7-2
Guide to Australia
Home Page

Exercise E: The City of Palo Alto, CA
`http://www.city.palo-alto.ca.us/home.html`

1. Open URL...

2. Click once in the **URL box**

3. Type `http://www.city.palo-alto.ca.us/home.html`

4. Click on **OK**

5. Use your up and down arrow keys (on the right-hand scroll bar) to learn an enormous amount of information about the City of Palo Alto, CA.

Figure 7-3 shows the home page that Palo Alto presents to the world.

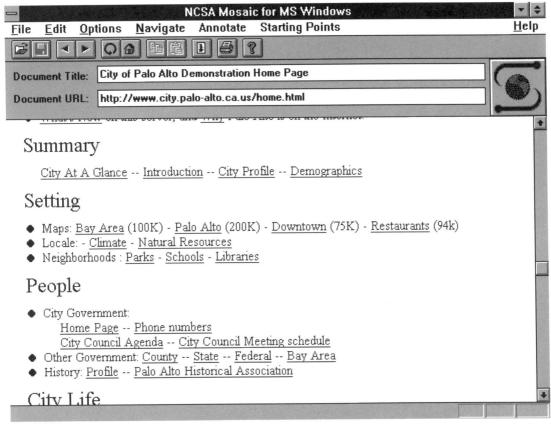

Summary

City At A Glance -- Introduction -- City Profile -- Demographics

Setting

- Maps: Bay Area (100K) - Palo Alto (200K) - Downtown (75K) - Restaurants (94k)
- Locale: - Climate - Natural Resources
- Neighborhoods : Parks - Schools - Libraries

People

- City Government:
  Home Page -- Phone numbers
  City Council Agenda -- City Council Meeting schedule
- Other Government: County -- State -- Federal -- Bay Area
- History: Profile -- Palo Alto Historical Association

City Life

Figure 7-3
City of Palo Alto Home Page

Exercise F: The Internet Book Information Center
`http://sunsite.unc.edu/ibic/IBIC-homepage.html`

1. Open URL...

2. Click once in the **URL box**

3. Type
    `http://sunsite.unc.edu/ibic/IBIC-homepage.html`

4. Click on **OK**

5. Use your up and down arrow keys (on the side) to learn an enormous amount about the amazing array of Internet resources that are related to books.

You should see a home page resembling the one in Figure 7-4.

182

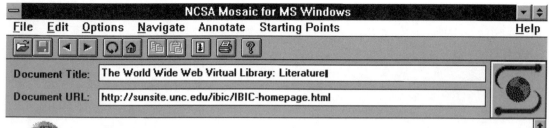

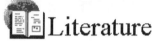 Literature

The World Wide Web Virtual Library: Literature is maintained at the Internet Book Information Center. Please mail ibic@sunsite.unc.edu to recommend additional resources for this page. For other subjects in the WWW Virtual Library, see the Subject Index at CERN.

What's New at the Internet Book Information Center

● I've broken the IBIC home page down into several smaller pages for ease of maintenance and use. Please let me know asap if I have inadvertently introduced bad html or bad links.

Internet Resources Related to Books and Literature

Figure 7-4
Internet Book
Information Center
Home Page

Exercise G: A Ton of Web Sites
`http://www.mit.edu:8001/people/mkgray/comprehensive.html`

Note: This exercise is included as a way of introducing you to the amazing array of http sites that exist on the World-Wide Web. As of June 18, 1994, there were 3,100 sites listed by Matthew Gray in this list (!!!!!).

Feel free to browse through this comprehensive http site list, using the tools that you have learned in the above exercises.

Here is how to do so:

1. Open URL...

2. Click once in the **URL box**

3. Type

`http://www.mit.edu:8001/people/mkgray/comprehensive.html`

4. Click on **OK**

5. Use your up and down arrow keys (on the right-hand scroll bar) to learn about all of the many http sites that are available to you. Your screen should resemble Figure 7-5.

Figure 7-5
http Site List Home
Page

THE URL HOTLIST

It quickly becomes apparent that URLs often are composed of extremely long lines of information. Certainly, it is possible to type the URL information each time that you need it. However, for many of us, this becomes a real chore, especially if there are URLs you find yourself using repeatedly. Therefore, NCSA Mosaic provides you with what is known as a Hotlist. Here is how to find it:

1. First connect to your Internet service provider. Then double-click on **NCSA Mosaic**

2. Click once on **File** and then click once on **Open URL...**

3. 3. When the Open URL window appears, it should resemble the one in Figure 7-6.

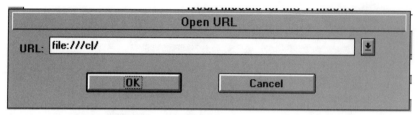

Figure 7-6
The Open URL WIndow

4. Click once on the **down arrow** on the right side of the Open URL window and a Hotlist should drop down. It should resemble the one in Figure 7-7.

Figure 7-7
The URL Hotlist

The URLs that are listed make up what is known as your Hotlist.

USING THE HOTLIST

To invoke any of the URLs that are listed

1. Click on your selection once to make it active

2. Click once on the **OK button** in the Open URL window

   Try doing this several times now to see how this works.

ADDING URLS TO THE HOTLIST

Should you wish to add a URL to your Hotlist, it is remarkably simple to do so.

1. When you are connected to a Web server, just click once on **Navigate**

   One of the menu items will say Add Current To Hotlist

2. Click on it once, and the current Web server will be added to your Hotlist.

HOME PAGES—GETTING STARTED

HANDS-ON
Activity 2

The key to the way in which many places (cities, states, companies, organizations) are presenting themselves on the World-Wide Web is through the use of what is known as a home page. This document is typically used to provide an overview of all the resources that a given entity wishes to provide to the world. The closest analogy might be the table of contents for a book. Using the table of contents, a reader should be able to

1. get a sense of what the whole book is all about

2. determine how the book has been organized

3. determine where in the book particular topics might be found

A well-designed home page should do all of the above, and more. For remember, we are working with hypertext and hyper-media. So, the reader of a home page really can choose to explore any or all of the topics listed on the home page in whatever order he or she might wish. Let's take the NCSA Home Page as an example. First, let's find it, and then we can take a look at it. Here is how to do that.

1. Begin by having the NCSA Mosaic for MS Windows main window on your screen.

2. Click once on **Starting Points**

3. Using the drop-down window, click once on **NCSA Mosaic Home Page** You should see a screen which resembles Figure 7-8.

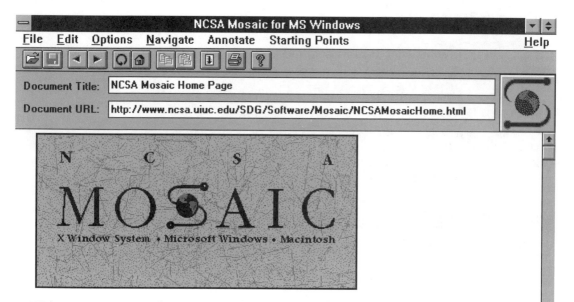

Welcome to NCSA Mosaic, an Internet information browser and World Wide Web client. NCSA Mosaic was developed at the National Center for Supercomputing Applications at the University of Illinois in Urbana-Champaign.

Each highlighted phrase (in color or underlined) is a hyperlink to another document or information resource somewhere on the Internet. *Single click* on any highlighted phrase to follow the link.

NCSA Mosaic Flavors

Figure 7-8
NCSA Mosaic Home Page

Let's spend a minute or two reading the screen.

1. There is a *Document Title* at the top of the home page. In this case, it is called NCSA Mosaic Home Page

2. There is a *Document URL* similar to those we have seen before. It is

```
http://www.ncsa.uiuc.edu/SDG/Software/Mosaic/NCSAMosaicHome.html
```

As we learned earlier, this tells us the following:

`http:` is a host computer which is using the Hypertext Transfer Protocol

`www.ncsa.uiuc.edu` is a World-Wide Web host computer, maintained by the National Center for Supercomputing Applications at the University of Illinois, Urbana- Champaign

`SDG` is a directory named SDG (which is used by the Software Development Group at NCSA)

`NCSAMosaicHome.html` is a document with the name NCSAMosaicHome, that was created using html

As we did earlier, if we wish to see more than just the first screen, we can click on the down or up arrows on the scroll bar on the right- hand side of the screen.

There are lots of words and phrases in blue on the screen. All of these phrases in blue type are hyperlinks, designed to take you to other documents, files, programs, and so forth.

3. Slide your cursor over to the phrase What's New with NCSA Mosaic and the Internet

    Notice that the cursor has become a hand with the forefinger extended.

4. Click once on the **hand** and a new document (whats-new.html) will be transferred from the http Server to your computer.

The Document Title is What's New With NCSA Mosaic

The Document URL is

`http://www.ncsa.uiuc.edu/SDG/Software/Mosaic/Docs/whats-new.html`

As before, you can use the up and down arrows on the right-hand scroll bar to see other parts of the document.

If you find an item on this screen of interest to you (and it has a word or phrase that appears in blue type), just slide your cursor to that word or phrase, and click once.

Navigation Notes

a. Each time you click on a blue word or phrase, you will be taken to the html document to which that blue word or phrase refers. In effect, you will be going deeper and deeper into the original home page.

b. When you get to this new page, if you find additional information that is of interest to you and there is a word or phrase in blue, just click on it to get to the next html document.

c. Should you decide to go back toward your original beginning, just click on the left-arrow button on the tool bar at the top of your screen. Clicking once on it will take you back to the preceding html document.

d. Using the left-arrow button on the tool bar at the top of your screen, you can return to the NCSA Mosaic Home Page where we began. Click on the left arrow as many times as necessary until you are back at the NCSA Mosaic Home Page.

e. Once there, click on **File** and then **Exit** to return to the NCSA Mosaic Icon.

*HANDS-ON
Activity 3*

HOME PAGES—CONTINUED

In this activity, we will look at four of the best known home pages. Here they are.

NASA's Jet Propulsion Lab

1. Double-click on the **NCSA Mosaic Icon**

2. When NCSA Mosaic appears, be sure to maximize it by clicking on the **up arrow** in the upper-right-hand corner.

3. Click once on File and then once on **Open URL...**

4. Click once on the URL box, and then type the following

`http://www.jpl.nasa.gov`

Then, click on **OK** and you will be taken to the NASA Jet Propulsion Laboratory.

Heads Up!

It is possible that you may get one or two error messages as the file is being loaded. Do *not* be concerned about this; just click on **OK** each time, and the rest of the file will be loaded. Sometimes there is network congestion. Another possibility is that an attempt was being made to load audio or video to your computer but the paths for the viewers have not yet been set. (We will return to this in greater detail in Session Eight.)

The NASA Jet Propulsion Laboratory home page should resemble the one in Figure 7-9.

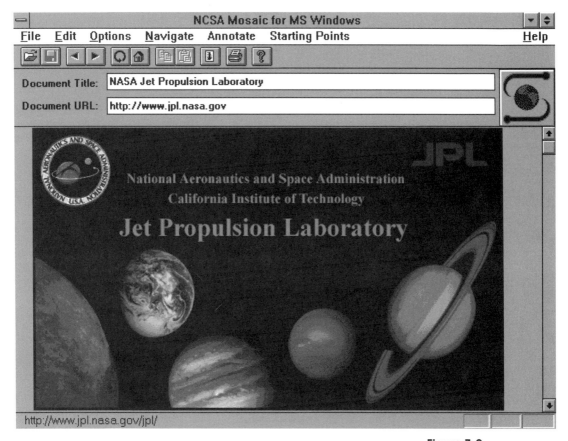

If you would like to save this Home Page, just do the following:

Figure 7-9
Jet Propulsion
Laboratory Home
Page

a. Click once on **Navigate**

b. Click once on **Add Current To Hotlist**

Spend some time exploring this home page. When you have finished, return to your NCSA Mosaic Icon.

CERN's World-Wide Web

This is an extremely important home page to know about, since CERN is the home of the World-Wide Web. As you will see momentarily, this home page will provide you with very valuable information about the Web and access to resources that you may desire. Here is how to get there:

1. Double-click on **NCSA Mosaic**
2. Be sure to maximize the NCSA Mosaic for Windows window by clicking on the **up arrow** in the upper-right-hand corner of the scroll bar.
3. With the NCSA Mosaic window open, click once on **Starting Points**
4. Then, click once on **Home Pages**
5. Then, click once on **Cern Home Page**

   If all goes according to plan, you should see a screen resembling the one in Figure 7-10.

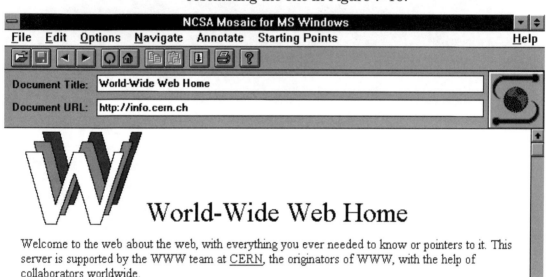

Figure 7-10
CERN Home Page

This initial screen provides you with a hint of the wonderful resources that are available. In particular, being able to learn quickly about the client and server software available for World-Wide Web users (and potential users) is invaluable.

Let's assume that you are interested in knowing more about client software for World-Wide Web usage. Follow along as we go through the steps—and, in the process, learn more about how to comfortably navigate your way through NCSA Mosaic screens. Here are the steps:

1. Click on **A list of client software, and documentation**
2. Click on the **right-hand down-arrow key** on the scroll bar until you come to the heading PC Running Windows
3. Click once on **Mosaic for Windows**

   Notice that on the NCSA Mosaic for Windows screen, we are provided with information about Availability. The hyperlink indicates that we may use Anonymous FTP from ftp.NCSA.uiuc.edu in PC/Mosaic

   Important: *Do not do this now.* We will return to this exercise shortly.

4. 4. Instead, click on the **left-arrow button** on the tool bar at the top of your screen.

   Click on it again, and you should be returned to the World-Wide Web Home Page.

A Little Bit Of History

1. You should be on the World-Wide Web Home Page.
2. Click once on **Navigate**
3. Click once on **History**

   When you do this, you should see the NCSA Mosaic - History window, which should resemble the one in Figure 7-11.

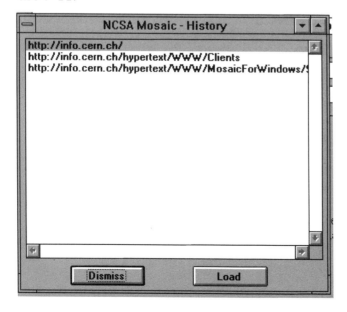

Figure 7-11
WWW History Window

NCSA Mosaic - History provides you with a record of the pages you have looked at during this session, as well as an ability to go quickly to any one of them. To do so

a. Highlight the page that interests you by clicking on it once

b. Then, click once on **Load** and you will be taken to that page

THE POWER OF HYPERLINKS

A good example of the power of hyperlinks is provided by the following:

1. Using the left-arrow button on the tool bar at the top of your screen, return to the World-Wide Web Home page.

2. Click once on **The definitive WWW project page**

3. Click once on **WWW Software Products**

4. Click once on **Client software**

5. Click on the **down arrow** on the scroll bar on the right-hand side of your screen until the heading PC Running Windows appears

Then, click on **Mosaic for Windows From NCSA**

Note: We will be taken to a screen which (again) provides us with an opportunity to use Anonymous ftp to retrieve NCSA Mosaic software.

Important: *Do not do this yet!*

The point of this exercise was to show you that by using hyper-media and hyperlinks, it is possible to get to the same end point (at least) two different ways.

This is all that we will do with the World-Wide Web Home page at this time.

Feel free to stay and browse, or just click once on **File** and then once on **Exit** to return to the NCSA Mosaic Icon.

UPDATING YOUR COPY OF **NCSA MOSAIC** _____

NCSA Mosaic has been particularly well received around the world since its release in late 1993. As you have seen by the examples, it is powerful, it is friendly, and it is, seemingly, limitless. In response to this, new versions of NCSA Mosaic software have been developed that include significant new features, and newer ones are under development. Therefore, it is reasonable to expect that no matter when you begin using NCSA Mosaic, there will always be a newer, better, more recent version of the software to be had. In the following activity, we will show you several ways to acquire and install the new software.

There are some technical issues affiliated with the newer versions of Mosaic. Specifically, in the software industry, there are versions which are known as *alpha* and *beta*. Typically, the latest version of NCSA Mosaic is Alpha software. This means that the product is *not* an official release. Here are some definitions of these terms.

Alpha software The stage of software development where features are added and bugs are identified and mostly fixed.

Beta software The stage of software development where bugs, stability, and cosmetic issues are addressed. No additional features will be added to this version in preparation for the official release version.

Official release Official release software will have a given number of functions, and it is supposed to be bug free and stable.

The formal name of the software which we will download is *wmos20a2.zip*; we will refer to it as Mosaic 2.2. You should be aware that the official version of NCSA Mosaic software which is to be released during the fall of 1994 may be somewhat different from this one.

Heads Up!

In Session Nine, we will show you how to download alpha version wmos20a7.zip (we shall call it Mosaic 2.7)that is the newest alpha version of NCSA Mosaic software as of September 9, 1994. In addition, we will show you how to download the additional Windows software which you will need to make Mosaic 2.7 run properly.)

GETTING NCSA MOSAIC VERSION 2.2

Using NCSA Mosaic 1.0 to get NCSA Mosaic 2.2 (`wmos20a2.zip`)

As you noticed earlier when we were working through the World-Wide Web information at CERN, we kept encountering opportunities to get NCSA Mosaic software using NCSA Mosaic. This time, we shall actually continue this activity, until we have done so.

At certain times of the day, it is sometimes very difficult to do the following activity. Both the NCSA Software Tools Home Page and the CERN Home page use the NCSA server as the source for NCSA Mosaic software. Often, as you might imagine, that server is extremely busy. It is possible that you will attempt to download the software, only to find that your computer will "hang" in the process of doing so. Should that occur to you, just re-boot your computer using CTRL-ALT-DEL. Before this activity is over, we will show you many other places and ways to get the desired software.

1.   Log in to your Internet service provider

2.   Double-click on the **NCSA Mosaic Icon**

3.   Click on **Starting Points**

4.   Click on **Windows Mosaic Home Page**

    If you don't have a Windows Mosaic Home Page, you may go to **File, Open URL** and type in

```
http://www.ncsa.uiuc.edu/SDG/Software/WinMosaic/HomePage.html
```

    (Be sure to use uppercase letters exactly as shown.)

A home page as shown in Figure 7-12 should appear. Note that home pages are continuously updated and you may possibly see variations from this figure.

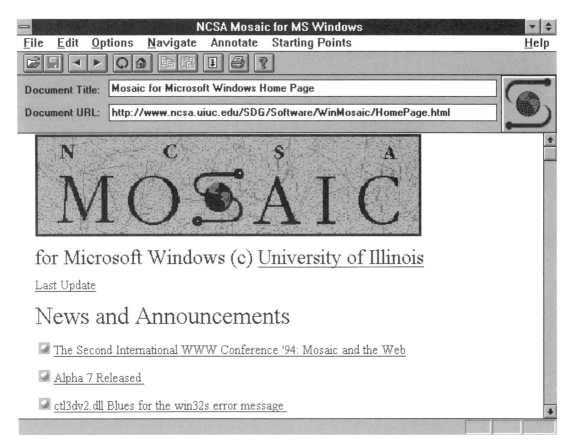

Figure 7-12
NCSA Mosaic for
Microsoft Windows
Home Page

5. Click on the **down-arrow** on the scroll bar

6. Move down the home page until you find the hyperlink called The Latest Release of Mosaic Click on it once. Your screen will look like Figure 7-13.

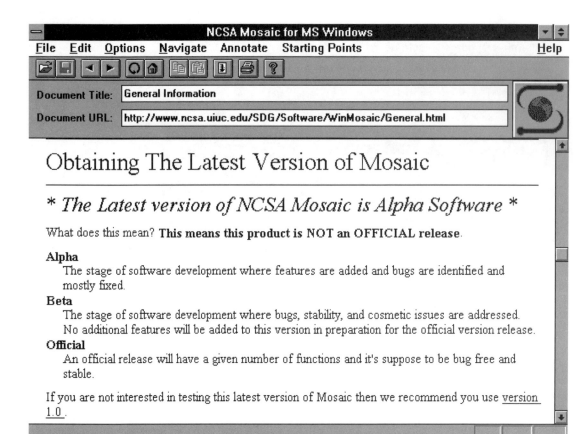

Obtaining The Latest Version of Mosaic

** The Latest version of NCSA Mosaic is Alpha Software **

What does this mean? **This means this product is NOT an OFFICIAL release**.

Alpha
The stage of software development where features are added and bugs are identified and mostly fixed.

Beta
The stage of software development where bugs, stability, and cosmetic issues are addressed. No additional features will be added to this version in preparation for the official version release.

Official
An official release will have a given number of functions and it's suppose to be bug free and stable.

If you are not interested in testing this latest version of Mosaic then we recommend you use version 1.0.

Figure 7-13
The Latest Version of Mosaic

7. Click on the down arrow on the scroll bar until you come to the screen which is labeled: Windows 3.1 and WfW Users

In Figure 7-14, notice the sentence which states:

Our last 16-bit version of Mosaic, v2.0alpha2, is available. Using Mosaic, select Options, Load to Disk, and click here to transfer it to your machine.

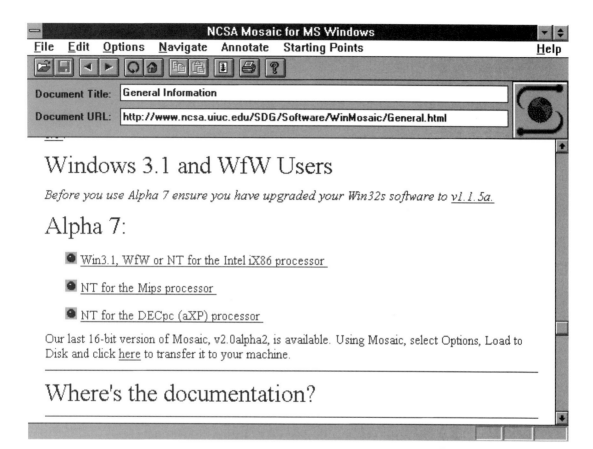

Figure 7-14
Windows 3.1 and WfW

We will do this now.

8. From the NCSA Mosaic Menu Bar, click on **Options**

9. Click on **Load to Disk**

10. Click on **here** as shown in Figure 7-14.

As soon as you move your cursor to the hyperlink **here** you will be shown where to find the file that we are seeking. If you look at the bottom of your screen, you will see that Mosaic is using ftp to get the file and that the ftp server information is

`ftp.ncsa.uiuc.edu/Mosaic/Windows/old/wmos20a2.zip`

If the following instructions do not work, you could certainly use ftp to get the file "manually," so to speak.

11. When the Save As dialog box appears, do the following:

a. When the File Name box appears, type

`c:\incoming\wmos20a2.zip`

b. Click on **OK**

Hopefully, NCSA Mosaic 20a2.zip will now be downloaded to your PC.

Important: Be sure to click on **Options** and **Load to Disk** when the file has been completely downloaded to your computer. This will turn the Load to Disk option off.

Later in this session, we will show you how to install this new version. First, we need to show you an alternate way to get this file.

Note: If you successfully downloaded wmos20a2.zip, then you do not have to complete the Archie search and ftp activities that follow. You may wish to join us later in this session when we install NCSA Mosaic 2.2.

Using Archie to Find NCSA Mosaic 2.2 (`wmos20a2.zip`)

It is certainly possible that you may be able to use NCSA Mosaic 1.0 to find a version of NCSA Mosaic 2.2 (wmos20a2.zip). However, due to the enormous popularity of NCSA Mosaic and the heavy demands on their file servers, this may be an exercise in frustration. So, it is helpful to have several other options available. Here is one of them.

As we did in Session Six, we will use Archie to help us to find host computers that have the NCSA Mosaic software. Here is a list of Archie servers that is valid as of this writing:

archie.ans.net (USA–NY)

archie.rutgers.edu (USA–NY)

archie.sura.net (USA–MD)

archie.unl.edu (USA–NE)

archie.mcgill.ca (Canada)

archie.funet.fi (Finland/Europe)

archie.au (Australia)

archie.doc.ic.ac.uk (Great Britain)

archie.wide.ad.jp (Japan)

archie.ncu.edu.tw (Taiwan)

1. Open Chameleon Sampler and double-click on **Telnet**

2. Click on **Settings** and then on **Preferences**

3. Set the Buffer Lines to **150**

4. Connect to the Archie server of your choice, for example, **archie.funet.fi**

5. Log in as `archie`

6. Once you are connected to the Archie server (we chose archie.funet.fi), type the following search specifications `prog wmos20a2.zip`

    wmos20a2.zip translates as Windows NCSA Mosaic Version 20a2 Compressed with PKZIP (This version of NCSA Mosaic was released on February 28, 1994.)

    When we did this, here is what we found:

```
Finnish University and Research Network FUNET
           Information Service
The following information services are available:
gopher     Menu-based global information tool
www        World Wide Web, Global hypertext web
wais       Wide Area Information Server, global databases
Host ftp.psg.com (147.28.0.33)
Last updated 09:18 22 Jun 1994
Location: /pub/ip-for-pc/windows
FILE -rw-r--r-- 243749 bytes 01:21 9 Jun 1994 wmos20a2.zip
Host olymp.wu-wien.ac.at (137.208.8.30)
Last updated 05:38 22 Jun 1994
Location: /pub/sgml/navysgml/www/NCSA Mosaic/PC
FILE -r--r--r-- 243749 bytes 00:24 28 May 1994
wmos20a2.zip
```

```
Host ftp.psg.com (147.28.0.33)
Last updated 09:18 22 Jun 1994
Location: /pub/ip-for-pc/RAINet.kit/windows
FILE -rw-r--r-- 243749 bytes 11:18 18 Apr 1994
wmos20a2.zip
Host pacific.mps.ohio-state.edu (128.146.37.18)
Last updated 02:04 22 Jun 1994
Location: /win3
FILE -rw-r--r-- 243749 bytes 17:53 8 Apr 1994 wmos20a2.zip
Host olymp.wu-wien.ac.at (137.208.8.30)
Last updated 05:38 22 Jun 1994
Location: /pub/email/quest/windows/winsock
FILE -r--r--r-- 243749 bytes 23:24 7 Apr 1994 wmos20a2.zip
Host tartarus.uwa.edu.au (130.95.128.3)
Last updated 03:42 2 Jul 1994
Location: /pub/spriggs/winsock
FILE -rw-r--r-- 243749 bytes 00:07 5 Apr 1994 wmos20a2.zip
Host ajk.tele.fi (131.177.5.20)
Last updated 06:01 2 Jul 1994 Location:
/PublicBinaries/msdos/winsock
FILE -rw-r--r-- 243749 bytes 15:13 24 Mar 1994
wmos20a2.zip
Host alf.uib.no (129.177.30.3)
Last updated 09:57 22 Jun 1994
Location: /pub/pc/WinSock
FILE -rwxr-xr-x 243749 bytes 15:58 18 Mar 1994
wmos20a2.zip
Host ucselx.sdsu.edu (130.191.1.100)
Last updated 01:55 22 Jun 1994
Location: /pub/ibm/winsock
FILE -rw-r--r-- 243749 bytes 04:53 4 Mar 1994 wmos20a2.zip
Host caip.rutgers.edu (128.6.19.83)
Last updated 03:40 2 Jul 1994
Location: /pub
FILE -rw-r--r-- 243749 bytes 14:43 2 Mar 1994 wmos20a2.zip
Host nic.switch.ch (130.59.1.40)
Last updated 10:33 22 Jun 1994
Location: /mirror/NCSA Mosaic/Windows/old
FILE -rw-rw-r-- 243749 bytes 19:41 1 Mar 1994 wmos20a2.zip
Host ftp.eunet.no (193.71.1.7)
Last updated 10:01 22 Jun 1994
```

```
Location: /networking/web/pc
FILE -r--r--r-- 243749 bytes 18:41 1 Mar 1994 wmos20a2.zip
Host olymp.wu-wien.ac.at (137.208.8.30)
Last updated 05:38 22 Jun 1994
Location: /pub/www/windows/old
FILE -r--r--r-- 243749 bytes 17:41 1 Mar 1994 wmos20a2.zip
Host ftp.ncsa.uiuc.edu (141.142.20.50)
Last updated 01:06 22 Jun 1994
Location: /PC/NCSA Mosaic/old
FILE -rw-rw-r-- 243749 bytes 17:41 1 Mar 1994 wmos20a2.zip
```

As you can tell from this list, there are many locations other than NCSA that have copies of NCSA Mosaic Version 2.0 available for you.

Once you have saved this information, disconnect from your Telnet server.

Using ftp to Get NCSA Mosaic 2.2 (`wmos20a2.zip`)

Note: If you were able to download wmos20a2.zip earlier from NCSA, you do not have to complete the following activity.

We are about to get a new file called wmos20a2.zip—we will continue to refer to it as NCSA Mosaic 2.2. Therefore, you might wish to create a new directory on your hard disk as we did earlier. We would suggest that you call it mosaic22

At your `c:` prompt, just type `md mosaic22`

1. With your Chameleon Sampler open, double-click on **FTP**

   It is important to

   a. Make sure that your Transfer mode is set to **Binary**

   b. Make sure that the Local Directory is c:\incoming

2. Click once on **Connect**

3. Add the following information:

   a. Host: `ftp.psg.com`

   b. User: `anonymous`

   c. Password: your full Internet address

   d. System: `Auto`

4. Then click on **OK**

5. Using the information obtained from our Archie search, we know that the file is located in pub/ip-for-pc/RAINet.kit/windows

Here is how to get there:

a. Double-click on **pub**

b. Double-click on **ip-for-pc**

c. Double-click on **RAINet.kit**

d. Double-click on **windows**

e. Click once on **wmos20a2.zip**

6. Once wmos20a2.zip is active, determine the drive and directory to which you would like to copy the file (for example, c:\incoming). Once you have done that, click on the **left copy button** and copy the 243,749 bytes of wmos20a2.zip to that directory.

7. Be sure to disconnect from ftp.psg.com when you have finished.

Congratulations! You now have (almost) a copy of NCSA Mosaic 2.0. In the next part of this activity, we will get the file ready to run.

Installing NCSA Mosaic 2.2
(`wmos20a2.zip`)

1. Copy wmos20a2.zip from c:\incoming to c:\mosaic22. Type `copy c:incoming\wmos20a2.zip c:\mosaic22`

2. In addition, you will need to have a copy of pkunzip.exe. This should be in your directory entitled pkware which you created earlier. Copy the file to the directory entitled mosaic22. To do this, type

`copy c:\pkware\pkunzip.exe c:\mosaic22`

Now we will unzip wmos20a2.zip with pkunzip.

3. Change to your mosaic22 directory. Type `cd mosaic22`

4. Type `pkunzip wmos20a2.zip`

Six files should be inflated:

MOSAIC.EXE
INSTALL.TXT
UPDATE.TXT
MOSAIC.INI
README.NOW
INSTALL.WRI

You should feel free to read the INSTALL.TXT and UPDATE.TXT files with your favorite word processor. However, for our purposes, we will focus on the MOSAIC.EXE and MOSAIC.INI files.

We are about to install NCSA Mosaic 2.2 into the directory (c:\netmanag) where you previously have had NCSA Mosaic 1.0. Also, we are about to install a new version of MOSAIC.INI into your Windows directory. To be safe, it would be good if you had a copy of NCSA Mosaic 1.0 (meaning MOSAIC.EXE and MOSAIC.INI) safely stored away elsewhere. To do this, type

```
c:\copy c:\netmanag\mosaic.exe c:\mosaic10
c:\copy c:\windows\mosaic.ini c:\mosaic10
```

---

5. We need to remove MOSAIC.EXE from the netmanag directory and MOSAIC.INI from the Windows directory. To do this, type the following

   a. `cd netmanag`

   b. `erase mosaic.exe`

   c. `cd\` (this will take you back to drive c:)

   d. `cd windows`

   e. `erase mosaic.ini`
   `cd\`

6. 6. Next, we need to copy the new MOSAIC.EXE file to the netmanag directory, and the new MOSAIC.INI file to the Windows directory. To do this, type

   ```
   copy c:\mosaic22\mosaic.exe c:\netmanag
   ```

   ```
   copy c:\mosaic22\mosaic.ini c:\windows
   ```

   Note: If you use DIR to scan the files in c:\netmanag, you should notice that the MOSAIC.EXE file is now 624,960 bytes, and is dated 02-28-94. This is the file which we shall call NCSA Mosaic 2.2.

Now, let's see if it works!

1. Open your Chameleon Sampler from Windows

2. Double-click on **Custom**, and log in to your Internet service provider

3. Double-click on **Mosaic**

If all is working correctly, the NCSA Mosaic for MS Windows screen should appear, just as it has done in the past. And, for the most part, it should look quite familiar.

There are some new features in wmos20a2.zip, but, for the most part, you should be able to use NCSA Mosaic 2.2 almost immediately with little or no coaching. We will explore some of the additional features in the activities to come.

**HANDS-ON
Activity 5**

EDITING YOUR MOSAIC.INI FILE

The first of the many interesting new features of NCSA Mosaic 2.2 is an editor for the MOSAIC.INI file. The MOSAIC.INI file resides in your Windows directory and is used by NCSA Mosaic and Windows to keep track of NCSA Mosaic's operations. In this activity, we will show you how to use NCSA Mosaic's Menu Editor and then show you how to use Windows Notepad to do the same thing. You will then have your choice.

You may be wondering why you should ever have to edit the MOSAIC.INI file. The answer is that the MOSAIC.INI file controls much of what you are able to do with NCSA Mosaic. There are choices you will wish to make; editing this file will permit you to have control over those choices. In all likelihood, you will need to edit this file sooner or later.

The first method (using NCSA Mosaic's Menu Editor) allows you to edit destinations (URLs). The second method (using Windows Notepad) allows you to edit the destinations (URLs), *plus* many other items in the MOSAIC.INI file.

Editing the MOSAIC.INI File Using NCSA Mosaic (First Method)

1. Double-click on **NCSA Mosaic** and move the mouse to Navigate on the top bar. Click on **Navigate**

2. Notice the Menu Editor item at the bottom of the list. Click on **Menu Editor...** and you will see a screen like the one in Figure 7-15 listing Personal Menus.

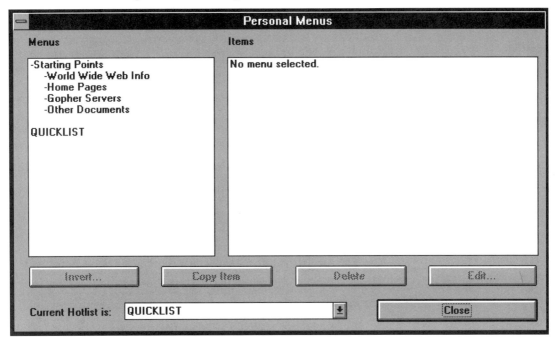

3. Click on **-Starting Points**

4. Then, double-click on **NCSA Mosaic's "What's New" Page** Your screen will resemble Figure 7-16.

Figure 7-15
Personal Menu Editor

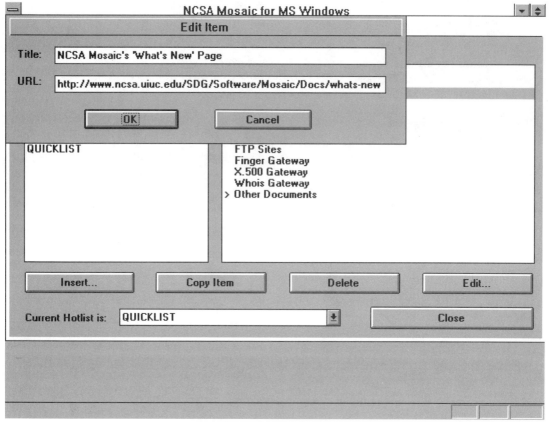

Figure 7-16
The "What's New"
Page

5. Click on **Edit** and you will see the screen in Figure 7-17.

```
─                          NCSA Mosaic for MS Windows              ▼ ♦
┌─────────────────────────── Edit Item ──────────────────────────┐
│                                                                 │
│  Title:  ┌──────────────────────────────────────────────────┐  │
│          │ NCSA Mosaic's 'What's New' Page                  │  │
│          └──────────────────────────────────────────────────┘  │
│                                                                 │
│  URL:    ┌──────────────────────────────────────────────────┐  │
│          │ http://www.ncsa.uiuc.edu/SDG/Software/Mosaic/Docs/whats-new│
│          └──────────────────────────────────────────────────┘  │
│                                                                 │
│          ┌──────────────────┐      ┌──────────────────┐         │
│          │       OK         │      │     Cancel       │         │
│          └──────────────────┘      └──────────────────┘         │
│                                                                 │
│  QUICKLIST                         FTP Sites                    │
│                                    Finger Gateway               │
│                                    X.500 Gateway                │
│                                    Whois Gateway                │
│                                  > Other Documents              │
│                                                                 │
│                                                                 │
│                                                                 │
│                                                                 │
│  ┌─────────────┐  ┌─────────────┐  ┌─────────────┐  ┌─────────────┐
│  │  Insert...  │  │  Copy Item  │  │   Delete    │  │   Edit...   │
│  └─────────────┘  └─────────────┘  └─────────────┘  └─────────────┘
│                                                                 │
│  Current Hotlist is:  ┌──────────────────────────┐ ♦  ┌──────────────┐
│                       │ QUICKLIST                │    │    Close     │
│                       └──────────────────────────┘    └──────────────┘
```

If you choose to do so, you will now be able to edit both
the title and the URL of this particular item.

Important: We will not edit this file at this time. Therefore, you should click on **Cancel**

Figure 7-17
Editing the "What's
New" Page

This method has been an illustration of how it is possible to edit the MOSAIC.INI file from within NCSA Mosaic using Menu Editor. This is one valid way to edit the file. Another way uses the Windows Notepad tool.

Editing the MOSAIC.INI File Using Windows Notepad (Second Method)

1. Minimize NCSA Mosaic
2. Click once on **Window** in the Program Manager drop-down menu bar
3. Click on the **Accessories Group**
4. Double-click on **Notepad**
5. Click on **File** and **Open...**
6. In the File Name: box, type `c:\windows\mosaic.ini`
7. Click on **OK** You will see a screen like the one in Figure 7-18.

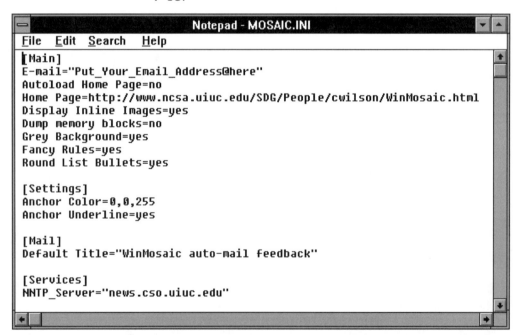

Figure 7-18
Getting the Notepad

You are seeing the top of the MOSAIC.INI file. Notice that there is a place where you may choose to put your E-mail address. You may wish to put your E-mail address here if you will be sending E-mail to NCSA, Mosaic's developers at the University of Illinois.

209

In Session Eight, after we have added some new software to
your computer, we will return to this screen so that we can edit
the section with the heading [Viewers]. For now, scroll down to a
screen which looks like Figure 7-19.

```
╔══════════════════════════════════════════════════════╗
║  —           Notepad - MOSAIC.INI              ▼ ▲   ║
╠══════════════════════════════════════════════════════╣
║  File   Edit   Search   Help                          ║
╟──────────────────────────────────────────────────────╢
║ [User Menu1]                                        ▲ ║
║ Menu_Name=Starting Points                             ║
║ Menu_Type=TOPLEVEL                                    ║
║ Item1=Starting Points Document,http://                ║
║ Item2=NCSA Mosaic Demo Document,http://www.ncsa.uiuc.edu/demoweb/demo ║
║ Item3=NCSA Mosaic's 'What's New' Page,http://www.ncsa.uiuc.edu/SDG/So ║
║ Item4=MENU,User Menu2                                 ║
║ Item5=MENU,User Menu3                                 ║
║ Item6=InterNIC Info Source,gopher://is.internic.net:70/11/infosource ║
║ Item7=MENU,User Menu4                                 ║
║ Item8=FTP Sites,http://hoohoo.ncsa.uiuc.edu:80/ftp-interface.html ║
║ Item9=Finger Gateway,http://cs.indiana.edu/finger/gateway ║
║ Item10=X.500 Gateway,gopher://umich.edu:7777/         ║
║ Item11=Whois Gateway,gopher://sipb.mit.edu:70/1B%3aInternet%20whois%2 ║
║ Item12=MENU,User Menu5                                ║
║                                                       ║
║ [User Menu2]                                          ║
║ Menu_Name=World Wide Web Info                         ║
║ Item1=Web Overview,http://info.cern.ch/hypertext/WWW/LineMode/Default ▼ ║
╟──────────────────────────────────────────────────────╢
║ ◄                                                   ► ║
╚══════════════════════════════════════════════════════╝
```

Figure 7-19
Editing the Notepad

You can see that NCSA Mosaic's Starting Points Menu is shown
here. This is where you can edit what you will see when you
start NCSA Mosaic. You may scroll through the various NCSA
Mosaic menus to add or delete URLs from each menu. The form
of each entry is

> Item Number=   Item Title,   Actual URL

Notice the use of the equal sign (=) and the comma (,) to
delimit each entry.

We are going to do one important editing activity at this time. It
is necessary that you do this so that you will be able to use
NCSA Mosaic to enable you to access telnet sites (which we will
do shortly). It is important that you change the *default* information which has been provided with NCSA Mosaic so that telnet
will work correctly. Here is how to do so:

1. Click on the **down arrow** on the scroll bar until you
   come to the [Viewers] section of MOSAIC.INI

2. Once you are there, scroll down a bit further until you can see the bottom lines of the [Viewers] section of MOSAIC.INI

It should resemble Figure 7-20.

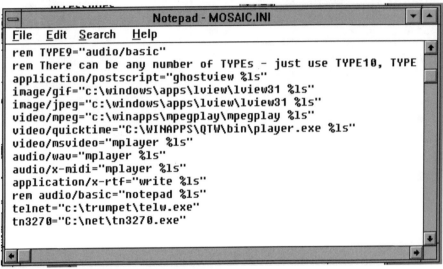

```
Notepad - MOSAIC.INI
File   Edit   Search   Help
rem TYPE9="audio/basic"
rem There can be any number of TYPEs - just use TYPE10, TYPE
application/postscript="ghostview %ls"
image/gif="c:\windows\apps\lview\lview31 %ls"
image/jpeg="c:\windows\apps\lview\lview31 %ls"
video/mpeg="c:\winapps\mpegplay\mpegplay %ls"
video/quicktime="C:\WINAPPS\QTW\bin\player.exe %ls"
video/msvideo="mplayer %ls"
audio/wav="mplayer %ls"
audio/x-midi="mplayer %ls"
application/x-rtf="write %ls"
rem audio/basic="notepad %ls"
telnet="c:\trumpet\telw.exe"
tn3270="C:\net\tn3270.exe"
```

Figure 7-20
Adding telnet Access

3. Move your cursor to the line that says
`telnet="c:\trumpet\telw.exe"`

4. Click once on the cursor. Delete all of the text after the c:

5. Type `\netmanag\telnet.exe"`

   Important: Be sure to type this exactly; make sure that you include the final quotes.

6. Proofread the telnet line. It should now read
`telnet="c:\netmanag\telnet.exe"`

7. Click on **File** and then on **Save**

When you have finished, just click on **File** and **Exit** to leave the Notepad.

At this point, we hope that you can recognize the value of both methods of editing your MOSAIC.INI file. In the next session, we will need to edit several items in your MOSAIC.INI file for sound, graphic, and video viewers.

Other Things You Can Do with NCSA Mosaic___

As you may have noticed earlier, NCSA Mosaic seemingly has the ability to permit you to do all of the Internet activities that are commonly described, including telnet, ftp, and gopher.

We will explore some of these now.

telnet

telnet addresses may be entered as you would enter other URL information. The format for this is always going to be telnet://address/ You will note that NCSA Mosaic permits you to enter the URL information and then switches you to telnet for the actual application. Here is one to try.

1. Click on **File** and then click on **Open URL...**

2. In the URL: box, type `telnet://www.njit.edu`

3. Click on **OK**

4. When you are prompted to log in, type: www Press **Enter**

This is the New Jersey Institute of Technology's text-only version of hypertext. You may make *Hypertext Action Choices*, as they are called, and you will be taken to the various documents that will provide you with information.

Notice two things:

a. The documents are retrieved quite quickly, since there are no graphics.

b. Many of the links that you are likely to see, are in the (by now) familiar URL form of http://info.cer n.ch/hypertext/ WWW/etc.

Important: This means that you may have already seen many of these documents, using these same hyperlinks, in the full NCSA Mosaic format; here they are presented in text-only fashion.

1. Pressing **X** followed by **Enter** will return you to a blank telnet screen

2. Click on **File** and then **Exit** to return to the NCSA Mosaic screen where you began.

ftp

An excellent illustration of the power of using NCSA Mosaic as the *front end* for ftp activities is provided in the following exercise. We will use our NCSA Mosaic front end to enable us to connect to an ftp server at the University of Illinois, Urbana-Champaign.

ftp addresses may be entered as you would enter other URL information. The format for this is always going to be ftp://address/ You will note that NCSA Mosaic permits you to enter the URL information but does not require you to add the other information which ftp traditionally requires such as a user name of anonymous and your actual Internet address as a password.

Here is how to do this:

1.Click on **File** and then on **Open URL...**

2.In the URL: box type: `ftp://ftp.ncsa.uiuc.edu`

3.Then click on **OK**

If this works successfully, you should be connected to the ftp server at UIUC and should see a screen resembling the one in Figure 7-21.

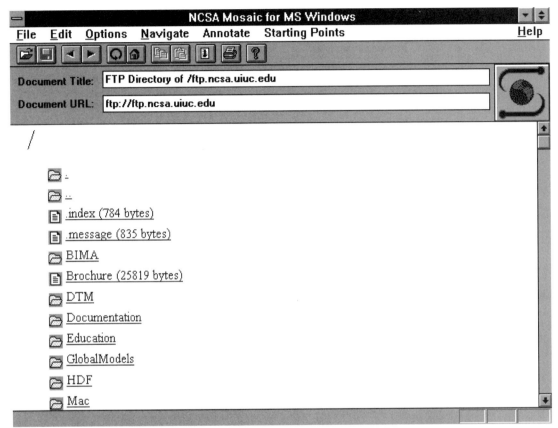

Notice several important facts:

Figure 7-21

UIUC's ftp Server

a. The ftp server contents are arrayed for you in a very visual fashion, with icons representing the text files, directories, and actual files of information.

b. Most significantly, you are provided with the number of bytes in various items before you download them!

c. Finally, you have hyperlinks to connect you to each of the items that is listed. In each instance, should you make a selection, the ftp server will swing into action. You will move to the selected subdirectory, or you will be able to retrieve the particular file you have chosen.

An extremely valuable resource has been included with NCSA Mosaic 2.2 that provides you with an amazingly detailed array of ftp sites. To access this, you will need to do the following:

1. Click on **Starting Points** and then **Other Documents**

2. Click on **FTP Sites**

Figure 7-22
FTP Interface Screen

You will see the FTP Interface screen, which is presented in Figure 7- 22.

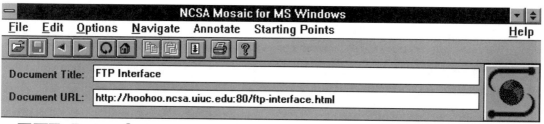

FTP Interface

Please note that it is a nontrivial problem for a World Wide Web browser like NCSA Mosaic to properly handle the wide range of datatypes residing on various FTP sites. Please go here for information on how Mosaic handles file typing.

- Introduction to the monster FTP list
- Sites with names A to E
- Sites with names F to K
- Sites with names L to O
- Sites with names P to S
- Sites with names T to Z

marca@ncsa.uiuc.edu

If you click on Sites with names A to E you will see the screen in Figure 7-23.

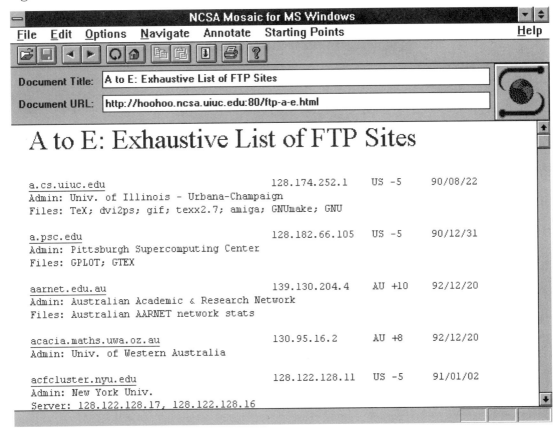

Not only do you have an amazing array of ftp sites at your disposal, but they are also all available using the hyperlinks that are presented to you via NCSA Mosaic. When you have lots of time available to you, you should feel free to explore this resource!

Figure 7-23
List of ftp Sites

gopher

gopher addresses may be entered as you would enter other URL information. The format for this is always going to be gopher://address/ You will note that NCSA Mosaic permits you to enter the URL information, and then switches you to gopher for the actual application. However, since you are now using NCSA Mosaic as your front end to gopher, you will find that your experience with gopher is much more graphical than it has been before.

In this exercise, we will use NCSA Mosaic as our front end to gopher. Let's try the following:

1.   With your NCSA Mosaic for MS Windows window open, click once on **File** and then once on **Open URL...**

2.   Click once on the **URL box** to make it active and then type gopher://ds.internic.net

3.   Click on **OK**

     You are quickly taken to a gopher server for the Internet Information Services which is provided by General Atomics. Select whichever items are of interest to you.

     When you have finished, click on **File** and then **Exit** to return to the NCSA Mosaic Icon.

Just as we discovered with the ftp resources listed above, there are also quite a few gopher resources that are accessible to you via NCSA Mosaic. A few of them have been included and many more are accessible via hyperlinks. Here is how to access them:

1.   With NCSA Mosaic for MS Windows open, click on **Starting Points**

2.   Click on **Gopher Servers**

3.   Double-click on **Gopherspace Overview**

     You should see a screen resembling the one in Figure 7-24.

217

```
┌─────────────────────────────────────────────────────────────────┐
│ ─              NCSA Mosaic for MS Windows              ▼ ▲        │
├─────────────────────────────────────────────────────────────────┤
│ File  Edit  Options  Navigate  Annotate  Starting Points   Help  │
├─────────────────────────────────────────────────────────────────┤
│ 🖿 🖫  ◄ ►  ○ ⌂  🖻 🖺  📩  🖶  ?                                   │
├─────────────────────────────────────────────────────────────────┤
│ Document Title: ┌────────────────────────────────────┐           │
│                 └────────────────────────────────────┘           │
│ Document URL:  ┌─────────────────────────────────────────────┐   │
│                │gopher://gopher.micro.umn.edu:70/11/Other%20Gopher%20and%20Information│
│                └─────────────────────────────────────────────┘   │
├─────────────────────────────────────────────────────────────────┤
│                                                                   │
│  Gopher Menu:                                                     │
│                                                                   │
│         All the Gopher Servers in the World                       │
│      🖻  Search All the Gopher Servers in the World               │
│         Search titles in Gopherspace using veronica               │
│         Africa                                                    │
│         Asia                                                      │
│         Europe                                                    │
│         International Organizations                               │
│         Middle East                                              │
│         North America                                            │
│         Pacific                                                   │
│         Russia                                                    │
│         South America                                            │
└─────────────────────────────────────────────────────────────────┘
```

Figure 7-24
Gopher Menu

It is beyond the scope of this book to explore in depth all of the
Gopher resources that are available to you via NCSA Mosaic.
However, when you have *lots of time*, you should feel free to do
some exploring on your own.

SESSION SUMMARY

As you have seen in sessions six and seven, there is an amazing
number of things that we can do with NCSA Mosaic. You have
complete access to all of the HyperText Transfer Protocol hosts
out there (3,100 as of June 18, 1994.) You also can use NCSA
Mosaic to access more traditional Internet tools such as ftp, telnet and gopher. In our next session, you will learn how to add
some additional software to NCSA Mosaic so that you might be
able to enjoy more of the multimedia capabilities of the Internet.

SESSION 8

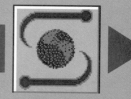

Pictures and Sounds

NCSA Mosaic's power to bring you text and images only begins to show you the power of the Internet and the World-Wide Web. What we will now introduce is NCSA Mosaic's ability to work with other packages to produce sound, brilliant images, and even video clips. This will allow you to access, view, and listen to information from all around the globe.

You can listen while corporate chief executives tell you about their companies. You can watch, in near real time, as space telescopes bring back planetary images. You can, with some patience, bring in film and animation clips to view at your leisure. You can look at some of the world's finest art treasures on your own PC.

As we write this, the range of sounds, images, and video clips is astounding. We can be sure that when you read this the range will have expanded tremendously. Let's look quickly at how NCSA Mosaic can get and show you all these things.

Using NCSA Mosaic to Get Sounds and Pictures

We have already looked briefly at the MOSAIC.INI file. This file, residing in your Windows directory, controls much of what NCSA Mosaic does. If you look in the first parts of this file, you will see something like the listing below. (We have edited the file shown here to highlight the relevant sections.)

 **Heads Up!**

One thing you may wish to change in your MOSAIC.INI file is the third line. As you can see, it tells NCSA Mosaic to go to the University of Illinois for the NCSA Mosaic Home Page each time you bring up NCSA Mosaic. You should probably change this to Autoload Home Page=no

This will bring up NCSA Mosaic faster for you and will take some load off the NCSA WWW server. You can use Windows Notepad to edit this file as we described in Session Seven. You can, of course, put another home page of your choice in the fourth line and leave Autoload set to =yes

Now let's look at the section of the MOSAIC.INI file headed [Viewers]. It is written in "near English" and tells us what types of audio, application, image, and video to expect.

```
[Main]
E-mail="Put_Your_Email_Address@here"
Autoload Home Page=yes
HomePage=http://www.ncsa.uiuc.edu/SDG/Software/NCSAMosaic
/NCSAMosaicHome.html
Display Inline Images=yes
Grey Background=yes
Fancy Rules=yes
Round List Bullets=yes

[Section edited out]

[Viewers]
TYPE0="audio/wav"
TYPE1="application/postscript"
TYPE2="image/gif"
TYPE3="image/jpeg"
TYPE4="video/mpeg"
TYPE5="video/quicktime"
TYPE6="video/msvideo"
TYPE7="application/x-rtf"
TYPE8="audio/x-midi"
TYPE9="application/zip"
rem TYPE9="audio/basic"
application/postscript="ghostview %ls"
```

```
image/gif="c:\windows\apps\lview\lview31 %ls"
image/jpeg="c:\windows\apps\lview\lview31 %ls"
video/mpeg="c:\winapps\mpegplay\mpegplay %ls"
video/quicktime="C:\WINAPPS\QTW\bin\player.exe %ls"
video/msvideo="mplayer %ls"
audio/wav="mplayer %ls"
audio/x-midi="mplayer %ls"
application/x-rtf="write %ls"
application/zip="C:\WINDOWS\APPS\ZIPMGR\ZM400.EXE %ls"
rem audio/basic="notepad %ls"
telnet="c:\netmanag\telnet.exe"

[Suffixes]
application/postscript=.ps,.eps,.ai,.ps
text/html=
text/plain=
application/x-rtf=.rtf,.wri
audio/wav=.wave,.wav,.WAV
audio/x-midi=.mid
image/x-tiff=.tiff,.tif
image/jpeg=.jpeg,.jpe,.jpg
video/mpeg=.mpeg,.mpe,.mpg
video/qtime=.mov
video/msvideo=.avi

[Rest of file edited out]
```

After the TYPES section, this file tells NCSA Mosaic where to look for viewers. A *viewer* is a program that can interpret an incoming file and play or display it on your PC.

The [Viewers] section is organized into two simple parts: The first part defines different TYPES of sounds or images. The second part points to directories and programs that will decode and play or display the incoming (or stored) files.

POSTSCRIPT AND JPEG

We will talk about playing sounds in a moment. Before that, we need to look at the bottom half of the [Viewers] section in the MOSAIC.INI file above and find two programs: ghostview and lview31.

Notice the directories for each of them. You do not have these directories yet, but we will create them as we go along.

ghostview

The first program, ghostview, is a PostScript viewer. *PostScript* is a text and image language that allows very complex documents to be described in plain ASCII text. Here is a sample of the first few lines of a PostScript file.

Note: You are not going to have to create anything like this file; it is provided here only to give you a sense of what a PostScript file looks like!

```
%!PS-Adobe-3.0
%%Title: (genbbb/wwww US)
%%Creator: (Microsoft Word: LaserWriter 8 8.1.1)
%%CreationDate: (10:47 AM Tuesday, April 26, 1994)
%%For: (Oliver McBryan)
%%Pages: 15
%%DocumentFonts: Palatino-Bold Palatino-Roman Palatino-Italic Courier
%%DocumentNeededFonts: Palatino-Bold Palatino-Roman Palatino-Italic Courier
%%DocumentSuppliedFonts:
%%DocumentData: Clean7Bit
%%PageOrder: Ascend
%%Orientation: Portrait
%ADO_PaperArea: -31 -31 761 581
%ADO_ImageableArea: 0 0 730 552
%%EndComments
```

Finally, the section entitled [Suffixes] in the MOSAIC.INI file tells NCSA Mosaic which viewer to use. As you can see, Post-Script file extensions are .ps, .eps, and .ai.

lview31

The extensions .jpeg, .jpe, and .jpg in the [Suffixes] section of the MOSAIC.INI file tell NCSA Mosaic to look for files that have been created in adherence to a standard called JPEG. *JPEG* stands for the *Joint Photographic Experts Group*. The key word *Photographic* might give you a hint that some of these images will be like photos. In addition, you might expect to find artistic paintings, and so on.

That's enough tutorial for now. Let's play some sounds.

If you already have a multimedia PC (or at least a soundboard such as SoundBlaster) you can play sounds right off of the Internet. Our first activity will do just that.

If you do not have a soundboard or multimedia PC, you can download a Microsoft Windows driver to send sounds to your PC speaker. In all honesty, the sound is generally pretty poor. On many PCs, you can just make out the words or music. However, it's better than silence. After the first activity, we will show you how to get this driver. If you have no sound capability, you may wish to skip ahead to the section entitled PC Speaker driver.

THE NCSA DEMO DOCUMENT

**HANDS-ON
Activity 1**

Figure 8-1 shows a portion of the NCSA Mosaic Demo Document. We have highlighted the Loudspeaker Icon. This icon, as explained by the screen text, will send a sound clip to your PC if you click on it. With your soundboard and speakers, you should then hear a clear and crisp audio clip.

We are venturing into tricky waters here, as there are many variations in PCs equipped with soundboards. The following activity may work flawlessly, or you may hear nothing. In the event that you hear nothing, you should use NCSA Mosaic's Options - Load to File and capture the sound clip. You can then try offline to find the problem by using NCSA Mosaic's File - Open Local File.

1. Connect to your Internet service provider and open NCSA Mosaic

2. Click on **Starting Points** and then click on **NCSA Mosaic Demo Document**

3. When the NCSA Mosaic Demo Document comes up, scroll down to show a screen similar to the one shown in Figure 8-1. Be sure that you are showing the bordered Loudspeaker Icon.

4. Click on the Loudspeaker Icon labeled *What is NCSA Mosaic?* (If that icon is no longer there, find the nearest Loudspeaker Icon.)

5. On the status bar at the bottom of your NCSA Mosaic screen, you should see a file coming in with the file extension .au

The file is many tens of thousands of bytes, but when the transfer has been completed, you should hear the audio clip.

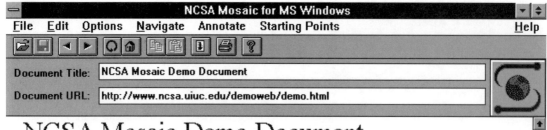

NCSA Mosaic Demo Document

In revision - July 20, 1994

Welcome to NCSA Mosaic, an information browser developed at the National Center for Supercomputing Applications at the University of Illinois, Urbana-Champaign. This document is an interactive hypermedia tour of Mosaic's capabilities.

Disclaimer:*This tour assumes that you have good network connectivity, that you have properly installed Mosaic and appropriate external viewers, and that the various information servers (at NCSA and elsewhere) the document references are alive and functioning well.*

Every time you see this icon: you can click on it to hear an audio clip narrating the current topic (if you have a workstation with appropriately configured audio hardware and software).

Introduction

Figure 8-1
NCSA Mosaic Demo
Document

PC SPEAKER DRIVER

If you do not have sound capabilities on your PC, you may wish to try the PC speaker as a sound driver. As we noted before, it will not produce very good sound, but you will be able to get a sense of the sound clip.

GETTING THE PC SPEAKER DRIVER

1. Connect to your Internet service provider and open NCSA Mosaic. We wish to go to the document whose title is External Viewer Information and whose URL is

```
http://www.ncsa.uiuc.edu/SDG/Software/WinMosaic/viewers.html
```

2. Click once on **File** and then click on **Open URL...**

3. Type the URL given above.

Your screen should resemble the one shown in Figure 8-2.

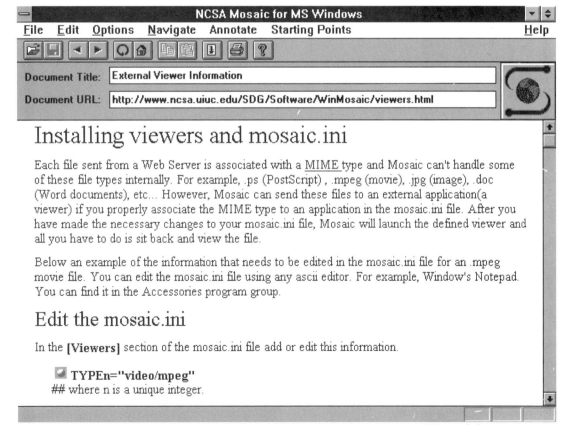

4. Click on the **down arrow** on the scroll bar down to Other Utilities. Your screen should be similar to Figure 8-3.

Figure 8-2
External Viewer
Information

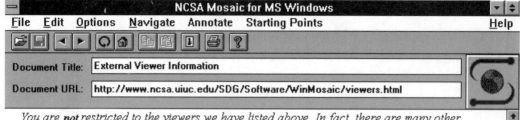

You are **not** restricted to the viewers we have listed above. In fact, there are many other viewers available from a number of ftp sites. As a rule of thumb if the viewer will accept command line instructions then Mosaic will be a ble to use it.

Other Utilities

PC Speaker driver

This product is a sound drive for the basic PC Speaker. It was developed by Microsoft and is freely available to licensed users of Windows 3.1. Please the read the <u>license agreement</u> for the terms of the products. You will also find a link to speak.exe at the bottom of the license agreement.

NOTE: *Since we did not develop these softwares we can not support them. If you are having problems with any of these viewers or other Utilities please contact the respective author.*

The National Center for Supercomputing Applications, mosaic-win@ncsa.uiuc.ed u

Figure 8-3
External Viewer
Information/Other
Utilities

5. Under PC Speaker driver find the hyperlink license agreement and click on it. You will receive a long license agreement document. As you read it, you will reach a single large here hyperlink at the bottom of the document.

    a. Click on **Options**

    b. Click on **Load to Disk**

    c. Click on **here**

        When you are prompted for a file name, type

        `c:\incoming\speak.exe`

        You will be downloading a file called speak.exe

    Important: Remember to click again on **Options** and then **Load to Disk** to turn off the file capture feature when you have finished.

6. Now, use the back arrow on NCSA Mosaic's Toolbar and return to the External Viewer Information Document.

7. Click on the **down arrow** on the scroll bar until you come to the hyperlink WPlany

    a. Click on **Options**

    b. Click on **Load to Disk**

    c. Double-click on **WPlany**

        When you are prompted for a file name, type

```
c:\incoming\wplny09b.zip
```

        This will download a file which is called, as of this writing, wplny09b.zip

    Important: Be sure to click on **Options** and then again on **Load to Disk** when you have finished.

    You have just downloaded two files, speak.exe and wplny09b.zip

8. Disconnect from your Internet service provider.

We will now prepare these two files for use.

INSTALLING THE PC SPEAKER DRIVER

1. Create a directory for your PC Speaker driver. For example, we created one called speaker (md speaker)

2. Copy the file speak.exe to this directory.

3. Change to the directory called speaker (cd\speaker), and type `speak`

    speak.exe will self-extract all of the PC Speaker driver files into this directory.

4. Using your favorite word processor, you should print copies of two files

        audio.txt
        speaker.txt

    These files will provide you with the information you will need to correctly install the PC Speaker driver.

5. We will follow the directions given by Microsoft to install the PC Speaker driver:

    a. In the Main Group, double-click on the **Control Panel Icon**

    b. In the Control Panel, double-click on **Drivers**

    c. In the Drivers dialog box, click on **Add...**

d. In the List of Drivers box, click on **Unlisted** or **Updated Driver**. Then, choose **OK**

e. The Install Driver box will appear. If you have installed the files into a subdirectory called speaker, then type

```
c:\speaker
```

Then, click on **OK**

f. The Add Unlisted or Undated Driver box will appear. You will be told that the name for your file is Sound Driver for PC-Speaker

g. Since this is correct, click on **OK**

You should hear a sound emanating from your PC!

Important: When you install the SPEAKER.DRV, you will be shown a PC-Speaker Setup box. Change the Seconds to limit playback from its default to No Limit (right end of the bar). Then, click on **OK**

h. Try hearing the sound, by clicking on **Test**

6. When you have finished installing your PC Speaker driver, you should click on **OK** and then **Cancel** to return to the Control Panel.

INSTALLING WINDOWS PLAY ANY FILE _____

1. Create a directory on your hard drive entitled wplayany

Type `md wplayany`

2. Copy the file wplny09b.zip to the wplayany directory

3. Copy the file pkunzip.exe to the wplayany directory

For example, type

```
copy c:\pkware\pkunzip.exe c:\wplayany
```

4. Use pkunzip to unzip wplny09b.zip by typing

```
pkunzip wplny09b.zip
```

5. Two files will be created:

```
WPLANY.DOC
WPLANY.EXE
```

6. Using your favorite word processor, print out WPLANY.DOC

7. Copy WPLANY.EXE to your Windows directory. Type

```
c:\wplayany\wplany.exe c:\windows
```

8. In the Main Group, double-click on **File Manager**. Then follow the directions in WPLANY.DOC

RUNNING WINDOWS PLAY ANY FILE (WPLANY) _____

You can run WPLANY either of two ways:

1. You can capture sound files from NCSA Mosaic by using Options and Load to Disk. Then, using Window's Program Manager - File - Run, you can type in
`WPLANY filename.au`

Be patient. The sound won't begin until the file has been loaded completely into the computer's memory.

2. You can change your MOSAIC.INI file. There are three steps to do this:

   a. Using Notepad, change the .INI file to include a new TYPE=audio/basic in the [Viewers] section. This will look like TYPE9="audio/basic"

   b. You will also need to add another line in this section:

   audio/basic= "wplany %ls"

   c. Finally, add the audio/basic file extension to the [Suffixes] section. This should look like audio/basic=.au

   d. Save the MOSAIC.INI file.

The next time you open NCSA Mosaic, you should be able to listen to sound clips from the NCSA Mosaic Demo Page or other locations that contain sound clips.

If you find that you are receiving other audio types (file extensions) from the Internet, modify your MOSAIC.INI file to handle them. Remember that the file must be fully received before it can play. For long sound bites, this may take many seconds.

Pointer

The directions above are a variation on those provided by NCSA in the External Viewer Information Document as shown in Figure 8-4.

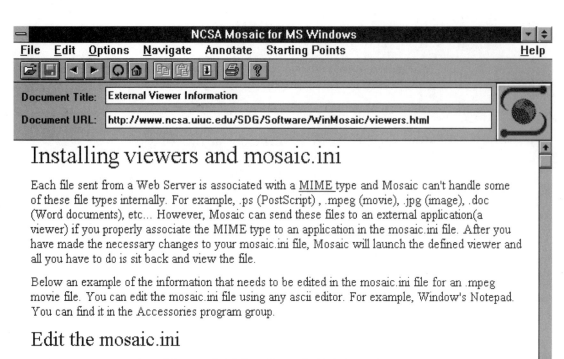

Figure 8-4
Installing Viewers

PLAYING A SOUND

A beautiful example of one of the many sounds that NCSA Mosaic permits you to hear is provided in this next example. We will go to Japan to the Nippon Telegraph and Telephone Corporation to hear the Japanese national anthem. Here is how to do this:

1. Click on **File** and then **Open URL...**

2. In the URL box, enter `http://www.ntt.jp`

    The Nippon Telegraph and Telephone Corporation Home Page will be downloaded to your computer.

3. Click on the hyperlink for **Japanese Information**

    Important: Click on **Options** and then on **Load to Disk**

4. Click on the hyperlink **Japanese National Anthem**

A Save As dialog box will appear. The name of the file is kimigayo.au

5. You will need to indicate where you would like to save the file. We suggest that you put a blank disk in drive A: and save it there since the file is about 400,000 bytes in length.

    Important: When the file has been transferred to your computer, be sure to remember to click once more on **Options** and **Load to Disk** to turn off that option.

6. Copy the kimigayo.au file to your Windows directory.

7. In your Program Manager window, click on **File** and then **Run...**

8. In the Command Line box, enter `wplany kimigayo.au`

9. Then click on **OK**

Congratulations! If all has gone according to plan, you should now be listening to all 400,419 bytes of the Japanese National Anthem.

Let's take a break. When we return, we will learn about the many graphics images that NCSA Mosaic permits us to see.

VIEWERS TO SEE THE PICTURES

On the worldwide Internet, you can find a marvelous variety of images and video clips that are freely available. For example, space photos from NASA, art from museums, photos of all descriptions, and near-real-time weather satellite views.

Some of the "art" available on the Internet may be objectionable to some people and some of it may be objectionable to almost everyone. To prevent this material from being shown to children, always exercise care and supervision in the use of the Internet.

Heads Up!

GIF, JPEG, AND POSTSCRIPT IMAGES

Many formats and standards have evolved for the PC presentation and storage of images and documents. A few have become quite popular and are more commonly found than are others. These more common formats are supported by NCSA Mosaic.

One of them, called *GIF* (and pronounced *jiff*), is supported directly by NCSA Mosaic. In fact, you have already seen NCSA Mosaic receiving GIF images and then converting them for presentation on your PC's screen. Others, however, require additional software before we are able to see them. Earlier, we mentioned JPEG. GIF and JPEG have become the most common formats for images found around the Internet.

Documents will often be found in PostScript format. If you have a PostScript printer, you can print these files directly. However, even if you have a PostScript printer, you may want to preview these documents before printing. For those without PostScript printers, viewing is the only option. The developers of NCSA Mosaic have found some viewers and have made them available. We will now get these viewers and help you to install them.

HANDS-ON
Activity 3

GETTING A JPEG VIEWER

1. Once again, connect to your Internet service provider and open NCSA Mosaic. As we did earlier in this session, we would like to go to the Document whose title is External Viewer Information. Its URL is

    `http://www.ncsa.uiuc.edu/SDG/Software/WinMosaic/viewers.html`

    Enter this information now, so you will return to the External Viewer Information Document.

2. Scroll down the page until you reach the section entitled Tested Viewers

3. To get Lview

    a. Click on **Options**

    b. Click on **Load to Disk**

    c. Double-click on **Lview**

4. When prompted for a file name, type
    `c:\incoming\lview31.zip`

5. Then click on **OK**

    lview31.zip (224,269 bytes) will be loaded to your disk.

Important: Be sure to click on **Options** and **Load to Disk** when the transfer has been completed.

6. Close your session with your Internet provider.

Heads Up!

A quick review of the particular part of the (Viewers) section of the NCSA MOSAIC.INI file that pertains to GIF and JPEG shows us the following:

```
[Viewers]
image/gif="c:\windows\apps\lview\lview31 %ls"
image/jpeg="c:\windows\apps\lview\lview31 %ls"
```

You will notice that the MOSAIC.INI file is set up to look for the file lview31 in a directory structure that goes from windows, to apps, to lview to lview31. We will construct such a directory structure in the following activity. However, you should be warned that should a newer version of MOSAIC.INI file change its default for lview31, you might have to construct a different path for your files.

PREPARING LVIEW FOR USE

1. Change to the Windows directory

2. Create a subdirectory called apps

3. Create a sub-subdirectory called lview

4. Then, copy LVIEW31.ZIP to the sub-subdirectory called lview

5. Copy pkunzip to the sub-sub-subdirectory called lview

6. Use PKUNZIP.EXE to unzip it as we have done before

If all goes according to plan, you should wind up with the file called LVIEW31.EXE in a sub-subdirectory called lview.

HANDS-ON Activity 4

SHOWING A JPEG PICTURE

After finishing modifications to MOSAIC.INI, we connected to San Francisco's Exploratorium and got the photo of a giant bubble, as shown in Figure 8-5.

Figure 8-5
Hand Bubble[1]

Here's how you can do it.

1. Connect to your Internet service provider and start NCSA Mosaic.

2. Click once on **File** and then on **Open URL...** and then type http://www.exploratorium.edu

3. Following hyperlinks, we reach the area where images are to be found.

    a. Click on **Digital Library**

    b. Click on **Other Interesting Images**

    c. Click on **just use your hands!**

    If you do this, the image called HAND_BUB.JPG will be transferred to your computer.

1. Reprinted by generous permission from the Exploratorium in San Francisco

4. By clicking on a series of hyperlinks, we received the photo shown in Figure 8-5 above. If all is configured properly, NCSA Mosaic will use Lview to display this (or any other GIF or JPEG) image.

You may now transfer other images and view them online. Or, you may use Options - Load to File and view them later.

To view files that have been loaded to a file, you have several options:

a. You can use NCSA Mosaic's File - Open Local File

b. You can use Lview directly from Program Manager - File - Run

c. You can choose to install Lview with its own icon in Windows

POSTSCRIPT DOCUMENTS AND IMAGES _____

To view PostScript documents, you need two tools: *Ghostscript* and *Ghostview*. Both are available using NCSA Mosaic and both are needed to display PostScript files. *Ghostscript* is a PostScript interpreter and *Ghostview* is a Windows-based viewer for Ghost-script. The following activity will help you to get, install, and test both programs.

POSTSCRIPT VIEWERS

HANDS-ON Activity 5

1. Once again, connect to your Internet service provider and open NCSA Mosaic. As we did earlier in this session, we would like to go to the Document whose title is External Viewer Information. Its URL is

`http://www.ncsa.uiuc.edu/SDG/Software/WinMosaic/viewers.html`

Enter this information now, so that you can return to the External Viewer Information Document.

2. As before, scroll down to the Tested Viewers section. Find the hyperlink for GhostScript v2.6 (or whatever the current version is called). This will be our PostScript viewer for Windows. You should see a screen resembling the one in Figure 8- 6.

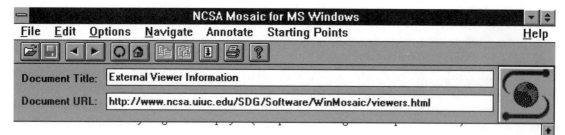

GhostScript v2.6

● A PostScript viewer for Windows.

*You are **not** restricted to the viewers we have listed above. In fact, there are many other viewers available from a number of ftp sites. As a rule of thumb if the viewer will accept command line instructions then Mosaic will be a ble to use it.*

Other Utilities

PC Speaker driver

This product is a sound drive for the basic PC Speaker. It was developed by Microsoft and is freely available to licensed users of Windows 3.1. Please the read the license agreement for the terms of the products. You will also find a link to speak.exe at the bottom of the license agreement.

NOTE: *Since we did not develop these softwares we can not support them. If you are having problems with any of these viewers or other Utilities please contact the respective author.*

Figure 8-6
GhostScript

Double-click on the **GhostScript v2.6 hyperlink**.

This will take you to a screen entitled PostScript Viewers for Windows. Its Document Title is Postscript Viewers for Windows. Its URL is

```
http://www.ncsa.uiuc.edu/SDG/Software/WinMosaic/ghostscript.html
```

3. Next,

    a. Click on **Options**

    b. Click on **Load to Disk**

    c. Double-click on **GhostScript**

    d. When prompted for a file name, type
        `c:\incoming\gs261exe.zip`

This is another very large file—over a million bytes. Be patient or decide to come back later. To view PostScript files, you will need this program.

Heads Up!

4.   When GhostScript has been downloaded,

   a.   Click on **Options**

   b.   Click on **Load to Disk**

5.   Now, it is time to download Ghostview. To do so,

   a.   Click on **Options**

   b.   Click on **Load to Disk**

   c.   Scroll down to the hyperlink Ghostview

Your screen will resemble Figure 8-7.

Figure 8-7
Ghostview

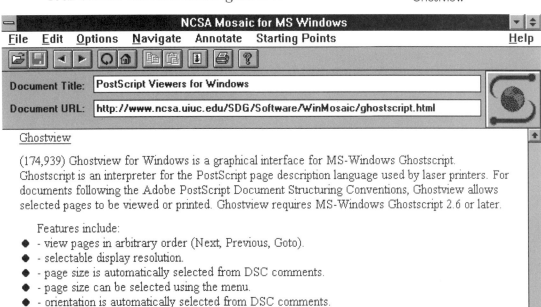

Ghostview

(174,939) Ghostview for Windows is a graphical interface for MS-Windows Ghostscript. Ghostscript is an interpreter for the PostScript page description language used by laser printers. For documents following the Adobe PostScript Document Structuring Conventions, Ghostview allows selected pages to be viewed or printed. Ghostview requires MS-Windows Ghostscript 2.6 or later.

   Features include:
◆ - view pages in arbitrary order (Next, Previous, Goto).
◆ - selectable display resolution.
◆ - page size is automatically selected from DSC comments.
◆ - page size can be selected using the menu.
◆ - orientation is automatically selected from DSC comments.
◆ - orientation can be selected using the menu (Portrait, Landscape).
◆ - print selected pages using Ghostscript.
◆ - extract selected pages to another file.
◆ - copy display bitmap to clipboard.
◆ - save clipboard bitmap as BMP file.
◆ - add bitmap preview to EPS file (Interchange, TIFF or Windows Metafile)
◆ - graphically select bounding box for EPS file.

d.   Double-click on **Ghostview**

    e.   When prompted for a file name, type `c:\incoming\gsview10.zip`

6.   When Ghostview has been downloaded

    a.   Click on **Options**

    b.   Click on **Load to Disk**

7.   Disconnect from your Internet service provider.

Now we will create a directory called GS and place these files in that directory one at a time. This sequence should be followed carefully to ensure that all of the programs work together.

1.   To create the directory GS,

    a.   At a DOS prompt, type `c:\mkdir gs`

    b.   Now, move to the directory cd\gs

2.   Copy GS261EXE.ZIP to the GS directory

    Note: We are using gs261exe.zip, but you may get a later version. It will be indicated by a number differing from 261.

3.   Copy pkunzip.exe to the GS directory.

4.   Use pkunzip.exe to unzip GS261EXE.ZIP. Read the files README and USE.DOC

5.   Now, copy GSVIEW10.ZIP to the GS directory and unzip it. (You may get a later version than number 10, which we found.)

6.   Open Windows and use File - New to add the GSVIEW program to a group of your choice. You may add it to the Chameleon Group or you may first wish to create a new Viewers group. Figure 8-8 shows an example.

Program Item Properties		
Description: GSView		OK
Command Line: c:\gs\gsview.exe		Cancel
Working Directory: c:\gs		Browse...
Shortcut Key: None		Change Icon...
☐ Run Minimized		Help

Figure 8-8
Installing Ghostview

7. Click on **OK** and double-click on the new **GSView Ghost Icon.**

Before attempting to read any files, there is one more step. We have to tell Ghostview how to talk to both GhostScript and to Windows.

8. With GSView open, click on **Options**

9. Click on **Ghostscript Command...**

10. Type in the following exactly
    C:\GS\GSWIN.EXE -IC:\GS
    Now, click on **OK**

    GSView should now be operational. You can test this with a PostScript image that comes with Ghostscript.

11. Click on **File - Open** and find GOLFER.PS in the GS directory. Double-click on this file and you should be rewarded with the image shown in Figure 8-9.

Figure 8-9
Golfer

You should edit your MOSAIC.INI file to make sure that it includes the following lines:

```
In [Viewers]
TYPE1="application/postscript"
application/postscript="c:\gs\gsview %ls"
In [Suffixes]
application/postscript=.ps,.eps,.ai,.ps
```

1. You can test all of this by opening NCSA Mosaic and clicking on **File** and then on **Open Local File...**

2. Go to the GS directory and open **GOLFER.PS**.

You should again see the figure of the golfer that was shown in Figure 8-9.

Congratulations! Your copy of NCSA Mosaic is now capable of receiving and displaying JPEG and PostScript files.

FINDING MUSIC, IMAGES, AND MULTIMEDIA

HANDS-ON Activity 6

Figures 8-10 through 8-13 are included to give you some ideas about where to go next for sounds and images. In each figure, the document name and document URL are shown by NCSA Mosaic. To explore these, we will just show you the figures and not give you our usual step-by-step instructions. By now, we believe, you know how to do this on your own. Happy exploring!

Music, Images, and Multimedia

Document
Title: Internet Resources List

Document
URL: http://www.eit.com/web/netservices.html

Once the Internet Resources Home Page appears, just click on the hyperlink **Music, Images, and Multimedia** to see the screen shown in Figure 8-10.

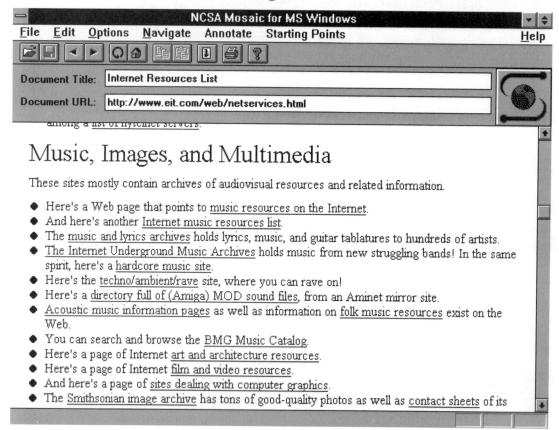

Figure 8-10
Music, Images, and
Multimedia

Guide to Film and Video

Document
      Title: Film and Video Resources

Document
      URL: `http://http2.sils.umich.edu/Public/fvl/film.html`

Click on **File** and then on **Open URL**. Type in the URL and then click. The Film and Video Resources Home Page shown in Figure 8-11 will appear.

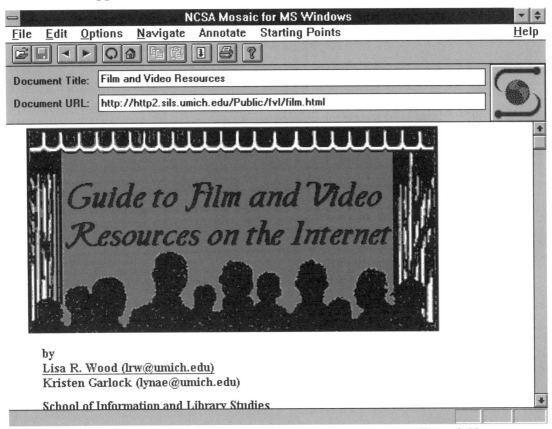

Figure 8-11
Film and Video
Resources

USG Current Weather Maps/Movies

Document
    Title: Current Weather Maps/Movies

Document
    URL: `http://clunix.cl.msu.edu:80/weather`

To see the screen in Figure 8-12, click on **File** and then on **Open URL**. Type the URL and then click on **OK**.

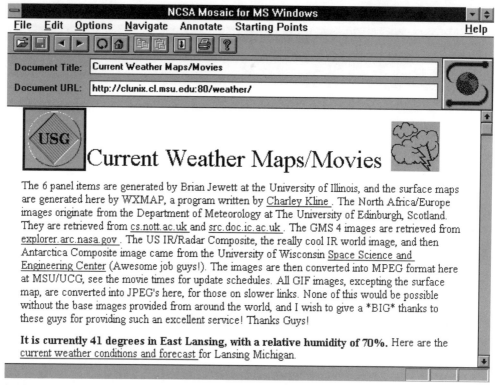

Figure 8-12
Current Weather
Maps/Movies

Krannert Art Museum, UIUC

Document

     Title: Krannert Art Museum

DocumentURL:
`http://www.ncsa.uiuc.edu/General/UIUC/KrannertArtMuseum/KrannertArtHome.html`

Click on **File** and **Open URL**. Then type in the URL and click on
OK to see the screen in Figure 8-13.

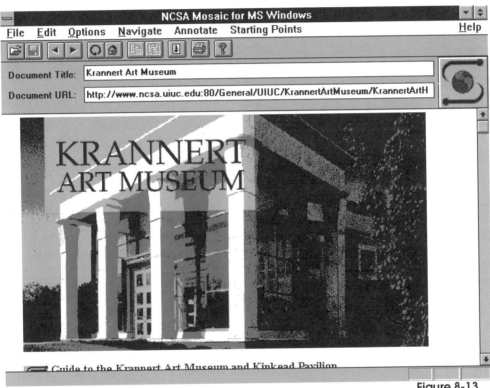

Figure 8-13
Krannert Art Museum

SESSION SUMMARY

In this session, you have begun to experience the multimedia
aspects of NCSA Mosaic and the World-Wide Web. You have
installed drivers that permit you to hear many of the audio
sounds that are available on the World-Wide Web. The viewers
that you have installed make it possible for you to see an amazing array of images on your PC. In addition, you can now preview PostScript files before printing them. As the last activity in
this session illustrated, the array of sights and sounds on the
World-Wide Web is limitless. We hope that you enjoy many pleasurable hours exploring the multimedia universe which NCSA
Mosaic and these new software programs make available to you.

SESSION 9

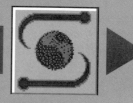

Activity 1: Finding the World-Wide Web Worm

Activity 2: The World-Wide Web Wanderer

Activity 3: Following Hyperlinks

Activity 4: Exploring CommerceNet

Activity 5: Commercial Services on the Web

Activity 6: Exploring MecklerWeb

Activity 7: Downloading and Installing WIN32s Software

Activity 8: Downloading and Installing NCSA Mosaic 2.7

Finding New Places, Exploring Internet Business, and Keeping Up-to-Date

THE WORLD-WIDE WEB WORM

As you have gathered by now, the World-Wide Web is an enormous place, filled with a tremendous and growing array of multimedia resources. To have access to this ever-changing world probably requires the help of a computer, as well as some talented individuals. Fortunately, both exist. For NCSA Mosaic users, the key to most organizations will be the home page. However, as you might imagine, with so many home pages to be found and so many new ones being added, just finding them all and having access to them is a daunting challenge.

Fortunately, Oliver McBryan at the University of Colorado in Boulder, has developed a resource to help us all. He calls it the *World-Wide Web Worm* (or *WWWW*, for short). We will begin our exploration of this amazing resource by first heading to the University of Colorado. Here is how to do so.

FINDING THE WORLD-WIDE WEB WORM

HANDS-ON Activity 1

1. Log in to your Internet service provider using the Chameleon Sampler

2. Double-click on the **Mosaic Icon**

3. Click on **File** and then on **Open URL...**

247

4. Move your cursor to the Open URL box and make it active. Type `http://www.cs.colorado.edu`

You should see a screen resembling Figure 9-1.

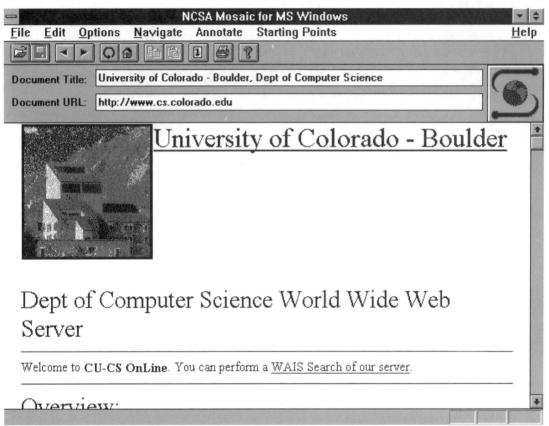

Figure 9-1
University of Colorado

While this is a very attractive home page, you cannot really tell much from this first screen about the treasures that await you.

Click on the **down arrow** on the scroll bar on the right-hand side of your window until Overview: and Other Resources: are visible. Your screen should look like the one in Figure 9-2.

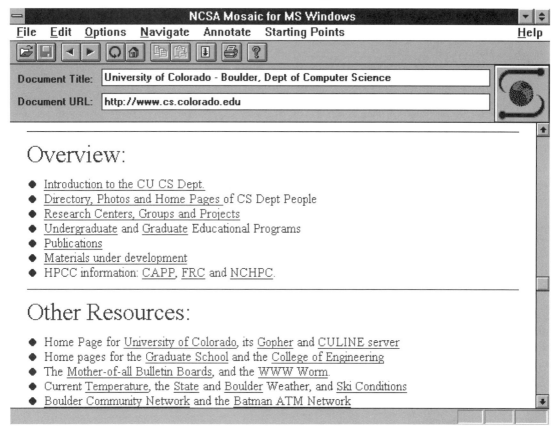

Figure 9-2
Overview: and Other
Resources

We are particularly interested in the item that is described as The Mother-of-all Bulletin Boards, including the WWW Worm. Click once on the hyperlink **WWW Worm**.

You should see the screen in Figure 9-3.

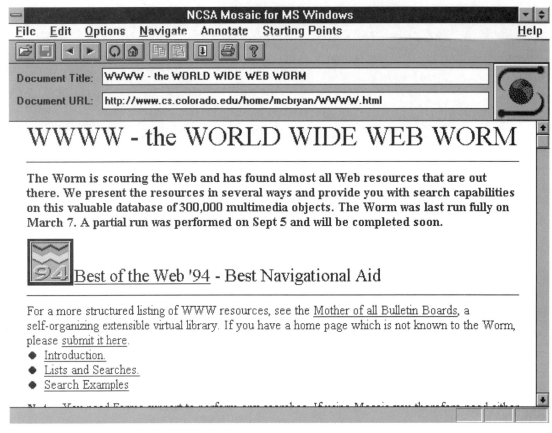

Figure 9-3
WWWW—the World-
Wide Web Worm

Oliver McBryan has put together an impressive and extensive set of resources for us. Let's see what it is all about. We will begin with the Introduction.

1. Click on the hyperlink **Introduction**. You should see a screen resembling the one in Figure 9-4.

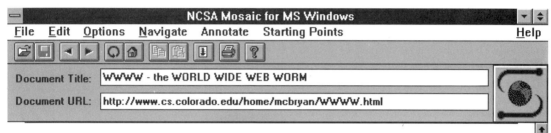

Figure 9-4
WWWW Introduction

Take a few minutes to read through the Introduction to WWWW. In some respects, the Introduction is just a reiteration of information you already know. However, it is worth taking the time to understand what Oliver McBryan has done and how he has done it.

Important: As you scroll down through this document, you will come to the following sentences which are not shown in Figure 9-4. They state that "WWWW provides a mechanism to search the WWW in any of the above ways. It also provides lists of all home pages and of all

URL's cited anywhere, although these are not really intended for viewing. Five sample searches are provided below."

Be aware that the word "below" should have been the word "above." When you have finished, return to the "top" of this current document, and we will show you how to get to the sample searches.

2.   Click on the hyperlink **Lists and Searches**. When you do so, you should a screen resembling the one in Figure 9-5.

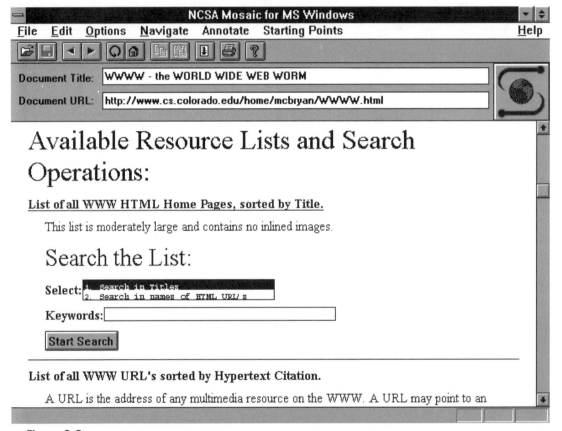

Figure 9-5
WWWW Available
Resource Lists and
Search Operations

The Available Resource Lists and Search Operations: is an important set of information. It is well worth your time to read through these screens carefully and to make sure that you understand all of the available options. Once you have done that, we will try a few searches together.

Search 1: Search in Titles

For example, suppose we are interested in learning more about the IBM Corporation. In this first search, we will begin with the 1. Search in Titles selection highlighted in blue.

1. Move your cursor to the Keywords: box and click once to make it active. Then just enter those three famous initials for your Keywords: IBM

2. Click on **Start Search**

When we did this, we were provided with three responses:

> IKE - IBM Kiosk for Education
> Projects Sponsored by IBM
> The IBM SP1

Notice how quick the search is and also that you may (or may not) have found what you were looking for with this first search.

If you are interested in any of these items, just click on them. Otherwise, click on **Return to Searching**

Search 2: Search in Names of HTML URL's

This time, we will try using the HTML URL as the field in which we will look.

1. First, click on **2. Search in names of HTML URL's** to make it active. (This line should turn blue.)

2. Now, make the Keywords: box active by clicking on it once and then enter those famous initials again: IBM

3. Then, click on **Start Search**

Again, the search is quite rapid. Note that this time we are provided with two responses: One of them is identical to the one we received previously (Projects Sponsored by IBM), but the other one is International Business Machines Corporation

4. Clicking once on **International Business Machines Corporation** should provide you with some information.

5. When you have finished, click on the **left-arrow button** at the top of your screen to return to the page in Figure 9-6.

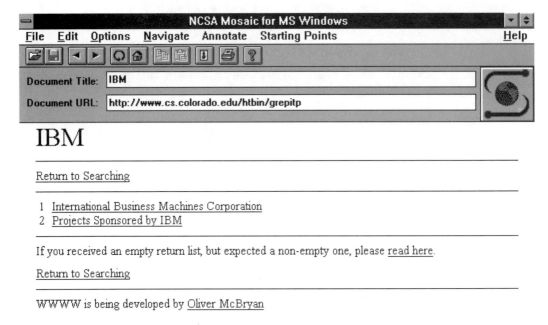

Figure 9-6
IBM

6. Click once on **Return to Searching**

HANDS-ON
Activity 2

THE WORLD-WIDE WEB WANDERER

This time we will use the World-Wide Web Worm to help us to find the World-Wide Web Wanderer. This happens to be a wonderful example of how the World-Wide Web Worm can become an invaluable resource. Follow along.

1. Begin on the World-Wide Web Worm Home Page and click on **Lists and Searches**

2. We will use the default that is provided to Search the List; we will select **1. Search in Titles**

3. Make the Keywords: box active, and type
`world wide web wanderer`

You should be taken quickly to a screen entitled world wide web wanderer

4. Click once on the hyperlink **1. World Wide Web Wanderers, Spiders, and Robots**

You should see a screen resembling Figure 9-7.

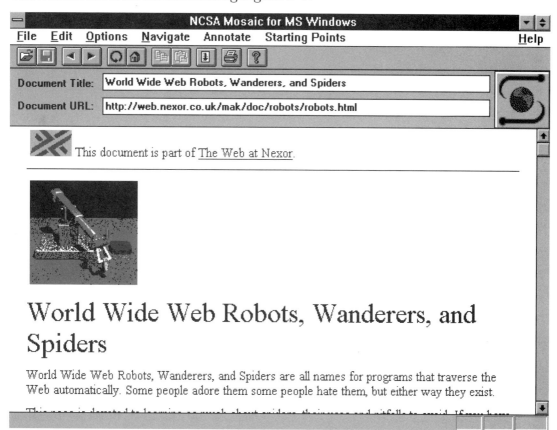

As you will discover, there is a wonderful world of World-Wide Web Robots, Wanderers, and Spiders which have been (and are being) developed by a variety of enterprising people who are continually trying to make the use of the Web easier for everyone else.

Figure 9-7
World-Wide Web Wanderers, Spiders, and Robots

If you have the time and the inclination, click on **A list of known robots** or **A list of other automated tools**. There is clearly a lot of creative thinking going on!

FOLLOWING HYPERLINKS

What you have been doing is following a freeform series of hyperlinks. That is, you found an interesting link to another topic, clicked on it, and were off. This process is what the World-Wide Web is all about—following hyperlinks to locate what you may want. It is also quite addictive in that you keep finding things that were not in your original search.

To illustrate, we will start you on your own freeform travels on the Web.

Warning: There is no end to this exercise. You can keep going until you are worn out. You can explore for a specific topic or you can just wander and see what appears.

In this exercise, we would like you to go off on your own and explore to see what you can find. You will pick the subject and you can then follow hyperlinks that interest you. Remember, the hyperlinks are usually indicated by blue underlines or blue borders.

Move your mouse to a hyperlink and notice the bottom of the NCSA Mosaic screen. As you put your mouse over each hyperlink, NCSA Mosaic will show you the URL associated with that link. If you click on the hyperlink, NCSA Mosaic will go off in search of that link.

This activity has no figures, as we don't know where you will be going. It's really up to you to explore. You can keep going until you get tired or you can set a time limit. Here we go.

1. Begin again on the World-Wide Web Worm Home Page and click on **Lists and Searches**

2. We will again use the default that is provided to Search the List; we will select **1. Search in Titles**

3. For Keywords, make the Keywords: box active and type a one- or two-word subject of interest to you.

4. When that page appears, find a hyperlink of interest and click on it.

5. When the next page appears, go off in search of something else.

And so on . . .

You have just run your own search. We hope this will give you confidence to begin greater explorations of the Internet on your own.

INTERNET BUSINESS AND COMMERCENET

As you may be aware, for many years the Internet was virtually free of commercial activity. Its primary use was to provide scientists and researchers with access to powerful host computers, and UNIX was the language of choice for Internet users. Consequently, the Internet was left in peace and quiet, as some would say.

However, during the past few years, the Internet has become exceedingly well known throughout the world. And, in the process, there are quite a few individuals and organizations that have begun to consider the commercial aspects of the Internet. There is considerable debate about the commercialization of the Internet, a debate that will probably continue for quite some time. However, no matter which side you are on, it is probably useful to know something about the business aspects of the Internet. We will focus on a few of the better-known examples in the following activities.

EXPLORING COMMERCENET

1. Click on **File** and then on **Open URL...**

2. Make the URL box active. Type
`http://www.commerce.net`

You should see a screen that resembles Figure 9-8.

HANDS-ON
Activity 4

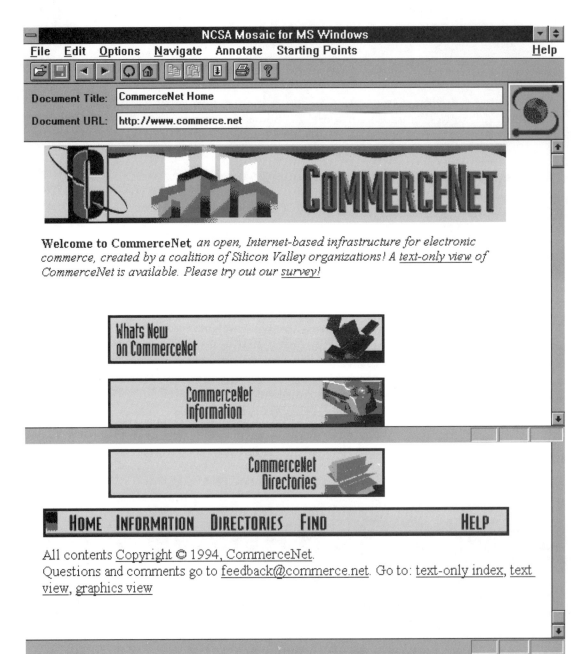

Figure 9-8
CommerceNet
Home Page

A list of the sponsors of CommerceNet includes many of the best-known corporations involved in the world of telecommunications and computers, as well as quite a few companies in other lines of business. Here is just a peek at the list. It includes only those sponsors in the index whose corporate names begin with A through D as of this writing.

> Advantis
> Amdahl Corporation
> Apple Computer, Inc.
> Association of Bay Area Governments
> Avex Electronics
> Bank of America, Inc.
> Bank One
> BARRNet
> California Department of General Services
> California Trade and Commerce Agency
> Citicorp Services, Inc.
> Commercial Internet Exchange (CIX) Association
> Dataquest
> Digital Equipment Corporation
> The Dun & Bradstreet Corporation

This list is impressive. However, the really compelling aspect of CommerceNet becomes clearer as we learn more about it. Let's use the available screens to help us to do so.

1. Begin with the initial CommerceNet Home Page (http://www.commerce.net)

2. Click once on **CommerceNet Information**

3. Click on **About CommerceNet**

4. Click on **Overview and Vision: What is CommerceNet?**

You should see a screen resembling Figure 9-9.

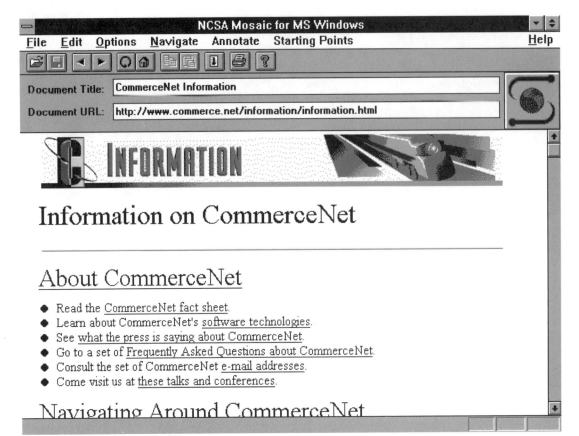

Figure 9-9
CommerceNet
Information

If you take some time to read the information that is provided about CommerceNet, you will begin to have a sense of how some responsible companies, governmental organizations, and others are beginning to think about the possible commercial utilization of the Internet. As they state:

> CommerceNet users will have access to a previously unimaginable range of products, services, and information—making them more competitive and expanding the potential of their marketplace.

We will leave you here for the moment. Feel free to take some time to explore CommerceNet in greater detail. The information provided is useful for those who are curious about possible commercial aspects of the Internet.

COMMERCIAL SERVICES ON THE WEB

HANDS-ON
Activity 5

A different way to understand the commercial potential of the Internet is to spend some time looking at the Commercial Sites on the Web Home Page that is located at the Massachusetts Institute of Technology. This list was begun in January 1994 by Henry Houh, a graduate student at MIT.

This resource lists the home pages of many companies. Some, such as AT&T and IBM, are quite well known. Others, such as Mighty Dog Designs and Grant's Florist and Greenhouse, are less well known (or at least that was true before they were listed here!).

Recently, a feature article about the Commercial Sites on the Web appeared in the *Internet Business Report,* a CMP Publication ®. In it, Henry Houh explains that the companies that have a commercial presence on the Web fall into three categories:

a.   Large companies that have a customer base that is clearly connected to the Internet. These companies use the Web to deliver marketing information and provide customer support.

b.   Companies—such as Branch Information Services, Internet Distribution Services, and InterNex Information Services—that provide Web sites for companies that don't have Internet access. Many commercial Web pages are based with one of these services.

c.   Local Internet access providers that are setting up their own Web servers for subscribers, signing up local businesses, and developing classified ad sections.

Let's take a look.

1.   Click on **File** and then **Open URL...**

2.   Type `http://tns-www.lcs.mit.edu/commerce.html`

If you have done this correctly, your screen should resemble the one in Figure 9-10

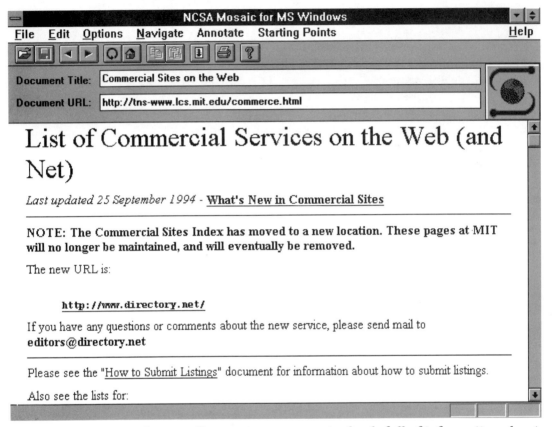

Figure 9-10
Commercial Sites on the Web

This rapidly growing resource is chock-full of information about an array of companies that are either using the Web for a competitive advantage, or are helping others to do so. It is interesting to take a "snapshot" of these companies by looking at a listing of some of the many companies that are listed in Commercial Sites on the Web. The variety of companies is intriguing, and the fact that they all have equal billing in this context certainly raises a myriad of issues.

Figure 9-11 is a listing of the companies whose names begin with the letter M and who were listing their services in July 1994.

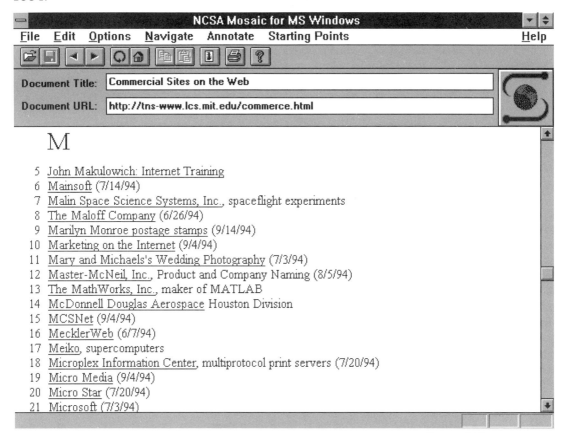

| — | NCSA Mosaic for MS Windows | ▼ ▲ |

File   Edit   Options   Navigate   Annotate   Starting Points   Help

Document Title: Commercial Sites on the Web

Document URL: http://tns-www.lcs.mit.edu/commerce.html

M

  5 John Makulowich: Internet Training
  6 Mainsoft (7/14/94)
  7 Malin Space Science Systems, Inc., spaceflight experiments
  8 The Maloff Company (6/26/94)
  9 Marilyn Monroe postage stamps (9/14/94)
10 Marketing on the Internet (9/4/94)
11 Mary and Michaels's Wedding Photography (7/3/94)
12 Master-McNeil, Inc., Product and Company Naming (8/5/94)
13 The MathWorks, Inc., maker of MATLAB
14 McDonnell Douglas Aerospace Houston Division
15 MCSNet (9/4/94)
16 MecklerWeb (6/7/94)
17 Meiko, supercomputers
18 Microplex Information Center, multiprotocol print servers (7/20/94)
19 Micro Media (9/4/94)
20 Micro Star (7/20/94)
21 Microsoft (7/3/94)

It is interesting to think that Mary and Michael's Wedding Photography is able to have equal billing with companies such as Microsoft. Now, if they can only do as well!

In addition, an important, and very useful feature of Commercial Sites on the Web is that it is possible to click on the name of the company or service which is of interest and be taken to it immediately. The popularity of this list is demonstrated by the meteoric rate at which it is being accessed by those who hear about it. It was first announced in early February 1994. By mid-June, it was receiving approximately 5,500 inquiries per week!

Figure 9-11
Commercial Sites on the Web/ Companies Beginning With M

EXPLORING MECKLERWEB

As you may be aware, Meckler Media is the publisher of Internet World. Recently, they have begun what they call *MecklerWeb*. As stated on the MecklerWeb Demonstration Home Page they believe that:

> MecklerWeb will be a very large Internet based corporate communication and marketing system serving the needs of business and commerce worldwide. It will enable companies to powerfully position themselves relative to fast-emerging, prequalified and highly attractive online market sectors. The MecklerWeb initiative has been developed in direct response to widespread business demand for a simple and effective way to intersect with these new online micro-markets.

Let's take a look.

1. Click on **File** and then on **Open URL...**

2. Make the Open URL box active and enter
   `http://www.mecklerweb.com/demo.html`

If you have done this correctly, you should see a screen resembling the one in Figure 9-12.

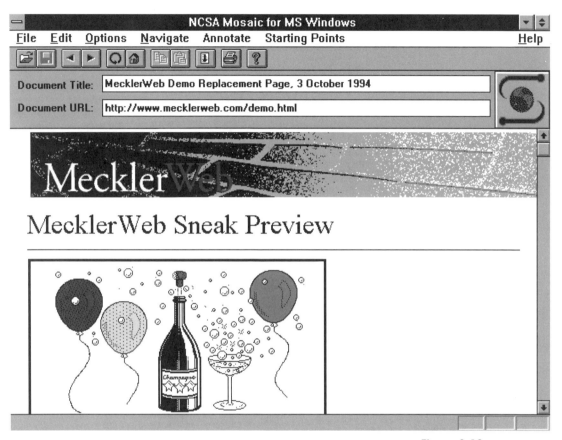

Figure 9-12
MecklerWeb
Demonstration

This screen is really just a way to begin the conversation with MecklerWeb. There is really a lot more to learn. To do so, click once on **Click here** and you will be taken to the MecklerWeb Home Page. It should look like Figure 9-13.

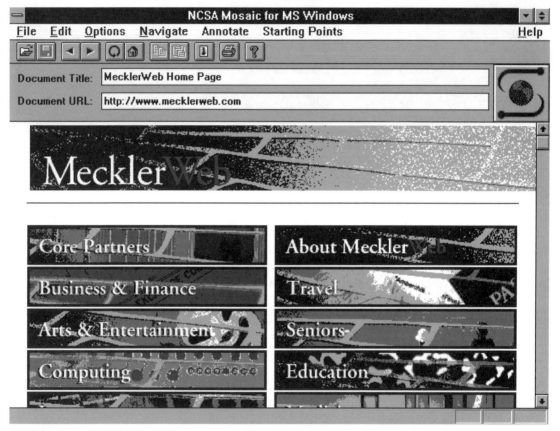

Figure 9-13
Learn about
MecklerWeb

The premise of MecklerWeb is an interesting one. As they say,

> MecklerWeb is a way of putting your company in front of customers and potential customers on the Internet. We call this "corporate presence." It's not about advertising—it's about offering the kind of value-added information that will attract and hold customers in the Nanosecond Nineties. Every corporation has such information already, and MecklerWeb is a way to realize its full value.

While their claims may or may not be true, what is true is that corporations which are participating on MecklerWeb are (as of this writing) paying $25,000 per year to do so. And, a significant number of corporations have already signed up. Clearly, the perception that the Internet can provide corporations with commercial opportunities is beginning to be a widely shared one.

In addition, the fact that the potential audience could be as many as 22 million is intriguing. Even more so is the fact that those who choose to look at the materials presented by a company have chosen to do so. The fact that this self-selected group has determined for themselves which topics they wish to explore is a compelling one.

A partial listing of those who are currently MecklerWeb partners provides some sense of the diversity that can be found among those who have chosen to participate in this new form of public relations. While the list does include some well-known, high-tech companies (Digital Equipment Corporation, EDS, Enterprise Integration Technologies, Sun Microsystems), it also includes companies such as Pharmaceutical Information Associates, Scudder Investor Services, Inc., and Tangerine ("A Steelcase Upstart").

The MecklerWeb Partners List includes the following list of companies, academic institutions, professional associations, and content providers who had already signed up as charter partners in MecklerWeb at the time this list was prepared:

> AlterNet (UUNET Technologies, Inc.)
> American Cybercasting
> BB9 Design, Inc.
> Bits & Bytes
> Bureau of National Affairs
> California Software
> Checkpoint Software Technologies, Ltd.
> The COOK Report on Internet -> NREN
> CommerceNet
> Commercial Internet eXchange (CIX)
> Cornell Legal Information Institute
> Crawford Communications, Inc.
> DBA Software, Inc.
> Demand Research Corporation
> Digital Equipment Corporation
> Dun & Bradstreet
> Edelman Public Relations Worldwide
> Educom

EDS
Enterprise Integration Technologies
Fast Company
Free Range Media, Inc.
GlasNews
IPC Software Services
Individual, Inc.
InfoPro
The Interface Group (producers of COMDEX)
Internet Guide Services
The Internet Group
Interleaf
Kaleidospace
KnowledgeWare
The Maloff Company
McGraw-Hill
NetManage
NovX
Ogilvy & Mather Direct
Passage Systems
Pharmaceutical Information Associates
The Reference Press, Inc. (an affiliate of Warner Books)
Scudder Investor Services, Inc.
SeniorNet
Spyglass, Inc.
Sun Microsystems
Tangerine ("A Steelcase Upstart")
Trusted Information Systems
WAIS, Inc.

As you have seen from the last few activities in this session, the commercialization of the Internet is just beginning. And, in the process, the ways in which that is happening are quite diverse. Commercial Sites on the Web is (so far) a free resource to those who have the ability to access it using an Internet Web browser. CommerceNet is a consortium of companies, and MecklerWeb is a service being offered. Each one has its strengths and weaknesses, and each one is a portent of the various ways in which the Internet will be used for commercial enterprise in the years to come.

KEEPING NCSA MOSAIC UP-TO-DATE _____

Now that you have traveled the Internet awhile with Chameleon and NCSA Mosaic, you must realize that everything is constantly changing. To stay current with the latest Internet tools and techniques is really quite easy thanks to the hard work of the folks at NCSA. In our final section, we will show you how to stay current.

Getting the Latest Versions

The latest versions of NCSA Mosaic will always be available from the NCSA at the University of Illinois. Probably the best way to stay current is to check the NCSA Mosaic Home Page, or, better yet, the NCSA Mosaic for Microsoft Windows Home Page. The URL is http://www.ncsa.uiuc.edu/SDG/Software/WinMosaic/HomePage.html

Figure 9-14
Mosaic for Microsoft
Windows Home Page

Figure 9-14 shows what we found on September 24, 1994.

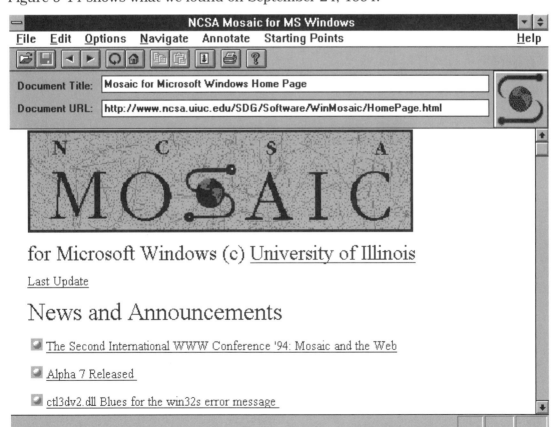

NCSA Mosaic for MS Windows is an ever-changing software program. When you first downloaded NCSA Mosaic in Session Six, you were downloading NCSA Mosaic 1.0, which is considered to be a well-tested, stable version of the program.

When you downloaded NCSA Mosaic 20a2.zip in Session Seven, you were retrieving a 16-bit version of NCSA Mosaic. It is reasonably stable and it is the final 16-bit version of NCSA Mosaic Windows.

However, as stated in Figure 9-15, an Alpha version of software is one in which "features are added and bugs are identified and mostly fixed." Note that "[t]his means the product is NOT an OFFICIAL release."

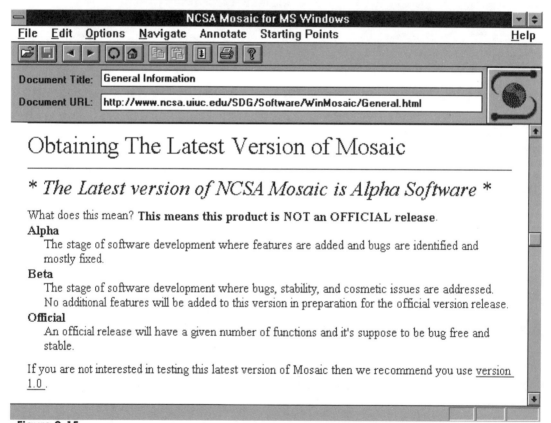

Figure 9-15
General Information

In addition to changes to NCSA Mosaic for MS Windows, there are also changes taking place in the Windows environment. Most significant is the fact that newer software is being developed to run in a 32-bit environment, not the 16-bit one that has been in effect for so long. This has particular significance for users of NCSA Mosaic for MS Windows. Please note:

NCSA Mosaic for MS Windows Version 1.0 runs in a 16-bit environment.

NCSA Mosaic for MS Windows Version 2.2 (wmos20a2.zip) runs in a 16-bit environment.

NCSA Mosaic for MS Windows Version 2.7 (it is actually called wmos20a7.zip) requires a system running Microsoft Windows 3.1 in enhanced mode, a 1.1 compliant winsock.dll, and Microsoft win32s software. This means that NCSA Mosaic 20a6 (and higher) software must be running in a 32-bit environment. These system requirements are explained in detail, as you can see in Figure 9-16.

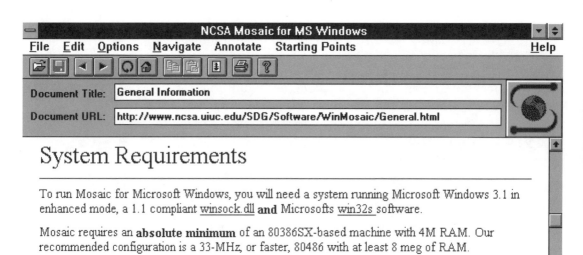

NCSA Mosaic for MS Windows

File   Edit   Options   Navigate   Annotate   Starting Points   Help

Document Title: General Information

Document URL: http://www.ncsa.uiuc.edu/SDG/Software/WinMosaic/General.html

System Requirements

To run Mosaic for Microsoft Windows, you will need a system running Microsoft Windows 3.1 in enhanced mode, a 1.1 compliant winsock.dll **and** Microsofts win32s software.

Mosaic requires an **absolute minimum** of an 80386SX-based machine with 4M RAM. Our recommended configuration is a 33-MHz, or faster, 80486 with at least 8 meg of RAM.

Obtaining The Latest Version of Mosaic

** The Latest version of NCSA Mosaic is Alpha Software **

What does this mean? **This means this product is NOT an OFFICIAL release.**
Alpha
   The stage of software development where features are added and bugs are identified and mostly fixed.
Beta

Figure 9-16
General Information/
System Requirements

Downloading and installing the required Windows software and the latest version of NCSA Mosaic will be the focus of our next few activities.

DOWNLOADING AND INSTALLING WIN32S SOFTWARE

HANDS-ON
Activity 7

As Figure 9-17 indicates, it is possible to acquire win32s software from a variety of locations. If the NCSA World-Wide Web server is hard to reach, then you may find it easier to use anonymous ftp to download the file from ftp servers at either

> Microsoft (ftp.microsoft.com)
>
> NCSA (ftp.ncsa.uiuc.edu)

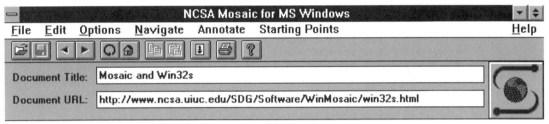

Mosaic is a 32-bit Application

Information for Windows 3.1 and Windows for Workgroup users

Mosaic is a 32-bit application and it requires you to install Microsoft's win32s software. Win32s allows you to run 32-bit Windows applications under Windows 3.1, Windows 3.11 and Windows for Workgroups 3.11. Win32s is a beta product developed by Microsoft and it's freely distributed to licensed Windows users. Since this is beta software there are periodic releases and updates, thus you will need to upgrade your Win32s software after these new releases. Win32s is available from Microsoft's anonymous ftp server, ftp.microsoft.com. You can find Win32s115a.Zip in the /developer/win32dk/sdk-public directory.

For the convenience of our users we keep a copy of this latest release on our ftp server, ftp.ncsa.uiuc.edu. However, we have added a readme.file and renamed the file win32s.zip .

Figure 9-17
Mosaic and Win32s

If you are able to use NCSA Mosaic to reach the page with the Document URL (http://www.ncsa.uiuc.edu/SDG/Software/WinMosaic/win32s .html) follow the step-by-step procedure below. If not, then use ftp as indicated above and get the file from either the Microsoft or NCSA ftp server. Then, rejoin us at step 3.

Heads Up!

The file that you are about to download, win32s.zip, is large (1,130,854 bytes). Be sure that the disk to which you intend to download it has ample room on it. Also, be prepared to wait a few minutes; even with a fast modem, this one takes some time!

1. Click on **Options** and then **Load to Disk**

2. Click on **win32s.zip**

3. When prompted for a file name, type
   `c:\incoming\win32s.zip`

4. Once the file has been downloaded, be sure to click on **Options** and then **Load to Disk**

5. Once you have downloaded the file, create a directory on your hard disk. We have called it win32s

6. Copy the file pkunzip.exe into the win32s directory. Type
   `copy c:\pkware\pkunzip.exe c:\win32s`

7. Now, unzip the file win32s.zip. Type
   `pkunzip win32s.zip`

8. If all is working correctly, you should now have three files in the win32s directory:

   > W32S1_1.BUG
   > README.TXT
   > W32S115A.ZIP

9. Now, unzip the file called W32S115A.ZIP

Important: You must use the -d extension with pkunzip, so that the unzip utility will put the files into their proper directories. To do so, type `pkunzip -d w32s115a`

If all has gone correctly, you should see the following files in your win32s directory:

> WIN32S.ZIP
> PKUNZIP.EXE
> W32S1_1.BUG

```
README.TXT
W32S115A.ZIP
DISK1      <DIR>
DISK2      <DIR>
```

If for any reason you don't, you might wish to erase all the files except WIN32S.ZIP and PKUNZIP.EXE and repeat this step.

10. Now, begin Windows.

    a. From the Program Manager, select **File** and then **Run...**

    b. In the Command Line box, type
```
c:\win32s\disk1\setup
```

    c. Then, click on **OK**

Heads Up!

At the end of the installation process, you will have the option of installing the Win32 game called Freecell. Freecell is a really neat game of solitaire; it is also a good way to test that your computer is working correctly. We would recommend that you choose to do this.

Once you have finished playing a few hands of Freecell, we will continue!

HANDS-ON Activity 1

DOWNLOADING AND INSTALLING NCSA MOSAIC 2.7 (WMOS20A7.ZIP)

1. Download wmos20a7.zip.

    a. One option is to return to General Information (see Figure 9-15). If you slide your cursor down the General Information Home Page, you will come to a section entitled Windows 3.1 and WfW Users. There, under Alpha 7, you may click on the hyperlink for **Win 3.1**, **WfW** or **NT for the Intel iX86** processor.

    b. Another option is to use ftp to "manually" download wmos20a7.zip. It is located at the NCSA ftp server. Here is the address
ftp.ncsa.uiuc.edu/Mosaic/Windows/wmos20a7.zip

Heads Up!

As was true when we installed Mosaic2.2 (wmos20a2.zip), the new NCSA Mosaic files (MOSAIC.EXE and MOSAIC.INI) will overwrite the ones that you have already installed in the NETMANAG directory. You may wish to copy them both to a safe place before continuing.

2. Create a directory on your hard drive for the new version of NCSA Mosaic. We have called ours wmos20a7

3. Copy the zipped version of NCSA Mosaic into it.

4. As you have done before, copy the pkunzip.exe file into the wmos20a7 directory, and then unzip the files. Type `copy c:\pkware\pkunzip.exe c:\wmos20a7` and, `pkunzip wmos20a7.zip`

If all has gone correctly, you should now have the following files in the wmos20a7 directory:

> WMOS20A7.ZIP
> PKUNZIP.EXE
> MOSAIC.EXE
> INSTALL.WRI
> MOSAIC.INI
> SLIP.TXT FAQ.WRI
> README.WRI
> UPDATE.WRI

All of the files ending with WRI are readable by Microsoft Write. The most important one, right now, is the one called INSTALL.WRI

In this file you will find step-by-step directions telling you how to install your new version of NCSA Mosaic. It is probably a good idea to print out this file at your earliest opportunity.

There are lots of options available to you. However, we will show you three simple steps that will have you immediately up and running:

1. Copy your MOSAIC.EXE and MOSAIC.INI files for NCSA Mosaic 2.2 (wmos20a2.zip) to a safe place. When you copy the new files for NCSA Mosaic 2.7, they will overwrite the files that are already present. In the process, you will lose the Hotlist, as well as the changes that you had made to your MOSAIC.INI file in Session Eight.

2. Copy the file MOSAIC.INI into your Windows directory. Typically, this directory is called c:\windows. Type
   `copy c:\wmos20a7\mosaic.ini c:\windows`

3. Copy the file MOSAIC.EXE into your NETMANAG directory, which is where we installed NCSA Mosaic initially. Type `copy c:\wmos20a7\mosaic.exe c:\netmanag`

If all has gone according to plan, you now should have a fully functioning copy of the program we will call Mosaic 2.7 (wmos20a7.zip) on your computer.

HOW TO STAY CURRENT WITH NCSA MOSAIC

As you use NCSA Mosaic for your multimedia travels about the Internet, you may wish to keep yourself current from time to time. Here are several suggestions:

1. When you discover newer versions, you may want to wait a little while until the bugs are worked out. It's probable that each new release will have many attractive new features. It's equally probable that there will be bugs in each release.

2. Newer versions of NCSA Mosaic will all be 32-bit versions. All of them will require win32s to run correctly on your computer. Be aware, however, that win32s changes from time to time. Earlier this year, the version that was available was win32s115; the version you installed earlier in this session was win32s115a.

   The good news is that the Software Development Group at NCSA has been attentive to making the newer win32s software available and posting prominent notices about the need to have it.

3. We strongly suggest that you back up the critical files on your PC before installing any new software. We have not experienced any problems as we have done this, but PCs differ and backing up files is always a good idea.

The best way to stay current with NCSA Mosaic is to use NCSA Mosaic to help you do so. Here is how:

1. Click on **Starting Points** on your NCSA Mosaic drop-down menu bar.

278

2. Click on **NCSA Mosaic's "What's New" Page**

You should see a screen with the Document Title What's New With NCSA Mosaic. It should resemble Figure 9-18.

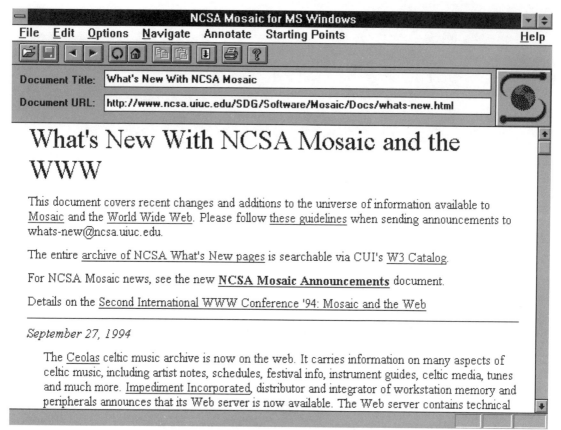

┌───┐
│ ▬   **NCSA Mosaic for MS Windows**   ▼ ▲ │
│ <u>F</u>ile <u>E</u>dit <u>O</u>ptions <u>N</u>avigate <u>A</u>nnotate Starting Points   <u>H</u>elp │
│   │
│ Document Title: │What's New With NCSA Mosaic   │   │
│ Document URL: │http://www.ncsa.uiuc.edu/SDG/Software/Mosaic/Docs/whats-new.html│ │
└───┘

What's New With NCSA Mosaic and the WWW

This document covers recent changes and additions to the universe of information available to <u>Mosaic</u> and the <u>World Wide Web</u>. Please follow <u>these guidelines</u> when sending announcements to whats-new@ncsa.uiuc.edu.

The entire <u>archive of NCSA What's New pages</u> is searchable via CUI's <u>W3 Catalog</u>.

For NCSA Mosaic news, see the new **<u>NCSA Mosaic Announcements</u>** document.

Details on the <u>Second International WWW Conference '94: Mosaic and the Web</u>

September 27, 1994

The <u>Ceolas</u> celtic music archive is now on the web. It carries information on many aspects of celtic music, including artist notes, schedules, festival info, instrument guides, celtic media, tunes and much more. <u>Impediment Incorporated</u>, distributor and integrator of workstation memory and peripherals announces that its Web server is now available. The Web server contains technical

Figure 9-18
What's New With
NCSA Mosaic

As you can tell, there is quite a bit of information available. Our first suggestion is that you spend some time browsing through the archive of NCSA What's New pages.

When you click on this hyperlink, you will see the screen in Figure 9-19.

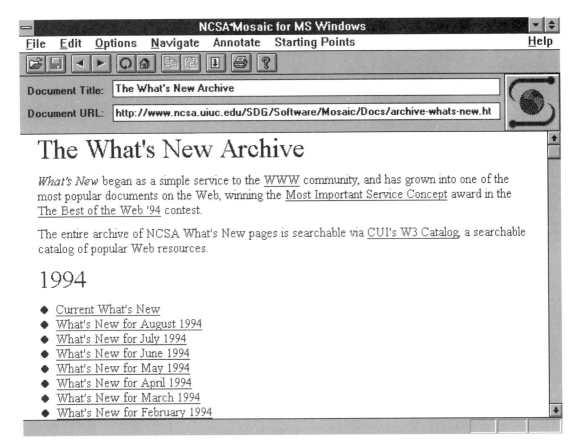

Figure 9-19
The What's New
Archive

If you have the time, a wonderful way to get a really good sense of what has been happening on the World-Wide Web is to browse through The What's New Archive. Begin with the Current What's New, and then work your way back. Each one of these screens is chock-full of interesting resources. You will learn about new services that are available, new World-Wide Web servers that have come online, as well as much other new and unanticipated information.

Also, be sure to look at the NCSA Mosaic News and Announcements. Figure 9-20 shows what we found in late August, 1994,

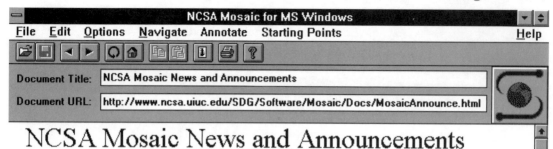

NCSA Mosaic for MS Windows
File Edit Options Navigate Annotate Starting Points   **Help**

Document Title: **NCSA Mosaic News and Announcements**

Document URL: **http://www.ncsa.uiuc.edu/SDG/Software/Mosaic/Docs/MosaicAnnounce.html**

NCSA Mosaic News and Announcements

August 26, 1994

The organizing committees of the first three International World Wide Web Conferences have formed the International World-Wide Web Conference Committee.

August 25, 1994

NCSA brings a new FTP Server online.

July 23, 1994

A new NCSA Mosaic Web Index is now available to help locate Mosaic-related information on our Web server. Links to HTTP-related tutorials are there.

June 22, 1994

A new Using and Licensing NCSA Mosaic FAQ is now online.

Mosaic for the Macintosh version 2.0 alpha2 is now available.

Figure 9-20
NCSA Mosaic News
and Announcements

If you are particularly interested in staying current with news about Windows Mosaic, then we suggest that you check the information on the Windows Mosaic Home Page from time to time. To do so is easy.

1. Click on **Starting Points**

2. Click on **Windows Mosaic home page**

Your screen will resemble Figure 9-21. The Document Title
should be Mosaic for Microsoft Windows Home Page.

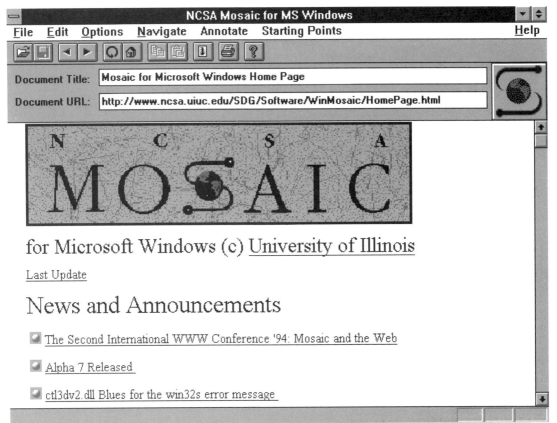

This page is very popular. You may encounter some difficulty
getting through to it. However, it is well worth the effort since
the information there will always be the most current.

Figure 9-21
Mosaic for Microsoft
Windows Home Page

Of particular importance are the Release Information and the User Support Information contained on this home page. Click on the **down arrow** on the scroll bar. You should see a screen that resembles the one in Figure 9-22.

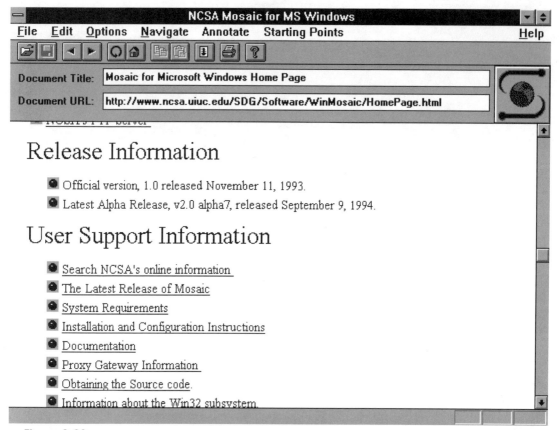

Figure 9-22
Release Information/
User Support
Information

New Alpha versions of NCSA Mosaic for MS Windows continue to be developed. In addition, it has been said that an Official Release Version of Mosaic 2 is to be available before the end of 1994. Of course, given what has happened during the past year, that probably means that the Alpha versions of Mosaic 3 should begin to appear soon after!

CHAMELEON, THE PRODUCT

We were very pleased that NetManage, Inc. allowed us to offer their Chameleon Sampler with this book. You may want to consider their product version of Chameleon. It is rich in additional features including a handsome Gopher Client, a news server, and additional E-mail tools.

As you have noticed, each time you have used Chameleon Sampler to connect to your service provider, you have been told that it is possible to receive information from NetManage by sending E-mail to sales@netmanage.com

You may also contact them at

> NetManage, Inc.
> 10725 North DeAnza Blvd.
> Cupertino, CA 95014
> Telephone: 408-973-7171 Fax: 408-257-6405

WHAT ELSE YOU MAY NEED

In addition to getting the latest in Chameleon and NCSA Mosaic software, you may also wish to stay current with the viewers we have discussed as they will be upgraded from time to time.

And, of course, the latest talk is: "Have you seen this URL?" You will want to stay alert to new destinations on the Internet as described by their URLs. As we go to print, new URLs are flooding both the Internet and the popular press. You will want to try them and add the most interesting to your Hotlist!

SESSION SUMMARY

In this session you have been introduced to some other aspects of the World-Wide Web. In particular, you have learned how to use tools such as the World-Wide Web Worm and the World-Wide Web Wanderer. You have also had a chance to learn about the commercialization of the World-Wide Web and several of the well-known providers of commercial services on the Web. Finally, you have upgraded your version of NCSA Mosaic to the latest one which is available as of this writing.

This completes our introduction to NCSA Mosaic and our limited tour of the Internet. In this expanding universe, there is no end to the exploring you can do. Our best wishes for a "Calm and Prosperous Journey!"

—David Sachs and Henry Stair

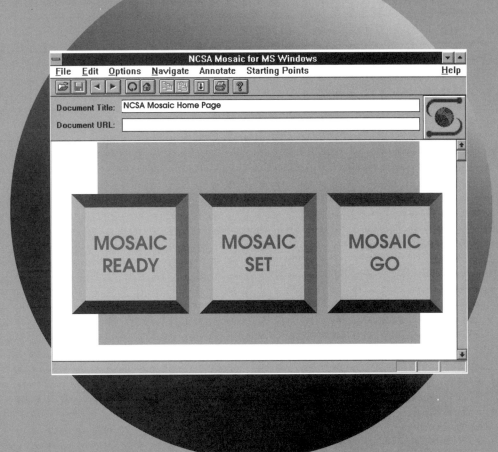

Internet Service Providers

Through the courtesy of the InterNIC, a project of the National Science Foundation, we have included their Internet Service Provider Listing. While not all of these providers offer SLIP or PPP connections, you may wish to contact those serving your area and inquire.

```
================================================================================
InterNIC Information Services
General Atomics (GA)                          Email: info@is.internic.net
P.O. Box #85608                               Phone: 619-455-4600
San Diego, CA 92186-9784                        FAX: 619-455-4640
================================================================================
Date Updated: 08/16/94


          INTERNIC INTERNET SERVICE PROVIDERS LIST


--------------------------------------------------------------------------------
Network                 Service Area(s)
  Contact Name(s)         Phone Number(s)
  Email Address             FAX Number


--------------------------------------------------------------------------------
Providers Based in the United States of America
--------------------------------------------------------------------------------


AlterNet            US and International
  A service of UUNET Technologies, Inc.
  alternet-info@uunet.uu.net  (800) 4UUNET3   (PHONE)
```

```
ANS                     US and International
   Sales and Information          (800) 456-8267   (PHONE)
   info@ans.net                 (703) 758-7717   (FAX)

BARRNet                 Northern/Central California, Nevada (CA, NV)
   Sales                        (415) 725-1790   (PHONE)
   info@barrnet.net             (415) 725-3119   (FAX)

California Online!      California (CA)
   Christopher Ward             (707) 586-3060   (PHONE)
   cward@calon.com              (707) 588-8642   (FAX)

CERFnet                 Western US and International
   CERFnet Hotline              (800) 876-2373 or (619) 455-3900 (PHONE)
   sales@cerf.net               (619) 455-3990   (FAX)

CICnet                  Midwest US (MN, WI, IA, IN, IL, MI, OH)
   Marketing and Sales Dept.    (800) 947-4754 or (313) 998-6703 (phone)
   info@cic.net                 (313) 998-6105   (FAX)

CO Supernet             Colorado (CO)
   Guy Cook                     (303) 273-3472   (PHONE)
   gcook@csn.org                (303) 273-3475   (FAX)

CONCERT                 North Carolina (NC)
   Naomi Courter                (919) 248-1999   (PHONE)
   info@concert.net             (919) 248-1405   (FAX)

CSUnet                  California (CA)
   Gary Jones                   (310) 985-9661   (PHONE)
   nethelp@csu.net

Digital Express Group, Inc.   United States
   John Todd                    (800) 969-9090   (PHONE)
   sales@access.digex.net       (301) 220-0477   (FAX)

EarthLink Network, Inc.        Los Angeles (CA)
   Sky Dayton                   (213) 644-9500   (PHONE)
   info@earthlink.net           (213) 644-9510   (FAX)

FXnet                   North and South Carolina (NC, SC)
                        (704) 338-4670   (PHONE)
   info@fx.net                  (704) 338-4679   (FAX)

HoloNet                 North America
   HoloNet Staff                (510) 704-0160   (PHONE)
   support@holonet.net          (510) 704-8019   (FAX)
```

```
Global Enterprise Services Inc. US and International
   Sergio Heker, President         (800) 35-TIGER   (PHONE)
   market@jvnc.net                 (609) 897-7310   (FAX)


IACNet                    Cincinnati Area (KY, IN, OH)
   Devon Sean McCullough        (513) 887-8877   (PHONE)
   info@iac.net


ICNet                     Michigan, Northern Ohio (MI, OH)
   Ivars Upatnieks              (313) 998-0090   (PHONE)
   info@ic.net


Interaccess               Chicago (IL)
   Tom Simonds                  (708) 498-2542   (PHONE)
   tom@interaccess.com


International Connections Manager (ICM) International
   Robert Collet                (703) 904-2230   (PHONE)
   rcollet@icm1.icp.net


Internetworks             US and Pacific Rim
   Internetworks, Inc.          (503) 233-4774   (PHONE)
   info@i.net               (503) 233-4773   (FAX)


Interpath                      North Carolina (NC)
   Tech Support Desk            (800) 849-6305 or (919) 890-6305 (PHONE)
   info@interpath.net           (919) 890-6319   (FAX)


Los Nettos                Los Angeles Area (CA)
   Joe Kemp                     (310) 822-1511   (PHONE)
   los-nettos-info@isi.edu      (310) 823-6714   (FAX)


MCSNet                    Greater Chicagoland (IL)
   Karl Denninger               (312) 248-8649   (PHONE)
   info@mcs.net                 (312) 248-8649   (FAX)


MichNet/Merit             Michigan (MI)
   Recruiting Staff             (313) 764-9430   (PHONE)
   info@merit.edu               (313) 747-3185   (FAX)


MIDnet                    Mid US (NE, OK, AR, MO, IA, KS, SD)
   Network Inf Ctr              (402) 472-7600   (PHONE)
   nic@westie.mid.net           (402) 472-5640   (FAX)


MRNet                     Minnesota (MN)
   Dennis Fazio                 (612) 342-2570   (PHONE)
   info@MR.Net                  (612) 342-2873   (FAX)
```

```
MSEN                      Michigan (MI)
  Owen Medd                   (313) 998-4562  (PHONE)
  info@msen.com                   (313) 998-4563  (FAX)


NEARNET                   Northeastern US (CT MA ME NH NJ NY RI VT)
  NEARNET Information Hotline    (617) 873-8730  (PHONE)
  nearnet-join@near.net         (617) 873-5620  (FAX)


NETCOM                    United States
  Business or Personal Sales    (800) 501-8649 or (408) 554-8649 (PHONE)
  info@netcom.com           (408) 241-9145  (FAX)


netILLINOIS               Illinois (IL)
  Peter Roll                  (708) 866-1825
  p-roll@nwu.edu              (708) 866-1857  (FAX)


NevadaNet            Nevada (NV)
  Braddlee                (702) 784-4827  (PHONE)
  braddlee@nevada.edu         (702) 784-1108  (FAX)


Northcoast Internet     Northern California
  Kevin Savetz             (707) 443-8696  (PHONE)
  support@northcoast.com


NorthwestNet            Northwestern US (WA OR ID MT ND AK)
  Member Relations            (206) 562-3000  (PHONE)
  info@nwnet.net              (206) 562-4822  (FAX)


NYSERNet            New York (NY)
                    (315) 453-2912  (PHONE)
  info@nysernet.org         (315) 453-3052  (FAX)


OARnet                  Ohio (OH)
  Alison Brown                (614) 292-8100  (PHONE)
  alison@oar.net              (614) 292-7168  (FAX)


PACCOM                  Hawaii (HI) and Australia, Japan, Korea,
                    New Zealand, Hong Kong
  Torben Nielsen              (808) 956-3499  (PHONE)
  torben@hawaii.edu


PREPnet                 Pennsylvania (PA)
  Thomas Bajzek               (412) 268-7870  (PHONE)
  twb+@andrew.cmu.edu         (412) 268-7875  (FAX)
```

```
PSCNET                  Eastern US (PA, OH, WV)
  Eugene Hastings         (412) 268-4960  (PHONE)
  pscnet-admin@psc.edu       (412) 268-5832  (FAX)

PSINet                  US and International
  PSI, Inc.               (800) 82PSI82 or (703) 620-6651 (PHONE)
  info@psi.com            (703) 620-2430  (FAX) (800) 79FAX79 (FAXBACK)

Red River Net           North Dakota, Minnesotra (ND, MN)
  Craig Lien              (701) 232-2227  (PHONE)
  lien@rrnet.com

SeaNet                  Seattle (WA)
  Igor Klimenko             (206) 343-7828  (PHONE)
  igor@seanet.com         (206) 628-0722  (FAX)

Sesquinet        Texas (TX)
  Farrell Gerbode         (713) 527-4988  (PHONE)
  farrell@rice.edu        (713) 527-6099  (FAX)

SprintLink              US and International
  SprintLink              (800) 817-7755  (PHONE)
  info@sprintlink.net       (703) 904-2680  (FAX)

SURAnet            S. East US (WV, VA, SC, NC, TN, KY, LA, MS, AL
                        GA, FL, DC, MD, DE), S.America, Puerto Rico
  Kimberly Donaldson        (301) 982-4600  (PHONE)
  kdonalds@sura.net       (301) 982-4605  (FAX)

Synergy Communications    United States
  Jamie Saker             (402) 346-4638
  jsaker@synergy.net        (402) 346-0208

THEnet                   Texas (TX)
  Frank Sayre               (512) 471-2444  (PHONE)
  f.sayre@utexas.edu        (512) 471-2449  (FAX)

VERnet                  Virginia (VA)
  James Jokl              (804) 924-0616  (PHONE)
  net-info@ver.net        (804) 982-4715  (FAX)

Westnet                 Western US (AZ, CO, ID, NM, UT, WY)
  Pat Burns               (303) 491-7260  (PHONE)
  pburns@yuma.acns.colostate.edu  (303) 491-1958  (FAX)

WiscNet                 Wisconsin (WI)
  Tad Pinkerton             (608) 262-8874  (PHONE)
  tad@cs.wisc.edu         (608) 262-4679  (FAX)
```

```
WVNET                    West Virginia (WV)
  Harper Grimm              (304) 293-5192  (PHONE)
  cc011041@wvnvms.wvnet.edu    (304) 293-5540  (FAX)
```

==
This material is based on work sponsored by the National Science Foundation
under Cooperative Agreement No. NCR-9218749. The Government has certain
rights to this material. Any opinions, findings, and conclusions or
recommendations expressed in this material are those of the author(s) and
do not necessarily reflect the views of the National Science Foundation,
General Atomics, AT&T, or Network Solutions, Inc.

The NIXPub Long Listing

Through the courtesy of Phil Eschallier of Bux Technical Services in Doylestown, PA, we can bring you his NIXPUB listing.

```
==============================================================================
NixPub Long Listing -- June 14, 1994
Public/Open Access UNIX (*NIX) Sites [both Fee and No Fee]
==============================================================================
Sites Listed <149>
** Sites with multiple locations are only counted once **

|   a2i         aa7bq       abode       actrix      admiral     agora     |
|   alphacm     amaranth    anomaly     anubis      aquila      bdt       |
|   bigtex      blkbox      bluemoon    btr         bucket      cellar    |
|   cg57        chinet      cinnet      clinet      cns         colmiks   |
|   conexch     coyote      cpumagic    crash       cruzio      cyber     |
|   cyberspace  ddsw1       debug       deeptht     dhw68k      digex     |
|   dircon      dorsai      echo        edsi        eskimo      ExNet     |
|   exuco1      fullfeed    gagme       genesis     gorn        grebyn    |
|   grex        halcyon     hcserv      HoloNet     iac         ibmpcug   |
|   ichlibix    indirect    infocom     intercom    isys-hh     ixgch     |
|   jabber      jack        kilowatt    kitana      kralizec    latour    |
|   loft386     lopez       lunapark    lunatix     m-net       m2xenix   |
|   madnix      magnus1     magpie      marob       maynard     medsys    |
|   melanie     metronet    micor       mindlink    mindvox     mixcom    |
|   mugnet      mv          ncoast      nervous     netcom      netlink   |
|   northshore  nuchat      nucleus     nyx         oaknet      odbffm    |
|   oldcolo     pacifier    pallas      panix       pnet51      portal    |
|   quack       quake       r-node      rgm         ritz        rock      |
```

```
|   sactoh0    sashimi    satelnet   schunix    scuzzy     sdf        |
|   seanews    sir-alan   sixhub     skypoint   solaria    stanton    |
|   stardust   starnet    sugar      sytex      szebra     teleport   |
|   telerama   telesys    tmsoft     tnc        tronsbox   tutor      |
|   ukelele    unixuser   uunet      uuwest     vicstoy    vpnet      |
|   wa9aek     wariat     wb3ffv     well       wet        WinNET     |
|   woodowl    world      wybbs      wyvern     xmission              |
```

==

```
Updated                 System                      Speed
Last   Telephone #      Name      Location          Range     Hours
-----  ----------------  ---------- ----------------- --------- -----
```

04/94 201-432-0060   ritz   Jersey City   NJ 300-FAST 24
  Gateway2000 486/66 EISA, 28mb RAM, 1 gig FAST SCSI-2 disk space (with
  2.1 gig of Barracuda FAST SCSI-2 disk on the way). BSDI/386 unix.
  8 dialins, all support MNP 3-5 and v.42/v.42bis. 7 modems are AT&T
  Dataport (14.4kbps/v.32bis) and one is a Telebit T2000 (19.2kbps/PEP).
  Shells supported: ash, csh, ksh, tcsh. **Full Internet access.** Our
  IP number is 165.254.109.51. All user accounts have complete internet
  access (FTP,IRC,Archie,Lynx(WWW),Gopher,Telnet, and more!) Mailers
  supported: elm,pine. Full USENET feed. Newsreaders supported: tin,trn,
  nn,rn. Editors supported: emacs,vi,jove, pico. RIP interface coming
  soon.
  Contact: ritz@mordor.com

03/94 201-759-8450   tronsbox Belleville   NJ 300-FAST 24
  Generic 386, UNIX 3.2; Provides shell for some users, USENET, E-Mail
  (feeds available) at $15 a month flat;
  Multiple line (-8568 300 - 2400 baud).

04/94 203-230-4848   colmiks   Hamden   CT 2400-FAST 24
  Linux. Public Access Unix site. Internet mail, Usenet news, FTP, Telnet,
  gopher, www, wais, archie, etc. are all available. News becomes stale in
  one week. Low monthly fee; no per hour connect charges and no setup fees.
  First two weeks free. Unix account with choice of two shells and three
  newsreaders. In addition, members can select new Usenet newsgroups that
  Colmik's is not currently receiving. Login as 'newuser'.
  Contact: mps@colmiks.com.

03/93 203-661-1279   admiral   Greenwich   CT 300-FAST 24
  SCO Unix 3.2.2. (HST/V32) 203-661-2873, (PEP/V32) 203-661-1279, (V32)
  203-661-0450, (MNP6) 203-661-2967. Magpie BBS for local conversation
  and Waffle for Internet mail/Usenet news. Interactive chat and games.
  BBS name is "The Grid." Willing to give newsfeeds and mail access.
  Shell (tcsh, ksh avail) accounts available at no charge. Direct connect
  to Internet site (Yale) via UUCP.230 megs disk space For more information
  contact uunet!admiral!doug (Doug Fields) or fields-doug@cs.yale.edu.

03/94 206-367-3837   eskimo   Seattle   WA 300-FAST 24
  Sun 3/180 SUN/OS 4.1.1_U1 - Everett Tel 206-742-1150 Fast 206-362-6731
  14 Lines including TB World:lazer and TB-3000. Free 2-week trial account.
  Rates $10/month or $96/year.Everybody gets their choice of sh, csh, tcsh,
  ksh, bash, or zsh. Full Usenet News feed 7 day expire. Unique real-time
  conference, message and files system. UUCP mail and news feeds available.
  Home of the Western Washington BBS List. Many applications online.
  Lots of Unix source code archived online.Internet ftp/telnet coming soon!

03/94 206-382-6245   halcyon   Seattle   WA 300-FAST 24
  ULTRIX 4.1, (PEP/V.32) 206-382-6245; monthly and annual fee schedules
  available. 56kBaud commercial Internet link to the T-3 backbone; NNTP
  news feed. Waffle bbs available. Irc server, archie and gopher clients,
  hytelnet, spop; dialup or telnet: login as 'bbs' and provide account
  information. For more information, contact: info@remote.halcyon.com,
  or call voice (PST, USA) +1 206 426 9298

06/94 206-693-0325   pacifier   Vancouver   WA 300-FAST 24
  ESIX 4.0.4, (V.32b) 206-693-0325; monthly and annual fee schedules
  available. 56kBaud commercial Internet link; SLIP/PPP & shell access.
  IRC, FTP, TELNET, GOPHER, hytelnet, lynx; dialup or telnet:login as 'new'
  to register or for further information contact register@pacifier.com
  or call voice (PST, USA) +1 206 693 2116

03/94 206-747-6397   seanews   Redmond   WA 1200-FAST 24
  Xenix 386 2.3.2. SEANEWS is a free public service, providing
  access to Usenet and Internet mail. There are no games, very limited
  files, etc. However SEANEWS does have up-to-date Usenet news and
  excellent mail-handling capability.

03/94 212-420-0527   magpie   NYC   NY 300-FAST 24
  ? - UNIX SYSV - 2, Magpie BBS, no fee, Authors: Magpie/UNIX; No Shell;
  Muli-line (using Telebit Worldblazers) plus anonymous uucp;
  Contact: Steve Manes, manes@magpie.com

03/94 212-675-7059   marob   NYC   NY 300-FAST 24
  386 SCO-XENIX 2.2, XBBS, no fee, limit 60 min; Telebit Trailblazer (9600
  PEP) only 212-675-8438;
  Contact: {philabs|rutgers|cmcl2}!phri!marob!clifford

03/94 212-787-3100   panix   New York City NY 1200-FAST 24
  2 Sparc10/40 & 2 Sparc2, 176MB RAM, 12GB disk, Cisco routers,
  Annex 64-port term servers. Use any of 6 shells or our own
  custom-written menu system. 119 dialins, all support MNP3-5 &
  V.42/V.42bis. 62 are V.32bis Zyxels (14.4kbps and higher), the rest
  2400bps. We are a full internet site with high-speed (T1)
  line- telnet to panix.com (198.7.0.2). Full UseNet; (t)rn, nn, GNUs,
  Tin. Elm, Pine, MM, other mail readers. Vi, Emacs, Jove, Pico, other

editors. Compile your own code (C/C++). $10/mn or 100/yr for basic, $9
per month add'l for telnet/ftp/gopher/www/etc. Feeds, domains, IP, more.
   NEW: SLIP or PPP service for only $35/month on 10 (soon 30) new lines.
      24 local numbers in Long island (516) 626-7863.
   COMING SOON: Local numbers in N.J. (201) and Westchester (914).
         4-processor CPU upgrade. And, as usual, more lines.
   Contact: Alexis Rosen (alexis@panix.com) 212-877-4854, or Jim Baumbach
(jsb@panix.com). Or email/finger info@panix.com, 212-787-6160.

03/94 212-989-4141   mindvox   New York   NY 1200-FAST 24
  Sparc10/51, SparcServer, 2 TurboSparcs, 256MB Ram, 15GB Disk, 96 dialups,

32 additional Hayes V.FC modems @ 212-645-8065. More high-speed lines
added every month. No startup fees. Conference-oriented system with
CyberPunk/Creative Arts focus. Custom Interface. Wired, Mondo 2000,
aXcess and others host online conferences. We are a full internet site
with a high-speed leased line connection, telnet to phantom.com
(198.67.3.2) and login as "guest" for a tour. Telnet, ftp, gopher, www,
lynx, wais, irc, ddial, SLIP, PPP, newsfeeds, QWK, POP3. Prices go from
$10-$17.50 per month for full access, discounts for pre-payment
are available.
   Contact: info@phantom.com, gopher phantom.com, or 800-MindVox

09/93 212-989-8411   echo   NYC   NY 300-FAST 24
  Equip ???, OS ???; A full Internet site with a highspeed leased line:
telnet to echonyc.com (198.67.15.1). Members have full access to shell,
Usenet, telnet, ftp, gopher et al. $19.95/month, $13.95/month for
students and seniors. We are a public computer conferencing system with
1500 members (40% female) and full Internet access.
Contact: horn@echonyc.com (Voice: (212) 255-3839)

03/94 214-248-9811   sdf   Dallas   TX 300-FAST 24
  i386/25 isc 2.0.1; sdf.lonestar.org; 8-line rotary, 2400 bps, 14.4k, PEP;
No Fees; Shell account and UUCP mail/news feeds available; Providing
access to Internet E-Mail, 1600+ USENET newsgroups, online games, programming utilities and more.
login 'info' for registration information.
contact: smj@sdf.lonestar.org

03/94 214-705-2901   metronet   Dallas   TX 300-FAST 24
  HP-UX 8.07, HP 9000/705; Texas Metronet Communications Service.
10 14.4k dialups (7052901), 10 2400 dialups (7052917). Offers shell
accounts w/ ftp, telnet, irc, UseNet, etc. Also UUCP and SLIP. Flat
monthly fees from $10-$50, depending on service type. telnet connections
to feenix.metronet.com welcome. For more information login as info/info,
. or mail info@metronet.com, or call voice at 7052900.

06/94 215-348-9727   jabber   Doylestown   PA 300-FAST 24
  80486DX/33, SunSoft ISC 4.01; V.32[bis]/[Turbo]PEP on dial-in,
  others lines V.32[bis]; No fee services: "Electronic Kiosk" conferencing
  BBS - currently evaluating AKCS - BBS users have read/post access to
  regional USENET groups and full Internet E-mail; Anonymous UUCP
  available for access to the latest nixpub lists, please see the footer of
  this list for more details; Fee services: UUCP feeds, providing access
  to Internet E-mail and USENET News (3000+ groups);
  Contact: Phil Eschallier (phil@bts.com) (+1 215 348 9721 voice).

02/94 216-481-9445   wariat   Cleveland   OH 300-FAST 24
  ISC Unix SysV/386; USR DS on 481-9445, T-3000 on 481-9425. Shell and
  UUCP/Internet mail access available. News and mail feeds are
  available; also, DOS and UNIX files. Anonymous uucp: login: nuucp,
  no password; request /x/files/ls-lR.Z; nuucp account does not allow
  mail exchange; UnixBBS distribution point. BBS free (with e-mail)
  for shell/uucp/newsfeed donation requested. For details, e-mail to:
  zbig@wariat.org (Zbigniew Tyrlik)

03/94 216-582-2460   ncoast   Cleveland   OH 1200-FAST 24
  80386 Mylex, SCO Xenix; 600 meg. storage; XBBS and Shell; USENET
  (newsfeeds available), E-Mail; donations requested; login as "bbs"
  for BBS and "makeuser" for new users.
  Telebit used on 216-237-5486.

03/93 217-789-7888   pallas   Springfield   IL 300-FAST 24
  AT&T 6386, 600 meg disk space; 4 lines w/ USRobotics Dual Standard
  modems; BBS available at no fee (UBBS), shell access for $50/year;
  E-Mail, Usenet; "guest" login available.

03/94 301-220-0462   digex   Greenbelt   MD 300-2400 24
  Express Access Online Communications. Local to Washington, Baltimore,
  Annapolis and Northern Virginia (area code 703); Baltimore dialup
  410-766-1855, Gaithersburg/Damascus 301-570-0001. SunOS shell, full
  Usenet, and e-mail $15/month or $150/year; Internet services incl.
  Telnet, FTP, IRC with news/mail $25/month or $250/year; includes
  unlimited usage 3am - 3pm and 1 hour between 3pm and 3am. Login as
  new (no password) for info and account application, major credit
  cards accepted. Telnet to digex.com or mail to info@digex.com for
  more info; voice phone 800-969-9090 (or 301-220-2020).

03/94 303-871-3324   nyx   Denver   CO 300-FAST 24
  A sort of "social experiment" aimed at providing Internet access to the
  public with minimal operational costs with a "friendly" front end (a
  home-made menu system). Completely donation and volunteer
  operated, no user fees at all. Log in as 'new' to create an account.
  Equipment: Sun SparcServer II + Pyramid 90x, ~6Gb disk space, 16 phone
  lines (+ network logins; usually ~50 users logged in). Public domain

298

file area, private file area, games, full USENET news, internet e-mail.
Provides shell and more network access with proof of identity.
Contact: Andrew Burt, aburt@nyx.cs.du.edu

06/94 305-587-1930   satelnet   Fort Lauderdale FL 300-FAST   24
MIPS RISCserver RC3260, UNIX (RISCos 4.52). Login "new" for
1 week of free access. Rates: $17/month or $60 for 4 months ($15/mo).
Full internet access (telnet, ftp, gopher, irc, etc), unix shell access,
usenet (nn, tin, rn, trn), e-mail (elm, pine, mail). Any other PD
software installed upon request. UUCP and SLIP connections available.
Contact: root@sefl.satelnet.org

03/94 309-676-0409   hcserv   Peoria   IL 300-FAST   24
SGI 4d70 SysV and 386BSD - Public Access UNIX Systems - Mult.Lines/ 1.8GB
Access fee structure based on usage and a $0.02 a minute connection with
a cap of $20.00 a month. Shells (sh,csh,bash,tcsh,zsh), Compilers C and
Fortran, games, File and Pic. Libs., UUCP and USENET access with various
news readers, U.S. Patent and USPS Stamp databases, general timesharing
and programmed on-line applications. Three gateways including AT&T mail
services with outgoing FAX. Self register.
     Contact: Victoria Kee {uunet!hcserv!sysop   sysop%hcserv@uunet.uu.net}

11/93 312-248-0900   ddsw1   Chicago   IL 300-FAST   24
Intel Machines, BSDI/DELL; guest users have free BBS access; fee for
shell, Usenet, Internet, unlimited use, and offsite mail; Authors
of AKCS bbs; 6.5GB storage, fee varies with service classification,
V.32bis & PEP available. Newsfeeds and mail connections available;
Full Internet services including SLIP, PPP, and leased circuits
Contact: Karl Denninger (karl@MCS.COM) or voice/fax at 312-248-UNIX

03/94 312-282-8606   gagme   Chicago   IL 300-FAST   24
80486 - Linux. World Wide Access (TM) Full Internet Access now
available! Full netnews, E-mail, ftp, telnet, IRC, MUD, and so much
more! Shell and BBS options. Multiple V.32bis and PEP lines. More
lines added as needed. UUCP feeds also available. Send mail to or
finger info@wwa.com for more information.

03/94 312-283-0559   chinet   Chicago   IL 300-FAST   24
'386, SysVr3.2.1; Multiple lines including Telebit and HST;
Picospan BBS (free), USENET at $50/year (available to guests on
weekends).

02/94 313-623-6309   nucleus   Clarkston   MI 1200-2400 24
AMI 80386 - ESIX 5.3.2, large online sources archive accessible by
anonymous UUCP, login: nuucp, nucleus!/user/src/LISTING lists
available public domain/shareware source code.
Contact: jeff@nucleus.mi.org

```
03/93 313-761-3000     grex      Ann Arbor      MI 300-FAST  24
   Sun 2/170 with SunOS 3.2.  Full Usenet feed, Internet e-mail, shell
   accounts, on-line games, PicoSpan, UUCP accounts.  Voluntary
   donation ($6/month or $60/year) for coop membership and Usenet
   posting access.  6 lines, 300MB.  Cooperatively owned & operated by
   Cyberspace Communications.
   Contact: info@cyberspace.org

03/94 313-996-4644     m-net     Ann Arbor      MI 300-2400  24
   486 - BSDI, open access; run by Arbornet, tax-exempt nonprofit; donations
   tax deductible; dues for extended access; user supported; 15 lines;
   Picospan conferencing; 500 MB disk; Internet e-mail; UUCP available;
   free shell access, C compiler, multiuser party, games (including nethack,
   empire, rotisserie baseball); M-Net 10 year anniversary in June, 1993!
   Access from the Internet:  telnet m-net.ann-arbor.mi.us
   contact:  help@m-net.ann-arbor.mi.us

03/93 401-455-0347     anomaly    Esmond        RI 300-FAST  24
   Informtech 486 mongrel; SCO Open Desktop 1.1; Trailblazer+ (0347) and
   v.32 T2500 (401-331-3706) dialins. Directly connected to the Internet:
   IP Address: 155.212.2.2, or 'anomaly.sbs.risc.net'. Current fees: $15/mo.
   includes complete Internet access. Mail and USENET Newsfeeds available,
   limited feeds for non-PEP sites. SCO software archive site, anonymous
   UUCP login: xxcp, pass: xenix. Anonymous FTP also supported. Software
   listing & download directions in anomaly!~/SOFTLIST

02/94 403-569-2882     debug     Calgary        AB 300-FAST  24
   386, SCO-Xenix; Login: gdx; Telebit, HST, V.32bis, MNP-5 supported;
   6 phone lines: (403) 569-2882, 569-2883, 569-2884, 569-2885, 569-2886;
   System runs modified GDX BBS software; Services: Usenet, Internet email,
   IRC, local-chat, 50+ games, legal-forms, programming, ftp-via-email,
   and much more; Fee: $10/month-3hrs/day to $25/month-24hrs/day;
   Visa & Amex accepted.  Demo accounts with limited access are free.
   Contact: Rob Franke root@debug.cuc.ab.ca

03/94 407-299-3661     vicstoy    Orlando       FL 1200-2400 24
   ISC 386/ix 2.0.2. Partial USENET, e-mail (feeds available);  Login as
   bbs, no passwd (8N1);  Free shell access;  Orlando BBS list, games;
   cu to Minix 1.5.10 system (weather permitting);  USENET includes
   Unix/Minix source groups.  Contact: uunet!tarpit!bilver!vicstoy!vickde
   or vickde@vicstoy.UUCP (Vick De Giorgio).

06/94 407-767-2583     stardust   Altamonte Sprin FL 300-FAST  24
   80386DX-40 SCO XENIX 2.3.4; XBBS bulletin board & conferencing system,
   no fee, login: bbs; partial Usenet newsfeed; amateur radio, H-P calc-
   ulator, embedded controllers and electronic design forums and files.
   Contact: kc4zvw@stardust.oau.org - David Billsbrough - 407/767-9310 (v)
```

03/94 408-241-9760   netcom   San Jose   CA 1200-FAST 24
  UNIX, Sun Network SunOS 4.1; Netcom - Online Communication Services;
  70 Telebit lines V.32/V.42 9600/2400/; USENET (16 days), Lrg archive,
  News/Mail Feeds, Shell, Internet (ftp, telnet, irc), Slip Connections,
  Local access via CALNet San Jose, Palo Alto, Red Wd Cty, San Fran,
  Oklnd, Berkly, Alameda, Pleasanton, Los Angeles, and Santa Cruz;
  Fee $17.50/mo + Reg fee of $15.00. Login: guest (510)865-9004,
  (408)241-9760,(408)459-9851,(310)842-8835,(415)424-0131,(510)426-6860;
  Just Say No to connect fees, Login as guest (no password).

03/94 408-245-7726   uuwest   Sunnyvale   CA 300-FAST 24
  SCO-XENIX, Waffle. No fee, USENET news (news.*, music, comics, telecom,
  etc) The Dark Side of the Moon BBS. This system has been in operation
  since 1985.
  Login: new Contact: (UUCP) ames!uuwest!request
  (Domain) request@darkside.com

03/94 408-249-9630   quack   Santa Clara   CA 300-FAST 24
  Sun 4/75, SunOS 4.1.3; 3 lines: First two are Zyxel U-1496E (300-2400,
  v.32bis/v.42bis), third is a Worldblazer (same and add PEP); Internet
  connectivity; Shell - $10/mo; New users should login as 'guest';
  Contact: postmaster@quack.kfu.com

06/94 408-293-9010   a2i   San Jose   CA 1200-FAST 24
  Usenet/Email/Internet/SunOS (Unix). 20 lines. Dial 408-293-9010
  (v.32bis, v.32) or 408-293-9020 (PEP) and log in as "guest". $15/month
  for 6-month. Also available via telnet, a2i.rahul.net, 192.160.13.1.
  Contact: info@rahul.net [daemon response] or voice 408-293-8078

04/93 408-423-4810   deeptht   Santa Cruz   CA 300-FAST 24
  4 dialin lines (2 2400 at 423-4810, 2 v32 at 423-1767), 486/40+32M,
  2 GB disk space including a large part of the uunet source archives,
  SCO UNIX 3.2v4.1, C/Pascal/Fortran/BASIC compilers, TinyMud, rn/trn.
  Domain name: deeptht.armory.com (and alias armory.com).

02/94 408-423-9995   cruzio   Santa Cruz   CA 1200-2400 24
  Tandy 4000, Xenix 2.3.*, Caucus 3.*; focus on Santa Cruz activity
  (ie directory of community and government organizations, events, ...);
  USENET Support; Multiple lines; no shell; fee: $15/quarter.
  Contact: ...!uunet!cruzio!chris

02/94 408-458-2289   gorn   Santa Cruz   CA 300-FAST 24
  Everex 386, SCO xenix 2.3.2; 2 lines, -2837 telebit for PEP connects;
  Standard shell access, games, email injection into the internet, up to
  date archive of scruz-sysops information, upload/download, usenet news
  including scruz.* hierarchy for santa cruz area information; UUCP set
  up on as-requested; No charge, donations accepted; newuser: log in as
  ``gorn'' and fill out online form.
  Contact: falcon@gorn.echo.com

03/94 408-725-0561   portal   Cupertino   CA 300-FAST 24
  Networked Suns (SunOS), multiple lines, shell or "online menu" access;
  Live Internet; fees: $19.95/mn; conferencing, multi-user chats,
  computer special interest groups; E-Mail/USENET; UUCP service
  also available.
  Contact: Customer Service (cs@portal.com).

06/94 408-739-1520   szebra   Sunnyvale   CA 300-FAST 24
  486PC, Linux; 4 lines, Telebit, V.FC, V32bis; Full Usenet News, email
  (Internet & UUCP), first time users login: new, shell access/files
  storage/email, FTP, gopher, archie, WWW available (registration
  required); GNU, X11R4 and R5 source archives. viet-net/SCV and VNese
  files/software archives. contact: admin@szebra.Saigon.COM or
  {claris,zorch,sonyusa}!szebra!admin

03/93 410-661-2598   wb3ffv   Baltimore   MD 1200-FAST 24
  80486, UNIX V.3.2.x; XBBS for HAM radio enthusiasts; 1.6 Gigabytes
  online; Multiple lines, dial in - TB WorldBlazer,
  2475 - USR HST DS V.32bis/42bis, 2648 - Tb+ PEP; Some USENET;
  Anon-UUCP available; Login as bbs (8-N-1).

12/93 410-893-4786   magnus1   Belair   MD 300-FAST 24
  Equip Unisys S/Series, UNIX 3.3.2; ksh, csh, sh; Multiple lines;
  $60.00/yr; E-Mail/USENET,ftp, telnet,finger; 'C', Pascal, Fortran,
  Cobol, Basic development systems; Interactive chat and games;
  Files for download; USA Today, Online Magazines, Daily Business News;
  PC Catalog; Local Online Forums as well; as Technical Help;
  Clarinet News; No limits.
  Contact cyndiw@magnus1.com

03/94 412-481-5302   telerama   Pittsburgh   PA 300-FAST 24
  Telerama Public Access Internet. 4.3 bsd. Multiple lines. Hourly fee
  includes telnet, ftp, e-mail, Usenet, ClariNet/UPI, gopher, IRC, games,
  compilers, editors, shell or menu navigation and 1 meg disk quota. Also
  offering SLIP, UUCP and commercial accounts. Fees: $20/mo (personal),
  $50/mo (commercial); Registration: login as new. FTP info from
  telerama.pgh.pa.us; /info/telerama.info
  Contact: Kristen McQuillin, info@telerama.pgh.pa.us. 412/481-3505 voice.

05/94 414-241-5469   mixcom   Milwaukee   WI 1200-FAST 24
  SVR4 UNIX; Services and features: Email, Usenet, ftp, telnet, irc,
  supports QWK and Zipnews off-line readers, easy to use menus; BBS,
  UUCP and personal SLIP/PPP services; Info server: info@mixcom.com;
  Info account (call or telnet to mixcom.com): login as "newuser";
  Contact: Dean Roth (sysop@mixcom.com) [414-228-0739 voice].

```
03/93 414-321-9287      solaria    Milwaukee      WI 300-2400  24
   Sun 3/60LE, SunOS 4.1.  Internet E-mail, limited USENET news,
   shell access, Telebit WorldBlazer soon.  Feeds available.
   Donations requested, registration required.  One hop off of the Internet.
   Contact: jgreco@solaria.mil.wi.us (Joe Greco) or log in as "help"

06/93 414-342-4847      solaria    Milwaukee      WI 300-FAST  24
   Sun 3/60LE, SunOS 4.1.  Internet E-mail, limited USENET news,
   shell access, feeds available, donations requested, registration
   required. One hop off of the Internet.
   Contact: jgreco@solaria.mil.wi.us (Joe Greco) or log in as "help"

06/93 414-734-2499      edsi       Appleton       WI 300-FAST  24
   IBM PS/2 Model 55SX, SCO Xenix 2.3.2;  Running STARBASE II Software.
   Enterprise Data Systems Incorporated (Non-profit).  100+ local rooms,
   PLUS USENET, Multi Channel Chat, 9 ports, $15 yr, flat rate for full
   access to net news (no alternet yet), mail.  The Fox Valley's only public
   access Unix based BBS.
   Contact: Chuck Tomasi (chuck@edsi.plexus.COM)

03/94 415-332-6106      well       Sausalito      CA 1200-FAST 24
   6-processor Sequent Symmetry (i386); Internet, UUCP and USENET
   access; multiple lines; access via CPN and Internet (well.sf.ca.us);
   PICOSPAN BBS; $15/mo + $2/hr (CPN or 9600 +$4/hr);
   Contact (415) 332-4335

03/94 415-826-0397      wet        San Francisco  CA 1200-FAST 24
   386 SYS V.3.  Wetware Diversions.  $15 registration, $0.01/minute.
   Public Access UNIX System:  uucp, PicoSpan bbs, full Usenet News,
   Multiple lines (6), shell access.  Newusers get initial credit!
   contact:{ucsfcca|hoptoad|well}!wet!editor (Eric Swanson)

03/94 415-949-3133      starnet    Los Altos      CA 300-FAST  24
   SunOS 4.1. 8-lines. MNP1-5 and v42/bis, or PEP on all lines.
   Shell access for all users.  USENET--900+ groups.  E-mail (feeds
   available).  smart mail.  Publically available software (pd/shareware).
   $12/mo. Contact: admin@starnet.uucp or ...!uunet!apple!starnet!admin

03/94 415-967-9443      btr        Mountain View  CA 300-FAST  24
   Sun (SunOS UNIX), shell access, e-mail, netnews, uucp, can access by
   Telenet PC Pursuit, multiple lines, Telebit, flat rate: $12.50/month.
   For sign-up information please send e-mail to Customer Service at
   cs@btr.com or ..!{decwrl,fernwood,mips}!btr!cs
   or call 415-966-1429 Voice.

03/93 416-249-5366      r-node     Etobicoke      ON 300-FAST  24
   80386, ISC SV386; SupraModem2400 on Dial-in line, Worldblazer and
   Cardinal2400 on other two lines; No fee services: Uniboard BBS for
```

BBS users; shell access for those who ask; Fee services: access
to subsequent lines, unlimited dl/ul access; full USENET News and
International E-mail access through Usenet/Internet mail; Free
UUCP connections;
Contact: Marc Fournier (marc@r-node.gts.org)

03/93 416-461-2608   tmsoft   Toronto   ON 300-FAST 24
  NS32016, Sys5r2, shell; news+mail $30/mo, general-timesharing $60/mo
  All newsgroups. Willing to setup mail/news connections.
  Archives:comp.sources.{unix,games,x,misc}
  Contact: Dave Mason <mason@tmsoft> / Login: newuser

06/94 503-220-1016   teleport   Portland   OR 300-FAST 24
  SPARCstations, SunOS 4.1.3, 10GB disk; 100+ lines and support PEP/V.32
  and V.32bis; E-Mail/USENET; Shell access for $120 / year includes
  choice of shell, full news feed, complete internet (ftp, telnet, irc,
  mud, SLIP, PPP) access; now supporting UUCP connections and with
  locations in Salem, OR (503) 364-2028 and Vancouver, WA (206) 260-0330;
  apply with "new" or email info@teleport.com

03/94 503-293-1772   agora   Portland   OR 1200-FAST 24
  Intel Unix V/386, $6/mo or $60/yr, news, mail, ftp, telnet, irc.
  Six lines with trunk-hunt, all V.32bis. Agora is part of RAINet.
  Contact: Alan Batie, batie@agora.rain.com

03/94 503-297-3211   m2xenix   Portland   OR 300-FAST 24
  '386/20, Xenix 2.3. 2 Lines (-0935); Shell accounts available, NO BBS;
  No fee; E-mail, USENET News, program development.
  Contact: ...!uunet!m2xenix!news or on Fido at 297-9145

03/94 503-632-7891   bucket   Portland   OR 300-FAST 24
  Tektronix 6130, UTek 3.0(4.2bsd-derived). Bit Bucket BBS no longer
  online. Modem is Telebit Trailblazer+ (PEP). Users interested in
  access to Unix should send EMail to rickb@pail.rain.com. $30/year
  access fee includes USENET News, EMail (fast due to local Internet
  access), and access to all tools/utilities/games. Internet 'ftp'
  available upon request. UUCP connections (1200, 2400, 9600V.32,
  9600PEP, 19200PEP) available (through another local system which is
  not publically available) to sites which will poll with reasonable
  regularity and reliability.

06/93 508-664-0149   genesis   North Reading MA 300-FAST 24
  SVR3 UNIX; Internet mail; Usenet News; No Fees; Shell access and menu
  system; Three lines; One hop from the Internet; HST and V.32bis; UUCP
  feeds available. Contact: steve1@genesis.nred.ma.us (steve belczyk).
  Automated reply: info@genesis.nred.ma.us

09/93 508-853-0340   schunix   Worcester   MA 2400-FAST 24
  Sparc 2, 1.9GB; Email, Shell, Full UseNet, C/C++, over 11GB on CD's,
  $5/month $3/hr, $10/mn 5hrs incl. $2/hr, uucp-feeds call,
  login:guest for info, Free BBS inside of schunix, login:pbbs,
  Contact: Robert Schultz (schu@schunix.com) 508-853-0258
  SCHUNIX 8 Grove Heights Drive, Worcester, MA 01605

03/93 510-294-8591   woodowl   Livermore   CA 1200-FAST 24
  Xenix/386 3.2.1. Waffle BBS, Usenet Access; Reasonable users welcome.
  No fee; For more information contact: william@woodowl.UUCP,
  lll-winken!chumley!woodowl!william, or call and just sign up on system.

06/94 510-530-9682   bdt   Oakland   CA 1200-FAST 24
  Sun 4, SunOS 4.1; BBS access to Usenet news, E-mail, with QWK support
  $35/year. Live Internet Access. Telnet to bdt.com. First time users
  login: bbs. SLIP/PPP starting at $20/month. Leased line connections,
  newsfeeds, POP3, domain mail services also available.
  Contact: david@bdt.com

03/94 510-623-8652   jack   Fremont   CA 300-FAST 24
  Sun 4/470 running Solaris 2.2 offers downloading of netnews archives
  and all uploaded software. Each user can log in as bbs or as the account
  which they create for themselves. This is a free Public Access Unix
  System that is part of a network of 4 machines. The primary phone line
  is on a rotary to five other lines.

02/94 510-704-1058   HoloNet   Berkeley   CA 1200-FAST 24
  DECstations, ULTRIX; Commercial network, over 850 cities; Custom shell;
  Full Internet, IRC, telnet, USENET, USA Today Decisionline, games;
  $2/hr off-peak; Telnet: holonet.net, Info sever: info@holonet.net,
  Contact: support@holonet.net

03/94 512-346-2339   bigtex   Austin   TX FAST   24
  SysVr3.2 i386, anonymous shell, no fee, anonymous uucp ONLY,
  Telebit 9600/PEP; Mail links available. Carries GNU software.
  anon uucp login: nuucp NO PASSWD, file list /usr3/index
  anon shell login: guest NO PASSWD, chroot'd to /usr3
  Contact: james@bigtex.cactus.org

03/93 513-779-8209   cinnet   Cincinnati   OH 1200-FAST 24
  80386, ISC 386/ix 2.02, Telebit access, 1 line; $7.50/Month; shell
  access, Usenet access; news feeds available;
  login: newacct password: new user to register for shell access

05/94 513-887-8855   iac   Cincinnati   OH 300-FAST 24
  Multiple Sun systems, offering shell access, USENET, FTP, TELNET IRC,
  MAIL; Also offer SLIP/PPP/UUCP feeds;
     login: new
  finger or mail info@iac.net for pricing and other info.

03/93 514-435-8896   ichlibix   Blainville Queb CA 300-FAST   24
  80386, ISC 2.2.1;   2400 bps modem on dial in, HST DS on -2650;   BBS
  program is Ubbs (RemoteAccess Clone) - named Soft Stuff, no shell;
  No fees required but are recommended for more access ($25 - $75/yr);
  Files for both dos and UNIX + a lot of binaries for ISC;   Possibility
  to send/receive UUCP mail from the BBS

02/94 515-945-7000   cyberspace Jefferson   IA 300-FAST   24
  SUNOS: FREE SERVICE, no time limits;   T1 (1.536MB) Internet Link, Full
  News Feed, Irc, Archie, Lynx, WWW, telnet
  ncftp, and more.   FREE Unix Shell, PPP & Slip Accounts.

06/93 516-586-4743   kilowatt   Deer Park   NY 2400-FAST 24
  Consensys SVR4 running on a clone 80486-33. 516-586-4743 for
  Telebit World-Blazer, 516-667-6142 for a Boca V.32bis. Providing FREE
USENET email/news to the general public. FREE feeds available with a
  selection of all of alt, biz, comp, rec, talk, sci, soc, and vmsnet
  newsgroups ... using UUCP or QWK-packets.
  Contact: Arthur Krewat 516-253-2805 krewat@kilowatt.UUCP
  or krewat@kilowatt.linet.org Telnet/Ftp not available here, so don't
  even ask!

03/93 517-487-3356   lunapark   E. Lansing   MI 1200-2400 24
  Compaq 386/20 SCO-UNIX 3.2, lunabbs bulletin board & conferencing
  system, no fee, login: bbs password: lunabbs. Primarily UNIX software
  with focus on TeX and Postscript, also some ATARI-ST and IBM-PC stuff
  2400/1200 --> 8 N 1
  Contact: ...!{mailrus,uunet}!frith!lunapark!larry

03/93 517-789-5175   anubis   Jackson   MI 300-1200   24
  Equip ???, OS ???; 1200 baud dial-in (planning on 19.2kbps);
  UUCP connections to the world, PicoSpan BBS software, Teleconferencing,
  C programming compiler, 3 public dial-in lines, Online games;
  Contact: Matthew Rupert (root@anubis.mi.org).

03/93 518-346-8033   sixhub   upstate   NY 300-2400   24
  PC Designs GV386. hub machine of the upstate NY UNIX users group (*IX)
  two line reserved for incoming, bbs no fee, news & email fee $15/year
  Smorgasboard of BBS systems, UNaXcess and XBBS online,
  Citadel BBS now in production. Contact: davidsen@sixhub.uucp.

09/93 602-274-9600   indirect   Phoenix   AZ 300-FAST   24
  Sun/SunOS + multiple 486/50's; Live internet, multiple lines
  (up to 14.4k); E-Mail/USENET, 5mb disk quota, shell or menu system,
  multi-user games, off-line news readers (personal $20/mo, business
  $30/mo); UUCP feeds available ($20-$45/mo); SLIP/PPP connection at
  speeds up to 14.4k - demand/dedicated lines (leased line connections
  to 24kbps) (basic rates $150/mo).
  Contact: info@indirect.com

```
03/93 602-293-3726      coyote    Tucson          AZ 300-FAST  24
   FTK-386, ISC 386/ix 2.0.2;  Waffle BBS, devoted to embedded systems
   programming and u-controller development software;  E-Mail/USENET;
   UUCP and limited USENET feeds available;
   Contact: E.J. McKernan (ejm@datalog.com).
      bbs: ogin: bbs    (NO PWD)
      uucp: ogin: nuucp  (NO PWD)

09/93 602-321-9600      indirect  Tucson          AZ 300-FAST  24
   Refer to primary entry (Phoenix, AZ) for system/services details.

03/94 602-649-9099      telesys   Mesa            AZ 1200-FAST 24
   SCO UNIX V/386 3.2.4; Telebit WorldBlazers; TeleSys-II Unix based BBS
   (no fee) login: bbs; Unix archives available via BBS or ANON UUCP;
   Shell Accounts available for full access USENET, email (fees);
   Phoenix Matchmaker with more than 9000 members (fees) login: bbs
   Regional supplier of USENET Newsfeeds; uucp-anon: nuucp NOPWD;
   Contact: kreed@tnet.com  or  ...!ncar!noao!enuucp!telesys!kreed

02/94 602-991-5952      aa7bq     Scottsdale      AZ 300-2400  24
   Sun 4, SunOS 4.1.2;  NB bbs system;  900 meg online;  Primarily Ham Radio
   related articles from usenet (Rec.radio.amateur.misc), complete Callsign
   Database, Radio and scanner modifications, frequency listings, shell
   access by permission, No fees, Free classified ads, Local e-mail only.
   Login: bbs (8N1) or
   Login: callsign for callsign database only.  Don't use MNP!
   For additional info contact Fred.Lloyd@West.Sun.COM

03/93 603-429-1735      mv        Litchfield      NH 1200-FAST 24
   80386; ISC UNIX; MV is on the Internet (mv.MV.COM, host 192.80.84.1);
   mail connections and news feeds via uucp; domain registrations;
   membership in "domain park" MV.COM; domain forwarding; archives of
   news and mail software for various platforms; mailing lists;
   area topics;  $7/month for 1 hour/month; $20/month for 3 hours/month
   $2/hour thereafter; blocks of 30 hours for $20 month - First month free
   up to 20 hours.
   Voice: 603-429-2223; USMail: MV Communications Inc, PO Box 4963
   Manchester NH 03108; Or dial the modem and login as "info" or "rates".

03/93 603-448-5722      tutor     Lebanon         NH 300-FAST  24
   Altos 386 w/ System V 3.1;  Limited newsfeed;  E-Mmail and USENET
   available via UUCP.
   Contact: peter.schmitt@dartmouth.edu

03/93 604-576-1214      mindlink  Vancouver       BC 300-FAST  24
   80386 w/ SCO Xenix;  14 lines, 660 Meg disk space, TB+ & 9600 HST
   available; No shell;  Fee of $45/year for BBS access;  E-Mail, USENET,
   hundreds of megs of file downloads;  Operating since 1986.
```

02/94 605-348-2738   loft386   Rapid City .   SD 300-FAST 24
  80386 SYS V/386 Rel 3.2, Usenet mail/news via UUNET, UUNET archive
  access. NO BBS! News feeds available. 400 meg hd. Fees: $10/month
  or $25/quarter.
  Call (605) 343-8760 and talk to Doug Ingraham to arrange an account or
  email uunet!loft386!dpi

03/93 606-233-2051   lunatix   Lexington   KY 300-2400 24
  SCO Unix 3.2.2. 2 2400 baud lines. V32bis later in the fall.
  Home grown Pseudo BBS software. Multiuser games, Full USENET Feed on
  tap, USENET Feeds available. Shells available, No Fees.

03/93 608-246-2701   fullfeed   Madison   WI FAST   24
  Sun SPARC station SLC, 16Mb RAM, 1Gb disk, SunOS 4.1.1, Telebit
  WorldBlazers; operated by FullFeed Communications; USENET/E-Mail,
  UUCP plus other digital communication services; login: fullfeed;
  UUCP starts at $24/month, shells cost $16/month; No-cost, limited-term,
  evaluation accounts are setup over the telephone; FullFeed plans to offer
  Internet connections (SLIP, PPP, 56Kbps) within 6 months.
  Contact "SYSop@FullFeed.Com" or call +1-608-CHOICE-9 (voice).

03/93 608-273-2657   madnix   Madison   WI 300-2400 24
  486, MST UNIX SysV/386, shell, no fee required, USENET news,
  mail, login: bbs
  Contact: ray@madnix.uucp

03/94 610-539-3043   cellar   Trooper/Oaks   PA 300-FAST 24
  DTK 486/33, SCO Unix 3.2, Waffle BBS - The Cellar BBS, no shell; USR
  Dual-Standard modems, five lines and growing. BBS is free; net news
  (full feed) and net mail by subscription. $10/mo, $55/6-mo, or $90/yr.
  Fancies itself to be more of a colorful "electronic community" than the
  best plug into the net, and as such, it features a lively local message
  base. But it also generally carries the latest Linux distribution,
  just to prove it hasn't forgotten its hacker roots.
  Contact: Tony Shepps (toad@cellar.org).

08/93 612-458-3889   skypoint   Newport   MN 300-FAST 24
  Unixware System V R4.2. VGA Graphics BBS/OIS using Sentience BBS
  software from Cyberstore - Sentience uses the RIP graphics protocol; 4
  lines are Courier 14.4 Modems, 1 Worldblazer; Full News Feed 7 day
  expire, Clarinet Feed Site, USA Today, Board Watch, News Bytes, Internet
  Mail, Real time games and conferences; Unix, DOS, Windows and OS/2
  source and binary archives on CDROMS and 2.1 Gigabytes of Disk;
  $45 dollars year basic services $85 dollars a year for full access,
  $100 a year for Unix shell account and access to full development tools;
   Will provide Clarinet and USENET News Feeds; Will add Fidonet and other
  networks in the near future;
  Login as 'guest'.
  Contact: info@skypoint.com

03/94 612-473-2295   pnet51   Minneapolis   MN 300-2400   24
   Equip ?, Xenix, multi-line, no fee, some Usenet news, email,
   multi-threaded conferencing, login: pnet id: new, PC Pursuitable
   UUCP: {rosevax, crash}!orbit!pnet51!admin

04/93 613-724-9817   latour   Ottawa   ON 300-FAST   24
   Sun 3/60, SunOS 4.1, 8meg Ram, 660 meg of disk; 2nd line v.32[bis];
   No BBS; Unix access rather than usenet; Login as guest for a shell
   (send mail to postmaster asking for an account);
   Anon uucp is login as 'anonuucp' (/bin/rmail is allowed) --
   Grab ~uucp/README[.Z] for an ls-lR.

03/93 613-837-3029   micor   Orleans   ON 300-FAST   24
   386/25, 600 Meg, Xenix 2.3.2, USENET, email, 2 phone lines
   fee required to get more than 15 mins/day of login and to access
   additional phone lines.
   Available: bbs accounts (waffle) or shell accounts.
   Contact: michel@micor.ocunix.on.ca or michel@micor.uucp, Michel Cormier.

03/94 614-868-9980   bluemoon   Reynoldsburg   OH 300-FAST   24
   Sun 4/75, SunOS; 2.2gb; Leased line to the Internet; Multiple lines,
   HST Dual on -9980 & -9982, Telebit T2500 on -9984; 2gb disk space;
   Bluemoon BBS -- supporting UNIX, graphics, and general interest; Full
   USENET, gated Fidonet conferences, E-Mail;
   Contact: grant@bluemoon.uucp (Grant DeLorean).

03/93 615-288-3957   medsys   Kingsport   TN 1200-FAST 24
   386 SCO-UNIX 3.2, XBBS; No fee, limit 90 min; Telebit PEP,
   USENET, 600mb;
   login: bbs   password: bbs
   anon uucp --> medsys Any ACU (speed) 16152883957 ogin: nuucp
   Request /u/xbbs/unix/BBSLIST.Z for files listing
   Contact: laverne@medsys (LaVerne E. Olney)

03/93 616-457-1964   wybbs   Jenison   MI 300-FAST   24
   386 - SCO-XENIX 2.3.2, two lines, XBBS for new users, mail in for shell
   access, usenet news, 150 meg storage, Telebit. Interests: ham radio,
   xenix AKA: Consultants Connection Contact: danielw@wyn386.mi.org
   Alternate phone #: 616-457-9909 (max 2400 baud) Anonymous UUCP available.

09/93 617-593-4557   northshore Lynn   MA 300-FAST   24
   Sun SPARCstation, SunOS 4.1.3; Telebit Worldblazer modems (v.32bis,
   v.32, 2400, 1200 baud); Eco Software, Inc; GNU, archie, gopher, wais,
   etc. - any software you need, we'll add it; $9/month for 10 hours
   connect time, 3 Mb disk quota (additional usage: connect - $1/hour,
   disk - $1/Mb/month); UUCP feeds available; Hours: 7 days/week,
   24 hours/day (except Friday 15:00-18:00 for backups).
   Contact: info@northshore.ecosoft.com (Voice: (617) 593-3110).

03/94 617-739-9753   world   Brookline   MA 300-FAST 24
   Sun 4/280, SunOS 4.0.3; Shell, USENET, E-Mail, UUCP, IRC, Alternet
   connection to the Internet, and home of the Open Book Initiative (text
   project), multiple lines; fees: $5/mo + $2/hr or $20/20hrs per month;
   Contact: geb@world.std.com

11/93 619-278-8267   cg57   San Diego   CA 1200-FAST 24
   i386 Unix ISC 3.2 R4.0, UniBoard BBS Software (login as bbs); Worldblaze
r
   on dial-in, -3905 Telebit Trailblazer Plus, -9837 Practical Peripherals
   (V32); BBS is free; Over 800 meg of downloadable software
   (UNIX/FreeBSD/386BSD/Linux/NETBSD and DOS systems + Soundblaster files);
   Shell accounts available for $30 for 3 months with access to ftp/telnet/
   irc/gopher/archie/etc. Full (USENET) news feed, and selected Fidonet
   uucp accounts available. cg57.esnet.com is on the internet
   (198.180.239.3) Anonymous uucp - login: nuucp (no password).
   Get file ls-lR.Z for complete files listing.
   Contact: steve@cg57.esnet.com

03/94 619-453-1115   netlink   San Diego   CA 1200-FAST 24
   The Network Information eXchange (NIX). i386 Unix system, provides
   access to email, over 1000 Usenet newsgroups, and file archives through
   Waffle BBS interface (no shell). Multiple lines, NO FEE for basic
   access (E-mail only). Higher access available to contributing members.
   Mail feeds available. Login: nix   Contact: system@netlink.nix.com

04/94 619-634-1376   cyber   Encinitas   CA 300-FAST 24
   Equip ???; Multiple lines [HST16.8/V.32]; The Cyberspace Station;
   On the Internet (telnet to CYBER.NET [192.153.125.1]); A Public Access
   Unix service with full Internet connectivity; E-Mail/USENET,
   International communications, hunting for files, and interactive chatting
;
   Login on as "guest" and send feedback (Don't forget to leave a phone
   number where you can be reached).
   Contact: info@cyber.net

03/94 619-637-3640   crash   San Diego   CA 12-FAST   24
   CTSNET Public Access Unix. A network of 486-66/DX2 64mb+32mb, SCO
   Unix 3.2v4.1 machines, 41 lines; HST: 619-593-6400, 637-3640,
   220-0836; V32/V32.bis: 619-593-7300, 637-3660, 220-0853; PEP:
   619-593-9500, 637-3680, 220-0857. V42.bis most lines, All modems at
   38,400bps, Telebits at 19,200/38,400bps. 8N1 only. International
   Usenet (6600+ groups), Clarinet News Service, Reuters News, worldwide
   email, shell and uucp accounts. 3.5gb disk. Direct Internet T1
   dedicated. Shell accounts $18 per month flat, newfeeds, SLIP, PPP,
   other svcs. Contact bblue@crash.cts.com, support@ctsnet.cts.com,
   info@crash.cts.com

03/94 703-281-7997   grebyn   Vienna   VA 300-2400 24
Networked Vax/Ultrix. $30/month for 25 hours. $1.20 connect/hr after 25
hours. 1 MB disk quota. $2/MB/month additional quota. USENET News.
Domain mail (grebyn.com). Full Internet IP connectivity expected in the
summer of 1992. Mail to info@grebyn.com, voice 703-281-2194.

04/93 703-528-4380   sytex   Arlington   VA 300-FAST 24
ISC Unix, UUCP, Waffle BBS, 5 lines. Login as "bbs". Mail, usenet news,
ftp available via ftp-requests though UUnet. Serving Washington DC,
Northern Virginia, Southern Maryland. First year startup Charter member
accounts available for $120. Gives fullest access as the system develops.

06/93 703-551-0095   ukelele   Woodbridge   VA 300-FAST 24
Genuine Computing Resources. SVR4/386. Calling area includes
District of Columbia, Fairfax Cty, Prince William Cty, Manassas, and
Dumfries, VA. Shell, Full Usenet, Internet E-Mail. $15/month
for access to (703)551 exchange, $10/month for (703)878 access.
All lines V.32bis or higher. You get 1 hour/day connect time and
1.5MB disk storage. Direct Internet connectivity expected soon
without rate increase for existing users. Login as 'guest' or
send mail to info@gcr.com for further details. For human interaction
send mail to cjl@gcr.com. News and mail feeds also considered.

03/94 703-803-0391   tnc   Fairfax Station VA 300-FAST 24
Zenith Z-386, SCO Xenix; 120 MB HDD; 12 lines, tb+ for UUCP only;
"The Next Challenge"; Usenet, mail, Unique (sysop written) multi-user
space game; No Shell; Free and user supported --> No fee for light mail
and usenet; Subscription required for game and unlimited mail and usenet
at $25 / year;
Contact: Tom Buchsbaum (tom@tnc.UUCP or uunet!tnc!tom).

03/94 708-367-1871   sashimi   Vernon Hills   IL 300-FAST 24
80486 - SVR4. World Wide Access (TM) Full Internet Access now
available! Full netnews, E-mail, ftp, telnet, IRC, MUD, and so much
more! Shell and BBS options. Multiple V.32bis lines. More
lines added as needed. UUCP feeds also available. Send mail to or
finger info@wwa.com for more information.

03/93 708-425-8739   oaknet   Oak Lawn   IL 300-FAST 24
386 Clone running AT&T System V release 3.2.1, no access charges.
Free shell accounts, USENET news, and internet email...
Contact: jason@oaknet.chi.il.us, Jason Vanick (708)499-0905 (human).

03/94 708-833-8126   vpnet   Villa Park   IL 1200-FAST 24
386 Clone - Interactive Unix R2.2 (3.2), Akcs linked bbs FREE, including many selected Usenet groups. Shells are available for a minimum
$60/year contribution; under 22, $30. Includes access to our FULL
Usenet feed. Well connected. Five lines including three Trailblazers.

Two hunt groups - V.32 modems call 708-833-8127 (contributors only).
Contact: lisbon@vpnet.chi.il.us, Gerry Swetsky (708)833-8122 (human).

03/93 708-879-8633   unixuser   Batavia   IL 300-FAST 24
   386, w/ Linux/Waffle; v.32[bis] support; Linux downloads; Limited free
   use; Paid subscribers get Internet mail access, some USENET groups;
   Subscription is $25/year; CDROM disk available - changes monthly;
   Shell accounts are available.

03/93 708-983-5147   wa9aek   Lisle   IL 1200-FAST 24
   80386, UNIX V.3.2.3; XBBS for HAM radio enthusiasts;
   1.5 Gigabytes online;
   Multiple lines, dial in - USR HST DS V.32bis/42bis, 8138 - Tb T2500;
   Login as bbs (8-N-1).

03/94 713-480-2686   blkbox   Houston   TX 300-FAST 24
   486/33, SCO Open Desktop; 5 lines, all V32[bis]/V42[bis]; E-Mail/USENET
   (4500+ groups); 25 online adventure games, IRC, SLIP/PP; $21.65 / month
   for full shell access.
   Contact: Marc Newman (mknewman@blkbox.com)

03/94 713-668-7176   nuchat   Houston   TX 300-FAST 24
   i486/25, UHC Unix SVR4, 2.5 Gigs online, ** 56kb internet connection
   **, 7 lines (2 Trailblazers, 5 Worldblazers), full Usenet news feed,
   personal accounts ($3/hour), UUCP feeds (several options), dedicated
   lines available w/ unlimited usage @$120/month (SLIP or any protocol
   you like). Full internet access (ftp, telnet, gopher, archie),

03/94 713-684-5900   sugar   Houston   TX 300-FAST 24
   486/AT, SCO UNIX, 16+ lines (V.22, V.32, PEP, TurboPEP), Usenet news,
   email, Clarinet, complete *.sources and *.binaries archives,
   dial-up SLIP, access to Internet (FTP, telnet, ...), varying fees for
   shell access, news feeds.

03/94 714-635-2863   dhw68k   Anaheim   CA 1200-FAST 24
   Unistride 2.1; Trailblazer access; 2nd line -1915;
   No fee; USENET News; /bin/sh or /bin/csh available

03/94 714-821-9671   alphacm   Cypress   CA 1200-FAST 24
   386 - SCO-XENIX, no fee, Home of XBBS, 90 minute per login, 4 lines,
   Trailblazer pluses in use.
      uucp-anon: ogin: nuucp NO PASSWD

03/94 714-842-5851   conexch   Santa Ana   CA 300-2400 24
   386 - SCO Xenix - Free Unix guest login and PC-DOS bbs login, one
   hour initial time limit, USENET news, shell access granted on request &
   $25/quarter donation. Anon uucp: ogin: nuucp NO PASSWD. List of
   available Unix files resides in /usr3/public/FILES.

```
03/94 714-894-2246      stanton    Irvine        CA 300-2400   24
   80386-25, SCO Xenix-386, 320mb disk, 2400/1200/300 MNP supported;
   E-Mail & USENET;  Fixed fee $20/yr;  X11R4 archive and many packages
   ported to Xenix 386;  C development system (XENIX/MSDOS), PROCALC
   1-2-3 clone, FOXBASE+;
   anon uucp: ogin: nuucp, no word

03/93 716-634-6552      exuco1     Buffalo        NY 300-FAST  -24
   SGI Iris Indigo;  2 Lines, both Telebit WorldBlazers (on a hunt) [PEP
   Answer sequence last];  "The Buffalo Computer Society", Western New
   York's first Public Access UNIX; Mon - Fri 6:00pm - 7:00am EST,
   24 Hours on Weekends;  No Fee;  E-Mail/USENET
   Come March '93 -- will be running on several DEC Vaxen running BSD 4.3,
   and MANY MANY MANY more lines.

04/94 718-252-6720      intercom   New York       NY 300-FAST   24
   Dell Pentium/60, SVR4.2, 64MB RAM, 4.8 gigabytes disk space, all 16
   dialups are Zyxel v.32bis, user-friendly menu system, 3000+ newsgroups,
   Internet mail, PINE, TIN, Games, DOS/Windows/OS2 CD-ROM with 5000+ files,
   PC/Mac/Amiga/Text Library, Gopher, WWW, IRC, Hytelnet, Lynx, WAIS, MUD.
   Fees: starting $5/month (standard access) and $10/month (full access).
   Contact: info@intercom.com

04/93 718-729-5018      dorsai     NYC            NY 300-FAST   24
   80386, ISC 386/ix, Waffle bbs;  Live Internet connection; 3 phone lines
   (V.32bis for contributors);  no shell (yet);  BBS with over 250
   non-Usenet newsgroups, 1.2 gb of mac, ibm, amiga, cp-m, appleII,
   cbm files;  BBS is free, $25/yr for UseNet access, (180 min/day),
   $50/yr for extended gold access (300 min/day);  $?? for platinum access
   (i.e. ftp/telnet/irc/etc); Full news and mail feed from uupsi; login
   through bbs.
   Contact: postmaster@dorsai.com

05/94 719-520-1700      cns        Colorado Spring CO 300-2400  24
   Sun 3/260,  SunOS;  22 lines (on rollover); $35 signup fee, CNS has
   national 800 service for $8/hr (incl Alaska, Hawaii, Virgin Islands and
   Puerto Rico), In Colo Springs/Denver (719/303) and telnet: $2.75/hr;
   CNS offers dialup, uucp, slip, xwindows xremote;  CNS offers 56K and T1
   access directly to the T3 ANS backbone nationally.
   Information at 1-800-748-1200 (voice)
      or write to info@cscns.com for automated response
      or write to service@cscns.com for operator response

05/94 719-632-4111      oldcolo    Colorado Spring CO 1200-FAST 24
   386 - SCO-XENIX frontend, 2 CT Miniframes backend, e-mail conferencing,
   databases, Naplps Graphics, USENET news;  7 lines 8N1, 2400 on -2906,
   USR Dual 9600 on -2658;  Self registering for limited free access
```

(political, policy, marketplace)
Subscriptions $10, $15, $18 per month for full use.
Dave Hughes SYSOP.

01/94 801-539-0900   xmission   Salt Lake City UT 300-FAST 24
  Sun Sparc Classic, Solaris; T1 Connection into Internet Backbone; 10 (at
  the moment) incoming phone lines (ZyXEL 19.2K 1496E+ modems on all
  lines); tin, nn, rn newsreaders; gopher, lynx, www navigators;
  hytelnet, telnet, ncftp, ftp; zmodem, ymodem, xmodem, kermit protocols;
  PPP and UUCP connections with all accounts; gnu software and compilers;
  assisted "menus" or shell access; "Big Dummy's Guide to the Internet"
  hypertexted online; nethack, mdg, and robohunt multiplayer games.
  $5 introductory rate for the first month ...
  Individuals: $19/mn ($102/6mns), Small businesses: $29/mn ($162/6mns),
  BBS accounts: $39/mn ($216/6mns). Voice Support at 801-539-0852

06/94 803-271-0688   melanie   Greenville   SC 2400-FAST 24
  80386, 130MB Linux 0.99p19; $1/hour connect time (minimum $10/month);
  Email and any USENET News group(s) requested. FREE: Will provide Waffle
  software and help setting it up within 50 miles of Greenville, SC. so
  you can get a feed at home or at work.
  Contact: uunet!melanie!peter   803-271-4034

04/93 804-627-1828   wyvern   Norfolk   VA 1200-FAST 24
  Multiple 486/66 networked, SVR4. Ten v.32bis lines. Shell accounts,
  mail, and news feeds available. Gigs of disk space with lots of
  games, programming languages, news. Modest fees. We provide full
  Internet services, including ftp, telnet, IRC, archie, etc. We can
  provide uucp email and news feeds, and can include your machine in
  our domain park.
  login as guest, no password, to register for full access.
  Contact: Wyvern Technologies, Inc. at (804) 622-4289,
                              or system@wyvern.wyvern.com
                              (uunet!wyvern!system)

03/93 812-333-0450   sir-alan Bloomington   IN 1200-FAST 24
  SCO UNIX 3.2; no fee; TB+ on 333-0450 (300-19.2K); archive site for
  comp.sources.[games,misc,sun,unix,x], some alt.sources,
  XENIX(68K/286/386) uucp-anon: ogin: nuucp password: anon-uucp uucp-
  anon directory: /u/pdsrc, /u/pubdir, /u/uunet, help in /u/pubdir/HELP
  Contact: miikes@iuvax.cs.indiana.edu
  (812-855-3974 days 812-333-6564 eves)

05/94 812-476-7564   aquila   Evansville   IN 2400-FAST 24
  SCO Unix; Email/News provider to the Tri-State area; Supports regional
  BBSs; Has satellite downlink for 2500+ Usenet newsgroups. No fee for
  mail, low fee for news;
  The Aquila System, PO Box 4912, Evansville IN 47724-0912.
  Contact: kilroy@aquila.nshore.org

```
03/93 814-353-0566      cpumagic   Bellefonte    PA 1200-FAST 24
   80386, ESIX 4.0.3a (SVR4);  Dual Standard (v.32/v.32bis/HST);
   The Centre Programmers Unit BBS, custom BBS software (Micro Magic);
   Files available: UNIX, GNU, X, ESIX, MSDOS tools and libraries;
   No fee but up/download ratios enforced.
   Contact: Mike Loewen at mloewen@cpumagic.scol.pa.us
                    or ... psuvax1!cpumagic!mloewen

11/93 815-874-3998      maynard    Rockford      IL 300-FAST   24
   USL UnixWare SysVr4.2;  Provides shell, USENET, E-Mail, uuftp
   sources, BBS, games, chat and more. $5 Email only
   $10 Email USENET.. UUCP available  Contact troy@maynard.chi.il.us

03/94 818-287-5115      abode      El Monte      CA 2400-FAST 24
   XENIX 2.3.3; 2400-9600 Baud (Telebit T1000 PEP); Fee of $40 per year;
   Users get access to shell account, C compiler, email, usenet news,
   games, etc. For more information send email to contact name below
   or login as 'guest'.
   Contact: eric@abode.ttank.com (cerritos.edu!ttank!abode!eric)

03/94 818-367-2142      quake      Sylmar        CA 300-FAST   24
   ESIX/386 3.2D running Waffle;  Telebit WorldBlazer on dial-in line,
   818-362-6092 has Telebit T2500;  Usenet (1000+ groups), Email
   (registered as quake.sylmar.ca.us), UUCP/UUPC connections;  Rare Bird
   Advisories, Technomads, more;  $5 a month if paid a year at a time.
   New users login as "bbs", then "new".  One week free to new users.

04/94 818-793-9108      kitana     Pasadena      CA 300-FAST   24
   LINUX; Internet E-mail, Usenet Newsgroups (5,400+), MUD, Chat.
   Contact: sysop@kitana.org; multi-lines V.32bis; login "mm"

06/93 900-468-7727      uunet      Falls Church  VA 300-FAST   24
   Sequent S81, Dynix 3.0.17(9);  UUNET Communication Services;  No Shell;
   Anonymous UUCP, fee $0.40/min -- billed by the telephone company,
   login: uucp (no passwd);  Multiple lines, PEP and V.32 available;
   grab "uunet!~/help for more info" ...
   Full internet mail and USENET access via subscriber UUCP accounts.
   Contact: info@uunet.uu.net or call [voice] 703-204-8000.

03/93 904-456-2003      amaranth   Pensacola     FL 1200-FAST 24
   ISC Unix V/386 2.2.1 TB+ on dialin.  XBBS no fee.  limited NEWS, E-mail
   For more info: Jon Spelbring jsspelb@amaranth.UUCP

03/93 906-228-4399      lopez      Marquette     MI 1200-2400 24
   80386, SCO Xenix 2.3.4; Running STARBASE II Software.  Great White North
   UPLink, Inc. (Non Profit) 100+ local rooms, PLUS USENET, Multi Channel
   Chat, 5 ports, $30 yr, flat rate for full access to net news, mail.
```

Upper Michigan's ORIGINAL BBS (since 1983)
Contact: Gary Bourgois ...rutgers!sharkey!lopez!flash (flash@lopez.UUCP)

08/93 908-937-9481   digex   New Brunswick   NJ 300-FAST 24
  Refer to primary entry (Greenbelt, MD) for system/services details.
  Telnet to cnj.digex.com or mail to info@cnj.digex.com for more info;
  voice phone 1-800-969-9090.

03/94 916-649-0161   sactoh0   Sacramento   CA 1200-FAST 24
  3B2/310 SYVR3.2; SAC_UNIX, sactoh0.SAC.CA.US; $2/month; 3 lines,
  v.32 on 722-6519, TB+ on 649-0161, 2400/1200 baud on 722-5068;
  USENET, E-Mail, some games; login: new
  Contact: root@sactoh0.SAC.CA.US   or   ..ames!pacbell!sactoh0!root

02/94 916-923-5013   rgm   Sacramento   CA 1200-FAST 24
  486SX-25. 200mb. Coherent 386 v4.0.1; Dedicated incoming HST line. Full
  Bourne/Korn shell access for all users. Internet mail, limited Usenet
  (requests encouraged). Mail & news feeds available. $2/mo. for light
  mail/news users. login: new; Contact root@rgm.com

03/94 919-248-1177   rock   RTP   NC 300-FAST 24
  SparcStation 1+, SunOS 4.1; Fee: $50 installation, $30/month. Full
  internet access (FTP, TELNET, etc). Netnews (includes vmsnet, u3b, alt)
  and E-Mail. No limit on time, 5 meg disk quotas enforced. 56Kbps and
  T1 internet connections also available. Phone number depends on location
  within North Carolina (PC Pursuit also available).
  Contact: info@concert.net

11/93 +31-1720-42580   mugnet   Alphen a/d Rijn NL 300-FAST 24
  386 PC/AT, LINUX -- Mugnet int. hobiest network, Worldblazer 300-19.2k
  + V42bis + V32; No Fee services : all good stuff for Linux Fee services:
  UUCP feeds, internet E-mail mugnet domain.
  SUITABLE FOR BUSINESS USE TOO
  Own distribution of Linux/Pro, supplied on disks/tape/removable pack
  or downloadable. Anonymous guest account. Bash Shell Access on Linux
  system, UUCP News and Mail Feeds.
  Contact: root@nic.nl.mugnet.org,
  Voice +31 1720 40005 , Fax: +31 1720 30979

04/93 +358-0-455-8331   clinet   Espoo   FI 300-FAST 24
  Sun 3/60 16M/1G + Motorola M8[48]00-hybrid 32M/300M (terminal server,
  mostly), SunOS (4.1.1); Multi-line -8331 (V32bisMNP), -8332 (V32MNP)
  & -8778 (V32), 4 lines starting at -8688 (V22bis); custom software
  (locally written), conferences, menu system, other stuff; TCP/IP
  connected with IRC, USENET (all groups), E-Mail, shell access, common
  UNIX software, programming; $10/mo including at least 1hr of daily
  time ($0.25/hr if all lines busy). login as 'new'. Since 1987.
  Contact: clinet@clinet.fi.

09/93 +39-541-27135   nervous   Rimini (Fo)   IT 300-FAST 24
   386/33, 1GB, Unix System V; Menu driven BBS, no shell. This system is
   the official UniBoard Development Site; latest UniBoard releases/fixes
   are available here. Also, lots of unix sources (& erotic images) as well
   as USENET & Fidonet conferences, are available on line.
   Contact: pizzi@nervous.com
   Foreign callers need to send email to the above address to gain access to
   most board options.

04/93 +41-61-8115492   ixgch   Kaiseraugst   CH 300-FAST 24
   80386, SCO XENIX SV2.3.3, USR-DS (-V.32); Host: ixgch.xgp.spn.com (Ixgate
   Switzerland); Organization: XGP Switzerland & SPN Swiss Public Network;
   Public UI: PubSh (Public Shell), free!; Services among others: UUCP feeds
   for Internet Mail and Usenet News, Swiss BBS-List Service, Ixgate-Archive
   (RFCs,NIC-docs,non-comp-areas etc.), anonymous UUCP, CHAT conference,
   TALK software and more. BTW: V.32bis connections soon!
   General info: mail to service@spn.com (Subject: help).
   Contact: sysadm@xgp.spn.com (...!gator!ixgch!sysadm)

04/93 +44-734-34-00-55 infocom   Berkshire   UK 300-FAST 24
   80486, SCO UNIX 3.2.2; BBS, Teletext pages; 2nd line 32-00-55; Internet
   Mail/USENET at HOME using FSUUCP (DOS)/UUCP; Max 60.00 + V.A.T. per annum
'
   this will also be the charge when internet access (i.e. ftp & telnet
   arrive shortly), this level includes UUCP Login & a BBS Login account, if

   you choose UUCP transfers this can save a lot of connection charges from
   those nasty telephone companies.
   File Upload & Download, no quotas; Some services are free and some are
   pay; login as 'new' (8-N-1) ... on-line registration, password sent
   by mail; Contact: sysop@infocom.co.uk or mail <information@infocom.co.uk>
   with "general" in the subject line or Fax +44 734 32 09 88

03/94 +44 81 244 6677   ExNet   London   UK 300-2400 24
   SunOS 4.1, V32/V42b soon. Mail, news and UNIX shell (/usr/ucb/mail,
   ream; rn; sh, csh, tcsh, bash) UK#5 per month. 500 USENET groups
   currently and expanding. All reasonable mail and USENET use free.
   Beginner's pack available. Mail for contract and charges documents.
   One month free trial period possible. ***Mail and news feeds.***
   SUITABLE FOR BUSINESS USE TOO.
   Contact: HelpEx@exnet.co.uk, or voice +44 81 244 0077 GMT 1300-2300.

08/93 +44-81-317-2222   dircon   London   UK 300-FAST 24
   UNIX SysV3.2; The Direct Connection multi-user on-line service; Full
   Internet Connectivity (including TELNET, FTP, GOPHER, IRC, etc), USENET
   News conferencing with a choice of newsreaders, Internet electronic mail
   with an outgoing FAX gateway, 24 hour computer newswire, download areas,

chat/talk facilities, personal file areas with access to a choice of
shells (including Unix). UUCP and TCP-IP (PPP or SLIP) connections
are also available. Login as 'demo' to sign-up.
EMAIL Contact: helpdesk@dircon.co.uk (+44-81-317 0100 [voice]).

12/93 +44-81-863-6646   ibmpcug   London   UK 300-FAST 24
    486 PC/AT, SCO Unix -- IBM-PC User Group; Multiple lines,
    300-19.2k + V42bis + V32; Fee: ~50 pounds sterling per year,
    unlimited use; Internet Access (FTP, Telnet and IRC) as well as News
    and Mail services via UUCP; Shell Access available as an option.
    UUCP News and Mail Feeds
    Contact: info@ibmpcug.co.uk, Voice +44 81 863 1191

12/93 +44-81-863-6646   WinNET   London   UK 300-FAST 24
    486 PC/AT, SCO Unix -- IBM-PC User Group; Multiple lines,
    300-19.2k + V42bis + V32; Fee: from 6.75 pounds sterling per month,
    (3.25 per hour) includes custom Windows 3.x Software;
    Software available for download vai anon ftp from ftp.ibmpcug.co.uk
    or via dial up link login as winnet (no password).
    Internet Access (optional FTP, Telnet and IRC) as well as News
    and Mail services via UUCP; Shell Access available as an option.
    UUCP News and Mail Feeds
    Contact: info@ibmpcug.co.uk, or request@win-uk.net Voice +44 81 863 1191

04/93 +49-30-694-61-82 scuzzy   Berlin   DE 300-FAST 24
    80486/33, ISC 3.0; HST 14400/v.42bis on the first, HST
    14400/V.32bis/V.42bis Modems on other dial-in lines; Large library of
    source code including 386BSD, GNU, TeX, and X11 -- will distribute
    on tapes (grab /src/TAPES for the order form, /src/SERVICE for info about
    support for Free Software). Bulletin Board System with possible full
    Internet access, i.e. email, USENET, IRC, FTP, telnet (grab /src/BBS for
    info, or login as 'guest'); Login as 'archive' for x/y/z-modem
    and kermit transfers; Anonymous UUCP available, grab /src/README for
    initial info;
    Contact: src@contrib.de (Heiko Blume)
       anon uucp: ogin: nuucp   word: nuucp

02/94 +49-40-4915655   isys-hh   Hamburg   DE 300-FAST 24
    Intel 2*80486 >2GB Disk - Unix System V 3.2v4.2 & Linux 0.99PL14,
    multiple lines w/ V.32bis, ISDN +49-40-40192183,
    Shells: msh, sh, csh, ksh, bash; nn & tin for newsreaders, ELM for mail,
    anon. UUCP: ogin: nuucp (no password) get ~/ls-lgR.[Z|z|F]
    Contact: mike@isys-hh.hanse.de (Michael 'Mike' Loth)

04/93 +49-69-308265   odbffm   Frankfurt/Main DE 300-FAST 24
    Altos 386/2000, Telebit Modem, Public Access Unix; only shell accounts,
    no bbs software. Mail and news access (currently via UUCP, Internet
    planned).
    Contact: oli@odb.rhein-main.de, voice +49 69 331461, fax +49 69 307682

```
06/94 +61-2-837-1183    kralizec   Sydney          AU 1200-FAST 24
   Sun 3/60, SunOS 4.0 + 386/40, Linux;  1.9GB disk; V.32bis/V.42bis modems;
   Dialup access to Full Internet services;  200+ Mb software for download +
   6 CD-ROMs online. Full C-shell access to all members;  No joining fee,
   Usage fee $1/hr (min $10/mn) connect time;  Home of IXgate - Internet
   to Fidonet gateway - also Fido 3:713/602.
   Contact: nick@kralizec.zeta.org.au

04/93 +64-4-389-5478    actrix     Wellington       NZ 300-FAST 24
   Zenith 386/33MHz w/ ISC 386/ix 2.02;  Actrix Information Exchange --
   New Zealand's first Public Access UNIX.  750 Mb disk; 3 lines, USR
   Courier HST (T2500 due December 1990, X25 in '91).  Fee: NZ$54 p.a. -
   offers heavily modified XBBS with USEnet and Fidonet, e-mail (elm),
   hundreds of file areas divided into sections for UNIX, MS-DOS, Amiga,
   Atari, Apple //, Macintosh, CP/M etc.  Shell w/ many extras available
   via `Enhanced subscription'.  Planned to join APC (PeaceNet/EcoNet);
   Contact: paul@actrix.gen.nz (Paul Gillingwater) PO Box 11-410, Wgtn, NZ


===============================================================================
NOTE: The information in this document is kept as current as possible ...
      however, you use this data at your own risk and cost.
===============================================================================
Lists are available via any of the following:
      o  Anonymous uucp from jabber.
            +1 215 348 9727 [Telebit access]
            login: nuucp  NO PWD   [no rmail permitted]
            long list: /usr/spool/uucppublic/nixpub.long
            short list: /usr/spool/uucppublic/nixpub.short
            (also available from the "*NIX Depot" BBS)
      o  Mail server on jabber
            mail to mail-server@bts.com
            body containing:
               get PUB nixpub.long
            or
               get PUB nixpub.short
      o  The nixpub-list electronic mailing list.  To subscribe to
         the list:
            mail to mail-server@bts.com
            body containing:
               subscribe NIXPUB-LIST Your Name
      o  USENET, regular posts to:
            alt.bbs
            comp.bbs.misc
            comp.misc
===============================================================================
```

The PDIAL Listing

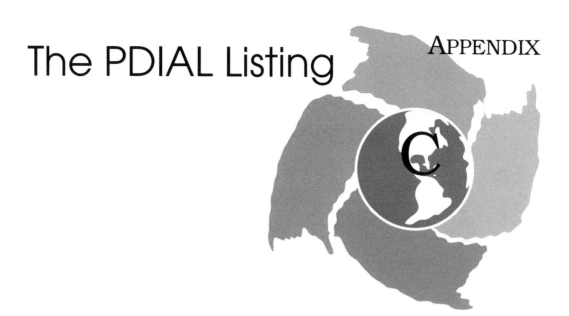

Peter Kaminski has generously given us permaission to reprint his PDIAL listing here.

```
        The Public Dialup Internet Access List (PDIAL)
        ================================================
File PDIAL015.TXT -- 09 December 1993

Copyright 1992-1993 Peter Kaminski.  Do not modify.  Freely distributable
for non-commercial purposes.  Please contact me if you wish to distribute
commercially or in modified form.

I make no representations about the suitability or accuracy of this document
for any purpose.  It is provided "as is" without express or implied
warranty. All information contained herein is subject to change.

Contents:

-00- Quick Start!
-01- Area Code Summary: Providers With Many Local Dialins (1-800, PDN)
-02- Area Code Summary: US/Canada Metro and Regional Dialins
-03- Area Code Summary: International Dialins
-04- Alphabetical List of Providers
-05- What *Is* The Internet?
-06- What The PDIAL Is
-07- How People Can Get The PDIAL (This List)
-08- Appendix A: Other Valuable Resources
-09- Appendix B: Finding Public Data Network (PDN) Access Numbers
-10- Providers: Get Listed in PDIAL!
```

Subject headers below are formatted so this list may be read as a digest by
USENET newsreaders that support digests. Example commands: rn, "control-G"
skips to next section; nn, "G%" presents as a digest.
Or, just skip to desired section by searching for the desired section number
string (e.g. "-01-") from the list above.

From: PDIAL -00-
Subject: Quick Start!

THE INTERNET is a global cooperative information network which can give you
instant access to millions of people and terabytes of data. Providers
listed in the PDIAL provide inexpensive public access to the Internet using
your regular modem and computer.

[Special note: the PDIAL currently lists only providers directly connected
to the Internet. Much of the Internet can still be explored through systems
with only Internet email and USENET netnews connections, but you need to
check other BBS lists to find them.]

GET A GUIDE: I highly recommend obtaining one of the many good starter or
guide books to the Internet. Think of them as travel guides to a new and
different country, and you wouldn't be far off. See section -08- below for
more details.

CHOOSING A PROVIDER: Phone charges can dominate the cost of your access to
the Internet. Check first for providers with metro or regional dialins
that are a local call for you (no per-minute phone charges). If there
aren't any, move on to comparing prices for PDN, 800, and direct-dial long
distance charges. Make sure to compare all your options. Calling long
distance out-of-state or across the country is often cheaper than calling
30 miles away.

If you're not in North America and have no local provider, you may still
be able to use one of the providers listed as having PDN access. Contact
the individual providers with PDN access (see listings below) to find out.

INFORMATION CHANGES: The information listed in the PDIAL changes and
expands rapidly. If this edition is more than 2 months old, consider
obtaining a new one. You can use the Info Deli email server, which will
provide you with updates and other information. Choose from the commands
below and just email them to <info-deli-server@netcom.com>.
    "Send PDIAL" -- receive the current PDIAL
    "Subscribe PDIAL" -- receive new editions of the PDIAL automatically
"Subscribe Info-Deli-News" -- news of Info Deli changes and additions
See section -07- below for more details and other ways to obtain the PDIAL.

CHECK IT OUT: Remember, the PDIAL is only a summary listing of the resources
and environment delivered by each of the various providers. Contact the
providers that interest you by email or voice phone and make sure you find
out if they have what you need.

Then GO FOR IT! Happy 'netting!

From: PDIAL -01-
Subject: Area Code Summary: Providers With Many Local Dialins (1-800, PDN)
      800 class cns crl csn dial-n-cerf-usa hookup.net IGC jvnc OARnet
PDN delphi holonet hookup.net IGC michnet millennium novalink portal
PDN psi-world-dial psilink tmn well world

"PDN" means the provider is accessible through a public data network (check
the listings below for which network); note that many PDNs listed offer
access outside North America as well as within North America. Check with
the provider or the PDN for more details.
"800" means the provider is accessible via a "toll-free" US phone number.
The phone company will not charge for the call, but the service provider
will add a surcharge to cover the cost of the 800 service. This may be
more expensive than other long-distance options.

From: PDIAL -02-
Subject: Area Code Summary: US/Canada Metro and Regional Dialins
If you are not local to any of these providers, it's still likely you are
able to access those providers available through a public data network
(PDN). Check the section above for providers with wide area access.

        201 jvnc-tiger
        202 CAPCON clarknet express michnet tmn
        203 jvnc-tiger
        205 nuance
        206 eskimo GLAIDS halcyon netcom nwnexus olympus
        212 echonyc maestro mindvox panix pipeline
        213 crl dial-n-cerf kaiwan netcom
        214 metronet netcom
        215 jvnc-tiger PREPnet
        216 OARnet wariat
        217 prairienet
        301 CAPCON clarknet express michnet tmn
        302 ssnet
        303 cns csn netcom nyx
        305 gate.net
        310 class crl dial-n-cerf kaiwan netcom
        312 InterAccess mcsnet netcom xnet

```
313 michnet MSen
401 anomaly ids jvnc-tiger
403 PUCnet UUNET-Canada
404 crl netcom
407 gate.net
408 a2i netcom portal
410 CAPCON clarknet express
412 PREPnet telerama
415 a2i class crl dial-n-cerf IGC netcom portal well
416 hookup.net UUNET-Canada uunorth
419 OARnet
503 agora.rain.com netcom teleport
504 sugar
508 anomaly nearnet northshore novalink
510 class crl dial-n-cerf holonet netcom
512 realtime
513 fsp OARnet
514 CAM.ORG UUNET-Canada
516 jvnc-tiger
517 michnet
519 hookup.net UUNET-Canada uunorth
602 crl Data.Basix evergreen indirect
603 MV nearnet
604 UUNET-Canada
609 jvnc-tiger
613 UUNET-Canada uunorth
614 OARnet
616 michnet
617 delphi nearnet netcom northshore novalink world
619 cg57 class crash.cts.com cyber dial-n-cerf netcom
703 CAPCON clarknet express michnet netcom tmn
704 concert Vnet
707 crl
708 InterAccess mcsnet xnet
713 blkbox nuchat sugar
714 class dial-n-cerf express kaiwan netcom
717 PREPnet
718 maestro mindvox netcom panix pipeline
719 cns csn oldcolo
804 wyvern
810 michnet MSen
814 PREPnet
815 InterAccess mcsnet xnet
817 metronet
818 class dial-n-cerf netcom
905 UUNET-Canada
906 michnet
907 alaska.edu
```

```
908 express jvnc-tiger
910 concert
916 netcom
919 concert Vnet
```

These are area codes local to the dialups, although some prefixes in the area codes listed may not be local to the dialups. Check your phone book or with your phone company.

From: PDIAL -03-
Subject: Area Code Summary: International Dialins

If you are not local to any of these providers, there is still a chance you are able to access those providers available through a public data network (PDN). Check section -01- above for providers with wide area access, and send email to them to ask about availability.

```
 +44 (0)81 Demon dircon ibmpcug
      +49 Individual.NET
   +49 23 ins
  +49 069 in-rhein-main
  +49 089 mucev
    +61 2 connect.com.au
    +61 3 connect.com.au
     +301 Ariadne
   +353 1 IEunet
```

From: PDIAL -04-
Subject: Alphabetical List of Providers

Fees are for personal dialup accounts with outgoing Internet access; most sites have other classes of service with other rate structures as well. Most support email and netnews along with the listed services.
"Long distance: provided by user" means you need to use direct dial long distance or other long distance services to connect to the provider.

```
<< a2i >>
name ----------> a2i communications
dialup --------> 408-293-9010 (v.32bis), 415-364-5652 (v.32bis), 408-293-
9020
            (PEP); login 'guest'
area codes ----> 408, 415
local access --> CA: West and South SF Bay Area
long distance -> provided by user
```

```
services ------> shell (SunOS UNIX and MS-DOS), ftp, telnet, irc, feeds,
          domains and host-less domains, virtual ttys, gopher
fees ---------->
$20/month or $45/3 months or $72/6 months
email ---------> info@rahul.net
voice ---------> 408-293-8078 voicemail
ftp more info -> ftp.rahul.net:/pub/BLURB


<< agora.rain.com >>
name ----------> RainDrop Laboratories
dialup --------> 503-293-1772 (2400) 503-293-2059 (v.32, v.32 bis) 'apply'
area codes ----> 503
local access --> OR: Portland, Beaverton, Hillsboro, Forest Grove, Gresham,
            Tigard, Lake Oswego, Oregon City, Tualatin, Wilsonville
long distance -> provided by user
services ------> shell, ftp, telnet, gopher, usenet
fees ----------> $6/month (1 hr/day limit)
email ---------> info@agora.rain.com
voice ---------> n/a
ftp more info -> agora.rain.com:/pub/gopher-data/agora/agora


<< alaska.edu >>
name ----------> University Of Alaska Southeast, Tundra Services
dialup --------> 907-789-1314
area codes ----> 907
local access --> All Alaskan sites with local UACN access -- Anchorage,
      Barrow, Fairbanks, Homer, Juneau, Keni, Ketchikan, Kodiak,
    Kotzebue, Nome, Palmer, Sitka, Valdez
long distance -> provided by user
services ------> Statewide UACN Mail, Internet, USENET, gopher, Telnet, FTP
fees ----------> $20/month for individual accounts, discounts for 25+ and
          50+ to public, gov't and non-profit organizations.
email ---------> JNJMB@acad1.alaska.edu
voice ---------> 907-465-6453
fax -----------> 907-465-6295
ftp more info -> n/a


<< anomaly >>
name ----------> Anomaly - Rhode Island's Gateway To The Internet
dialup --------> 401-331-3706 (v.32) or 401-455-0347 (PEP)
area codes ----> 401, 508
local access --> RI: Providence/Seekonk Zone
long distance -> provided by user
services ------> shell, ftp, telnet, SLIP
fees ----------> Commercial: $125/6 months or $200/year; Educational: $75/6
          months or $125/year
email ---------> info@anomaly.sbs.risc.net
voice ---------> 401-273-4669
```

```
ftp more info -> anomaly.sbs.risc.net:/anomaly.info/access.zip


<< Ariadne >>
name ----------> Ariadne - Greek Academic and Research Network
dialup --------> +301 65-48-800 (1200 - 9600 bps)
area codes ----> +301
local access --> Athens, Greece
long distance -> provided by user
services ------> e-mail, ftp, telnet, gopher, talk, pad(EuropaNet)
fees ----------> 5900 drachmas per calendar quarter, 1 hr/day limit.
email ---------> dialup@leon.nrcps.ariadne-t.gr
voice ---------> +301 65-13-392
fax -----------> +301 6532910
ftp more info -> n/a


<< blkbox >>
name ----------> The Black Box
dialup --------> (713) 480-2686 (V32bis/V42bis)
area codes ----> 713
local access --> TX: Houston
long distance -> provided by user
services ------> shell, ftp, telnet, SLIP, PPP, UUCP
fees ----------> $21.65 per month or $108.25 for 6 months
email ---------> info@blkbox.com
voice ---------> (713) 480-2684
ftp more info -> n/a


<< CAM.ORG >>
name ----------> Communications Accessibles Montreal
dialup --------> 514-931-7178 (v.32 bis), 514-931-2333 (2400bps)
area codes ----> 514
local access --> QC: Montreal, Laval, South-Shore, West-Island
long distance -> provided by user
services ------> shell, ftp, telnet, gopher, wais, WWW, irc, feeds, SLIP,
         PPP, AppleTalk, FAX gateway
fees ----------> $25/month Cdn.
email ---------> info@CAM.ORG
voice ---------> 514-931-0749
ftp more info -> ftp.CAM.ORG


<< CAPCON >>
name ----------> CAPCON Library Network
dialup --------> contact for number
area codes ----> 202, 301, 410, 703
local access --> District of Columbia, Suburban Maryland & Northern
Virginia
long distance -> various plans available/recommended; contact for details
services ------> menu, archie, ftp, gopher, listservs, telnet, wais, whois,
```

```
                 full day training and 'CAPCON Connect User Manual'
       fees -----------> $35 start-up + $150/yr + $24/mo for first account from an
                  institution; $35 start-up + $90/yr + $15/mo for additional
                  users (member rates lower); 20 hours/month included,
                  additional hours $2/hr
       email ---------> capcon@capcon.net
       voice ---------> 202-331-5771
       fax -----------> 202-797-7719
       ftp more info -> n/a


       << cg57 >>
       name ----------> E & S Systems Public Access *Nix
       dialup --------> 619-278-8267 (V.32bis, TurboPEP), 619-278-8267 (V32)
           619-278-9837 (PEP)
       area codes ----> 619
       local access --> CA: San Diego
       long distance -> provided by user
       services ------> shell, ftp, irc, telnet, gopher, archie, bbs (UniBoard)
       fees ----------> bbs (FREE), shell - $30/3 months, $50/6 months, $80/9
                   months, $100/year
       email ---------> steve@cg57.esnet.com
       voice ---------> 619-278-4641
       ftp more info -> n/a


       << clarknet >>
       name ----------> Clark Internet Services, Inc. (ClarkNet)
       dialup --------> 410-730-9786, 410-995-0271, 301-596-1626, 301-854-0446,
            301-621-5216 'guest'
       area codes ----> 202, 301, 410, 703
       local access --> MD: Baltimore; DC: Washington; VA: Northern VA
       long distance -> provided by user
       services ------> shell, menu, ftp, telnet, irc, gopher, hytelnet, www,
            WAIS, SLIP/PPP, ftp space, feeds (UUCP & uMDSS), dns, Clarinet
       fees ----------> $23/month or $66/3 months or $126/6 months or $228/year
       email ---------> info@clark.net
       voice ---------> Call 800-735-2258 then give 410-730-9764 (MD Relay Svc)
       fax -----------> 410-730-9765
       ftp more info -> ftp.clark.net:/pub/clarknet/fullinfo.txt


       << class >>
       name ----------> Cooperative Library Agency for Systems and Services
       dialup --------> contact for number; NOTE: CLASS serves libraries and
                  information distributors only
       area codes ----> 310, 415, 510, 619, 714, 818, 800
       local access --> Northern and Southern California or anywhere (800) service
                   is available
       long distance -> 800 service available at $6/hour surcharge
       services ------> menus, mail, telnet, ftp, gopher, wais, hytelnet, archie,
```

```
                      WWW, IRC, Unix shells, SLIP, etc.  Training is available.
fees ----------> $4.50/hour + $150/year for first account + $50/year each
                 additional account + $135/year CLASS membership.  Discounts
                      available for multiple memberships.
email ---------> class@class.org
voice ---------> 800-488-4559
fax -----------> 408-453-5379
ftp more info -> n/a


<< cns >>
name ----------> Community News Service
dialup --------> 719-520-1700 id 'new', passwd 'newuser'
area codes ----> 303, 719, 800
local access --> CO: Colorado Springs, Denver; continental US/800
long distance -> 800 or provided by user
services ------> UNIX shell, email, ftp, telnet, irc, USENET, Clarinet,
       gopher, Commerce Business Daily
fees ----------> $2.75/hour; $10/month minimum + $35 signup
email ---------> service@cscns.com
voice ---------> 719-592-1240
ftp more info -> cscns.com


<< concert >>
name ----------> CONCERT-CONNECT
dialup --------> contact for number
area codes ----> 704, 910, 919
local access --> NC: Asheville, Chapel Hill, Charlotte, Durham, Greensboro,
            Greenville, Raleigh, Winston-Salem, Research Triangle Park
long distance -> provided by user
services ------> UUCP, SLIP
fees ----------> SLIP: $150 educational/research or $180 commercial for
                 first 60 hours/month + $300 signup
email ---------> info@concert.net
voice ---------> 919-248-1999
ftp more info -> ftp.concert.net


<< connect.com.au >>
name ----------> connect.com.au pty ltd
dialup --------> contact for number
area codes ----> +61 3, +61 2
local access --> Australia: Melbourne, Sydney
long distance -> provided by user
services ------> SLIP, PPP, ISDN, UUCP, ftp, telnet, NTP, FTPmail
fees ----------> AUS$2000/year (1 hour/day), 10% discount for AUUG members;
       other billing negotiable
email ---------> connect@connect.com.au
voice ---------> +61 3 5282239
fax -----------> +61 3 5285887
```

```
ftp more info -> ftp.connect.com.au

<< crash.cts.com >>
name ----------> CTS Network Services (CTSNET)
dialup --------> 619-637-3640 HST, 619-637-3660 V.32bis, 619-637-3680 PEP
          'help'
area codes ----> 619
local access --> CA: San Diego, Pt. Loma, La Jolla, La Mesa, El Cajon,
        Poway,Ramona, Chula Vista, National City, Mira Mesa, Alpine, East
            County, new North County numbers, Escondido, Oceanside, Vista
long distance -> provided by user
services ------> Unix shell, UUCP, Usenet newsfeeds, NNTP, Clarinet,
                Reuters,FTP, Telnet, SLIP, PPP, IRC, Gopher, Archie, WAIS,
                POPmail, UMDSS, domains, nameservice, DNS
fees ----------> $10-$23/month flat depending on features, $15 startup,
        personal $2-> /month flat depending on features, $25
                  startup, commercial
email ---------> info@crash.cts.com (server), support@crash.cts.com
              (human)
voice ---------> 619-637-3637
fax -----------> 619-637-3630
ftp more info -> n/a

<< crl >>
name ----------> CR Laboratories Dialup Internet Access
dialup --------> 415-389-UNIX
area codes ----> 213, 310, 404, 415, 510, 602, 707, 800
local access --> CA: San Francisco Bay area + San Rafael, Santa Rosa, Los
        Angeles, Orange County; AZ: Phoenix, Scottsdale, Tempe, and
      Glendale; GA: Atlanta metro area; continental US/800
long distance -> 800 or provided by user
services ------> shell, ftp, telnet, feeds, SLIP, WAIS
fees ----------> $17.50/month + $19.50 signup
email ---------> info@crl.com
voice ---------> 415-381-2800
ftp more info -> n/a

<< csn >>
name ----------> Colorado SuperNet, Inc.
dialup --------> contact for number
area codes ----> 303, 719, 800
local access --> CO: Alamosa, Boulder/Denver, Colorado Springs, Durango,
                Fort Collins, Frisco, Glenwood Springs/Aspen, Grand Junction,
      Greeley, Gunnison, Pueblo, Telluride; anywhere 800 service is available
long distance -> provided by user or 800
services ------> shell or menu, UUCP, SLIP, 56K, ISDN, T1; ftp, telnet, irc,
              gopher, WAIS, domains, anonymous ftp space, email-to-fax
fees ----------> $1/hour off-peak, $3/hour peak ($250 max/month) + $20
```

```
 signup, $5/hr surcharge for 800 use
email ---------> info@csn.org
voice ---------> 303-273-3471
fax -----------> 303-273-3475
ftp more info -> csn.org:/CSN/reports/DialinInfo.txt
off-peak ------> midnight to 6am

<< cyber >>
name ----------> The Cyberspace Station
dialup --------> 619-634-1376 'guest'
area codes ----> 619
local access --> CA: San Diego
long distance -> provided by user
services ------> shell, ftp, telnet, irc
fees ----------> $15/month + $10 startup or $60 for six months
email ---------> help@cyber.net
voice ---------> n/a
ftp more info -> n/a

<< Data.Basix >>
name ----------> Data Basix
dialup --------> 602-721-5887
area codes ----> 602
local access --> AZ: Tucson
long distance -> provided by user
services ------> Telnet, FTP, NEWS, UUCP; on-site assistance
fees ----------> $25 monthly, $180 yearly; group rates available
email ---------> info@Data.Basix.com (automated);
                 sales@Data.Basix.com (human)
voice ---------> 602-721-1988
ftp more info -> Data.Basix.COM:/services/dial-up.txt

<< Demon >>
name ----------> Demon Internet Systems (DIS)
dialup --------> +44 (0)81 343 4848
area codes ----> +44 (0)81
local access --> London, England
long distance -> provided by user
services ------> ftp, telnet, SLIP/PPP
fees ----------> GBPounds 10.00/month; 132.50/year (inc 12.50 startup
     charge).  No on-line time charges.
email ---------> internet@demon.co.uk
voice ---------> +44 (0)81 349 0063
ftp more info -> n/a

<< delphi >>
name ----------> DELPHI
dialup --------> 800-365-4636 'JOINDELPHI password:INTERNETSIG'
area codes ----> 617, PDN
```

```
local access --> MA: Boston; KS: Kansas City
long distance -> Sprintnet or Tymnet: $9/hour weekday business hours, no
          charge nights and weekends
services ------> ftp, telnet, feeds, user groups, wire services, member
          conferencing
fees ----------> $10/month for 4 hours or $20/month for 20 hours + $3/month
            for Internet services
email ---------> walthowe@delphi.com
voice ---------> 800-544-4005
ftp more info -> n/a

<< dial-n-cerf >>
name ----------> DIAL n' CERF or DIAL n' CERF AYC
dialup --------> contact for number
area codes ----> 213, 310, 415, 510, 619, 714, 818
local access --> CA: Los Angeles, Oakland, San Diego, Irvine, Pasadena, Palo
          Alto
long distance -> provided by user
services ------> shell, menu, irc, ftp, hytelnet, gopher, WAIS, WWW,
            terminal service, SLIP
fees ----------> $5/hour ($3/hour on weekend) + $20/month + $50 startup OR
            $250/month flat for AYC
email ---------> help@cerf.net
voice ---------> 800-876-2373 or 619-455-3900
ftp more info -> nic.cerf.net:/cerfnet/dial-n-cerf/
off-peak ------> Weekend: 5pm Friday to 5pm Sunday

<< dial-n-cerf-usa >>
name ----------> DIAL n' CERF USA
dialup --------> contact for number
area codes ----> 800
local access --> anywhere (800) service is available
long distance -> included
services ------> shell, menu, irc, ftp, hytelnet, gopher, WAIS, WWW,
            terminal service, SLIP
fees ----------> $10/hour ($8/hour on weekend) + $20/month
email ---------> help@cerf.net
voice ---------> 800-876-2373 or 619-455-3900
ftp more info -> nic.cerf.net:/cerfnet/dial-n-cerf/
off-peak ------> Weekend: 5pm Friday to 5pm Sunday

<< dircon >>
name ----------> The Direct Connection
dialup --------> +44 (0)81 317 2222
area codes ----> +44 (0)81
local access --> London, England
long distance -> provided by user
services ------> shell or menu, UUCP feeds, SLIP/PPP, ftp, telnet, gopher,
          WAIS, Archie, personal ftp/file space, email-to-fax
```

```
fees ----------> Subscriptions from GBPounds 10 per month, no
                   on-line charges. GBPounds 7.50 signup fee.
email ---------> helpdesk@dircon.co.uk
voice ---------> +44 (0)81 317 0100
fax -----------> +44 (0)81 317 0100
ftp more info -> n/a


<< echonyc >>
name ----------> Echo Communications
dialup --------> (212) 989-8411 (v.32, v.32 bis) 'newuser'
area codes ----> 212
local access --> NY: Manhattan
long distance -> provided by user
services ------> shell, ftp, telnet, gopher, archie, wais, SLIP/PPP
fees ----------> Commercial: $19.95/month; students/seniors: $13.75/month
email ---------> horn@echonyc.com
voice ---------> 212-255-3839
ftp more info -> n/a


<< eskimo >>
name ----------> Eskimo North
dialup --------> 206-367-3837 300-14.4k, 206-362-6731 for 9600/14.4k,
     206-742-1150 World Blazer
area codes ----> 206
local access --> WA: Seattle, Everett
long distance -> provided by user
services ------> shell, ftp, telnet
fees ----------> $10/month or $96/year
email ---------> nanook@eskimo.com
voice ---------> 206-367-7457
ftp more info -> n/a


<< evergreen >>
name ----------> Evergreen Communications
dialup --------> (602) 955-8444
area codes ----> 602
local access --> AZ
long distance -> provided by user or call for additional information
services ------> ftp, telnet, gopher, archie, wais, www, uucp, PPP
fees ----------> individual: $239/yr; commercial: $479/yr;
                   special educational rates
email ---------> evergreen@libre.com
voice ---------> 602-955-8315
fax -----------> 602-955-5948
ftp more info -> n/a


<< express >>
name ----------> Express Access - A service of Digital Express Group
```

```
dialup --------> 301-220-0462, 410-766-1855, 703-281-7997, 714-377-9784,
                 908-937-9481 'new'
area codes ----> 202, 301, 410, 703, 714, 908
local access --> Northern VA, Baltimore MD, Washington DC, New Brunswick NJ,
                 Orange County CA
long distance -> provided by user
services ------> shell, ftp, telnet, irc, gopher, hytelnet, www, Clarinet,
        SLIP/PPP, archie, mailing lists, autoresponders, anonymous
    FTP archives
fees ----------> $25/month or $250/year
email ---------> info@digex.net
voice ---------> 800-969-9090, 301-220-2020
ftp more info -> n/a


<< fsp >>
name ----------> Freelance Systems Programming
dialup --------> (513) 258-7745 to 14.4 Kbps
area codes ----> 513
local access --> OH: Dayton
long distance -> provided by user
services ------> shell, ftp, telnet, feeds, email, gopher, archie, SLIP, etc.
fees ----------> $20 startup and $1 per hour
email ---------> fsp@dayton.fsp.com
voice ---------> (513) 254-7246
ftp more info -> n/a


<< gate.net >>
name ----------> CyberGate, Inc
dialup --------> 305-425-0200
area codes ----> 305, 407
local access --> South Florida, expanding in FL
long distance -> provided by user
services ------> shell, UUCP, SLIP/PPP, leased, telnet, FTP, IRC, archie,
         gopher, etc.
fees ----------> $17.50/mo on credit card; group discounts; SLIP/PPP:
     $17.50/mo + $2/hr
email ---------> info@gate.net or sales@gate.net
voice ---------> 305-428-GATE
fax -----------> 305-428-7977
ftp more info -> n/a


<< GLAIDS >>
name ----------> GLAIDS NET (Homosexual Network)
dialup --------> 206-322-0621
area codes ----> 206
local access --> WA: Seattle
long distance -> provided by user
services ------> BBS, Gopher, ftp, telnet
```

```
fees ----------> $10/month.  Scholarships available. Free 7 day trial.
      Visitors are welcome.
email ---------> tomh@glaids.wa.com
voice ---------> 206-323-7483
ftp more info -> GLAIDS.wa.com


<< halcyon >>
name ----------> Halcyon
dialup --------> 206-382-6245 'new', 8N1
area codes ----> 206
local access --> Seattle, WA
long distance -> provided by user
services ------> shell, telnet, ftp, bbs, irc, gopher, hytelnet
fees ----------> $200/year, or $60/quarter + $10 start-up
email ---------> info@halcyon.com
voice ---------> 206-955-1050
ftp more info -> halcyon.com:/pub/waffle/info


<< holonet >>
name ----------> HoloNet
dialup --------> 510-704-1058
area codes ----> 510, PDN
local access --> Berkeley, CA
long distance -> [per hour, off-peak/peak] Bay Area: $0.50/$0.95; PSINet A:
          $0.95/$1.95; PSINet B: $2.50/$6.00; Tymnet: $3.75/$7.50
services ------> ftp, telnet, irc, games
fees ----------> $2/hour off-peak, $4/hour peak; $6/month or $60/year minimum
email ---------> info@holonet.net
voice ---------> 510-704-0160
ftp more info -> holonet.net:/info/
off-peak ------> 5pm to 8am + weekends and holidays


<< hookup.net >>
name ----------> HookUp Communication Corporation
dialup --------> contact for number
area codes ----> 800, PDN, 416, 519
local access --> Ontario, Canada
long distance -> 800 access across Canada, or discounted rates by HookUp
services ------> shell or menu, UUCP, SLIP, PPP, ftp, telnet, irc, gopher,
          domains, anonymous ftp space
fees ----------> Cdn$14.95/mo for 5 hours; Cdn$34.95/mo for 15 hrs;
             Cdn$59.95/mo for 30 hrs; Cdn$300.00/yr for 50 hrs/mo;
          Cdn$299.00/mo for unlimited usage
email ---------> info@hookup.net
voice ---------> 519-747-4110
fax -----------> 519-746-3521
ftp more info -> n/a
```

```
<< ibmpcug >>
name ----------> UK PC User Group
dialup --------> +44 (0)81 863 6646
area codes ----> +44 (0)81
local access --> London, England
long distance -> provided by user
services ------> ftp, telnet, bbs, irc, feeds
fees ----------> GBPounds 15.50/month or 160/year + 10 startup (no time charges)
email ---------> info@ibmpcug.co.uk
voice ---------> +44 (0)81 863 6646
ftp more info -> n/a


<< ids >>
name ----------> The IDS World Network
dialup --------> 401-884-9002, 401-785-1067
area codes ----> 401
local access --> East Greenwich, RI; northern RI
long distance -> provided by user
services ------> ftp, telnet, SLIP, feeds, bbs
fees ----------> $10/month or $50/half year or $100/year
email ---------> sysadmin@ids.net
voice ---------> 401-884-7856
ftp more info -> ids.net:/ids.net


<< IEunet >>
name ----------> IEunet Ltd., Ireland's Internet Services Supplier
dialup --------> +353 1 6790830, +353 1 6798600
area codes ----> +353 1
local access --> Dublin, Ireland
long distance -> provided by user, or supplied by IEunet
services ------> DialIP, IPGold, EUnet Traveller, X400, X500, Gopher, WWW,
                 FTP, FTPmail,SLIP/PPP, FTP archives
fees ----------> IEP25/month Basic
email ---------> info@ieunet.ie, info@Ireland.eu.net
voice ---------> +353 1 6790832
ftp more info -> ftp.ieunet.ie:/pub


<< IGC >>
name ----------> Institute for Global Communications/IGC Networks
                 (PeaceNet, EcoNet, ConflictNet, LaborNet, HomeoNet)
dialup --------> 415-322-0284 (N-8-1), 'new'
area codes ----> 415, 800, PDN
local access --> CA: Palo Alto, San Francisco
long distance -> [per hour, off-peak/peak] SprintNet: $2/$7; 800: $11/$11
services ------> telnet, local newsgroups for environmental, peace/social
                 justice issues; NO ftp
fees ----------> $10/month + $3/hr after first hour
email ---------> support@igc.apc.org
```

```
voice ---------> 415-442-0220
ftp more info -> igc.apc.org:/pub
```

```
<< indirect >>
name ----------> Internet Direct, Inc.
dialup --------> 602-274-9600 (Phoenix); 602-321-9600 (Tucson); 'guest'
area codes ----> 602
local access --> AZ: Phoenix, Tucson
long distance -> provided by user
services ------> Shell/menu, UUCP, Usenet, NNTP, FTP, Telnet, SLIP, PPP,
        IRC, Gopher, WAIS, WWW, POP, DNS, nameservice, QWK (offline
    readers)
fees ----------> $20/month (personal); $30/month (business)
email ---------> info@indirect.com (automated); support@indirect.com (human)
voice ---------> 602-274-0100 (Phoenix), 602-324-0100 (Tucson) ftp more
info -> n/a
```

```
<< Individual.NET >>
name ----------> Individual Network e.V. (IN)
dialup --------> contact for number
area codes ----> +49
local access --> Germany: Berlin, Oldenburg, Bremen, Hamburg, Krefeld, Kiel,
        Duisburg, Darmstadt, Dortmund, Hannover, Ruhrgebiet, Bonn,
    Magdeburg, Duesseldorf, Essen, Koeln, Paderborn, Bielefeld,
 Aachen, Saarbruecken, Frankfurt, Braunschweig, Dresden, Ulm,
Erlangen, Nuernberg, Wuerzburg, Chemnitz, Muenchen,
Muenster, Goettingen, Wuppertal, Schleswig, Giessen,
Rostock, Leipzig and other
long distance -> provided by user
services ------> e-mail, usenet feeds, UUCP, SLIP, ISDN, shell, ftp, telnet,
            gopher, irc, bbs
fees ----------> 15-30 DM/month (differs from region to region)
email ---------> in-info@individual.net
voice ---------> +49 2131 64190 (Andreas Baess)
fax -----------> +49 2131 605652
ftp more info -> ftp.fu-berlin.de:/pub/doc/IN/
```

```
<< in-rhein-main >>
name ----------> Individual Network - Rhein-Main
dialup --------> +49-69-39048414, +49-69-6312934 (+ others)
area codes ----> +49   069
local access --> Frankfurt/Offenbach, Germany
long distance -> provided by user
services ------> shell (Unix), ftp, telnet, irc, gopher, uucp feeds
fees ----------> SLIP/PPP/ISDN: 40 DM, 4 DM / Megabyte
email ---------> info@rhein-main.de
voice ---------> +49-69-39048413
ftp more info -> n/a
```

```
<< ins >>
name ----------> INS - Inter Networking Systems
dialup --------> contact for number
area codes ----> +49 23
local access --> Ruhr-Area, Germany
long distance -> provided by user
services ------> e-mail,uucp,usenet,slip,ppp,ISDN-TCP/IP
fees ----------> fees for commercial institutions and any others:
 uucp/e-mail,uucp/usenet:$60/month; ip:$290/month minimum
email ---------> info@ins.net
voice ---------> +49 2305 356505
fax -----------> +49 2305 25411
ftp more info -> n/a

<< InterAccess >>
name ----------> InterAccess
dialup --------> 708-671-0237
area codes ----> 708, 312, 815
local access --> Chicagoland metropolitan area
long distance -> provided by user
services ------> ftp, telnet, SLIP/PPP, feeds, shell, UUCP, DNS, ftp space
fees ----------> $23/mo shell, $26/mo SLIP/PPP, or $5/mo +$2.30/hr
email ---------> info@interaccess.com
voice ---------> (800) 967-1580
fax -----------> 708-671-0113
ftp more info -> interaccess.com:/pub/interaccess.info

<< jvnc >>
name ----------> The John von Neumann Computer Network - Tiger Mail &
                 Dialin' Terminal
dialup --------> contact for number
area codes ----> 800
local access --> anywhere (800) service is available
long distance -> included
services ------> email and newsfeed or terminal access only
fees ----------> $19/month + $10/hour + $36 startup (PC or Mac SLIP software
             included)
email ---------> info@jvnc.net
voice ---------> 800-35-TIGER, 609-897-7300
fax -----------> 609-897-7310
ftp more info -> n/a

<< jvnc-tiger >>
name ----------> The John von Neumann Computer Network - Dialin' Tiger
dialup --------> contact for number
area codes ----> 201, 203, 215, 401, 516, 609, 908
local access --> Princeton & Newark, NJ; Philadelphia, PA; Garden City, NY;
```

                Bridgeport, New Haven, & Storrs, CT; Providence, RI
long distance -> provided by user
services ------> ftp, telnet, SLIP, feeds, optional shell
fees ----------> $99/month + $99 startup (PC or Mac SLIP software included --
                shell is additional $21/month)
email ---------> info@jvnc.net
voice ---------> 800-35-TIGER, 609-897-7300
fax -----------> 609-897-7310
ftp more info -> n/a

<< kaiwan >>
name ----------> KAIWAN Public Access Internet Online Services
dialup --------> 714-539-5726, 310-527-7358
area codes ----> 213, 310, 714
local access --> CA: Los Angeles, Orange County
long distance -> provided by user
services ------> shell, ftp, telnet, irc, WAIS, gopher, SLIP/PPP, ftp
                space, feeds, dns, 56K leasd line
fees ----------> $15.00/signup + $15.00/month or $30.00/quarter (3 month)
                or $11.00/month by credit card
email ---------> info@kaiwan.com
voice ---------> 714-638-2139
ftp more info -> kaiwan.com:/pub/KAIWAN

<< maestro >>
name ----------> Maestro
dialup --------> (212) 240-9700 'newuser'
area codes ----> 212, 718
local access --> NY: New York City
long distance -> provided by user
services ------> shell, ftp, telnet, gopher, wais, irc, feeds, etc.
fees ----------> $15/month or $150/year
email ---------> info@maestro.com (autoreply); staff@maestro.com,
        rkelly@maestro.com, ksingh@maestro.com
voice ---------> 212-240-9600
ftp more info -> n/a

<< mcsnet >>
name ----------> MCSNet
dialup --------> (312) 248-0900 V.32, 0970 V.32bis, 6295 (PEP), follow prompts
area codes ----> 312, 708, 815
local access --> IL: Chicago
long distance -> provided by user
services ------> shell, ftp, telnet, feeds, email, irc, gopher, hytelnet, etc.
fees ----------> $25/month or $65/3 months untimed, $30/3 months for 15
        hours/month
email ---------> info@genesis.mcs.com
voice ---------> (312) 248-UNIX

```
ftp more info -> genesis.mcs.com:/mcsnet.info/

<< metronet >>
name ----------> Texas Metronet
dialup --------> 214-705-2901/817-261-1127 (V.32bis),214-705-2929(PEP),
               'info' or 214-705-2917/817-261-7687 (2400) 'signup'
area codes ----> 214, 817
local access --> TX: Dallas, Fort Worth
long distance -> provided by user
services ------> shell, ftp, telnet, SLIP, PPP, uucp feeds
fees ----------> $5-$45/month + $10-$30 startup
email ---------> info@metronet.com
voice ---------> 214-705-2900, 817-543-8756
fax -----------> 214-401-2802 (8am-5pm CST weekdays)
ftp more info -> ftp.metronet.com:/pub/metronetinfo/

<< michnet >>
name ----------> Merit Network, Inc. -- MichNet project
dialup --------> contact for number or telnet hermes.merit.edu and type
       'help' at 'Which host?' prompt
area codes ----> 202, 301, 313, 517, 616, 703, 810, 906, PDN
local access --> Michigan; Boston, MA; Wash. DC
long distance -> SprintNet, Autonet, Michigan Bell packet-switch network
services ------> telnet, SLIP, PPP, outbound SprintNet, Autonet and Ann
               Arbor dialout
fees ----------> $35/month + $40 signup ($10/month for K-12 & libraries in
          Michigan)
email ---------> info@merit.edu
voice ---------> 313-764-9430
ftp more info -> nic.merit.edu:/

<< millennium >>
name ----------> Millennium Online
dialup --------> contact for numbers
area codes ----> PDN
local access --> PDN private numbers available
long distance -> PDN
services ------> shell, ftp, telnet, irc, feeds, gopher, graphical bbs
      (interface required)
fees ----------> $10 monthly/.10 per minute domestic .30 internationally
email ---------> jjablow@mill.com
voice ---------> 800-736-0122
ftp more info -> n/a

<< mindvox >>
name ----------> MindVOX
dialup --------> 212-989-4141 'mindvox' 'guest'
area codes ----> 212, 718
```

```
local access --> NY: New York City
long distance -> provided by user
services ------> conferencing system ftp, telnet, irc, gopher, hytelnet,
        Archives, BBS
fees ----------> $15-$20/month.  No startup.
email ---------> info@phantom.com
voice ---------> 212-989-2418
ftp more info -> n/a

<< MSen >>
name ----------> MSen
dialup --------> contact for number
area codes ----> 313, 810
local access --> All of SE Michigan (313, 810)
long distance -> provided by user
services ------> shell, WAIS, gopher, telnet, ftp, SLIP, PPP, IRC, WWW,
        Picospan BBS, ftp space
fees ----------> $20/month; $20 startup
email ---------> info@msen.com
voice ---------> 313-998-4562
fax -----------> 313-998-4563
ftp more info -> ftp.msen.com:/pub/vendor/msen

<< mucev >>
name ----------> muc.de e.V.
dialup --------> contact for numbers
area codes ----> +49 089
local access --> Munich/Bavaria, Germany
long distance -> provided by user
services ------> mail, news, ftp, telnet, irc, gopher, SLIP/PPP/UUCP
fees ----------> From DM 20.-- (Mail only) up to DM 65.-- (Full Account with
        PPP)
email ---------> postmaster@muc.de
voice ---------> 
ftp more info -> ftp.muc.de:public/info/muc-info.*

<< MV >>
name ----------> MV Communications, Inc.
dialup --------> contact for numbers
area codes ----> 603
local access --> Many NH communities
long distance -> provided by user
services ------> shell, ftp, telnet, gopher, SLIP, email, feeds, dns,
     archives, etc.
fees ----------> $5.00/mo minimum + variable hourly rates.  See schedule.
email ---------> info@mv.com
voice ---------> 603-429-2223
ftp more info -> ftp.mv.com:/pub/mv
```

```
<< nearnet >>
name ----------> NEARnet
dialup --------> contact for numbers
area codes ----> 508, 603, 617
local access --> Boston, MA; Nashua, NH
long distance -> provided by user
services ------> SLIP, email, feeds, dns
fees ----------> $250/month
email ---------> nearnet-join@nic.near.net
voice ---------> 617-873-8730
ftp more info -> nic.near.net:/docs


<< netcom >>
name ----------> Netcom Online Communication Services
dialup --------> 206-547-5992, 214-753-0045, 303-758-0101, 310-842-8835,
        312-380-0340, 404-303-9765, 408-241-9760, 408-459-9851,
        415-328-9940, 415-985-5650, 503-626-6833, 510-274-2900,
        510-426-6610, 510-865-9004, 617-237-8600, 619-234-0524,
        703-255-5951, 714-708-3800, 818-585-3400, 916-965-1371
area codes ----> 206, 213, 214, 303, 310, 312, 404, 408, 415, 503, 510,
                617, 619, 703, 714, 718, 818, 916
local access --> CA: Alameda, Irvine, Los Angeles, Palo Alto, Pasadena,
        Sacramento, San Diego, San Francisco, San Jose, Santa Cruz,
      Walnut Creek; CO: Denver; DC: Washington; GA: Atlanta; IL:
    Chicago; MA: Boston; OR: Portland; TX: Dallas; WA: Seattle
long distance -> provided by user
services ------> shell, ftp, telnet, irc, WAIS, gopher, SLIP/PPP, ftp
                space, feeds, dns
fees ----------> $19.50/month + $20.00 signup
email ---------> info@netcom.com
voice ---------> 408-554-8649, 800-501-8649
fax -----------> 408-241-9145
ftp more info -> ftp.netcom.com:/pub/netcom/


<< northshore >>
name ----------> North Shore Access
dialup --------> 617-593-4557 (v.32bis, v.32, PEP) 'new'
area codes ----> 617, 508
local access --> MA: Wakefield, Lynnfield, Lynn, Saugus, Revere, Peabody,
        Salem, Marblehead, Swampscott
long distance -> provided by user
services ------> shell (SunOS UNIX), ftp, telnet, archie, gopher, wais,
                www, UUCP feeds
fees ----------> $9/month includes 10 hours connect, $1/hr thereafter,
                higher volume discount plans also available
email ---------> info@northshore.ecosoft.com
voice ---------> 617-593-3110 voicemail
```

```
ftp more info -> northshore.ecosoft.com:/pub/flyer


<< novalink >>
name ----------> NovaLink
dialup --------> (800) 937-7644 'new' or 'info', 508-754-4009 2400, 14400
area codes ----> 508, 617, PDN
local access --> MA: Worcester, Cambridge, Marlboro, Boston
long distance -> CPS: $1.80/hour 2400, 9600; SprintNet $1.80/hour nights
          and weekends
services ------> ftp, telnet, gopher, shell, irc, XWindows, feeds, adult,
          user groups, FAX, Legends of Future Past
fees ----------> $12.95 sign-up (refundable and includes 2 hours), +
              $9.95/mo (includes 5 daytime hours) + $1.80/hr
email ---------> info@novalink.com
voice ---------> 800-274-2814
ftp more info -> ftp.novalink.com:/info


<< nuance >>
name ----------> Nuance Network Services
dialup --------> contact for number
area codes ----> 205
local access --> AL: Huntsville
long distance -> provided by user
services ------> shell (Unix SVR4.2), ftp, telnet, gopher, SLIP, PPP, ISDN
fees ----------> personal $25/mo + $35 start-up, corporate: call for options
email ---------> staff@nuance.com
voice ---------> 205-533-4296 voice/recording
ftp more info -> ftp.nuance.com:/pub/NNS-INFO


<< nuchat >>
name ----------> South Coast Computing Services, Inc.
dialup --------> (713) 661-8593 (v.32) - (713) 661-8595 (v.32bis)
area codes ----> 713
local access --> TX: Houston metro area
long distance -> provided by user
services ------> shell, ftp, telnet, gopher, Usenet, UUCP feeds, SLIP,
      dedicated lines, domain name service, FULL time tech support
fees ----------> dialup - $3/hour, UUCP - $1.50/hour or $100/month
        unlimited, dedicated - $120, unlimited access
email ---------> info@sccsi.com
voice ---------> 713-661-3301
ftp more info -> sccsi.com:/pub/communications/*


<< nwnexus >>
name ----------> Northwest Nexus Inc.
dialup --------> contact for numbers
area codes ----> 206
local access --> WA: Seattle
```

```
long distance -> provided by user
services ------> UUCP, SLIP, PPP, feeds, dns
fees ----------> $10/month for first 10 hours + $3/hr; $20 start-up
email ---------> info@nwnexus.wa.com
voice ---------> 206-455-3505
ftp more info -> nwnexus.wa.com:/NWNEXUS.info.txt


<< nyx >>
name ----------> Nyx, the Spirit of the Night; Free public internet access
        provided by the University of Denver's Math & Computer
 Science Department
dialup --------> 303-871-3324
area codes ----> 303
local access --> CO: Boulder/Denver
long distance -> provided by user
services ------> shell or menu; semi-anonymous accounts; ftp, news, mail
fees ----------> none; donations are accepted but not requested
email ---------> aburt@nyx.cs.du.edu
voice ---------> login to find current list of volunteer 'voice' helpers
ftp more info -> n/a


<< OARnet >>
name ----------> OARnet
dialup --------> send e-mail to nic@oar.net
area codes ----> 614, 513, 419, 216, 800
local access --> OH: Columbus, Cincinnati, Cleveland, Dayton
long distance -> 800 service
services ------> email, ftp, telnet, newsfeed
fees ----------> $4.00/hr to $330.00/month; call for code or send email
email ---------> nic@oar.net
voice ---------> 614-292-8100
fax -----------> 614-292-7168
ftp more info -> n/a


<< oldcolo >>
name ----------> Old Colorado City Communications
dialup --------> 719-632-4111 'newuser'
area codes ----> 719
local access --> CO: Colorado Springs
long distance -> provided by user
services ------> shell, ftp, telnet, AKCS, home of the NAPLPS conference
fees ----------> $25/month
email ---------> dave@oldcolo.com / thefox@oldcolo.com
voice ---------> 719-632-4848, 719-593-7575 or 719-636-2040
fax -----------> 719-593-7521
ftp more info -> n/a


<< olympus >>
```

```
name ----------> Olympus - The Olympic Peninsula's Gateway To The Internet
dialup --------> contact voice number below
area codes ----> 206
local access --> WA:Olympic Peninsula/Eastern Jefferson County
long distance -> provided by user
services ------> shell, ftp, telnet, pine, hytelnet
fees ----------> $25/month + $10 startup
email ---------> info@pt.olympus.net
voice ---------> 206-385-0464
ftp more info -> n/a


<< panix >>
name ----------> PANIX Public Access Unix
dialup --------> 212-787-3100 'newuser'
area codes ----> 212, 718
local access --> New York City, NY
long distance -> provided by user
services ------> shell, ftp, telnet, gopher, wais, irc, feeds
fees ----------> $19/month or $208/year + $40 signup
email ---------> alexis@panix.com, jsb@panix.com
voice ---------> 212-877-4854 [Alexis Rosen], 212-691-1526 [Jim Baumbach]
ftp more info -> n/a


<< pipeline >>
name ----------> The Pipeline
dialup --------> 212-267-8606 'guest'
area codes ----> 212, 718
local access --> NY: New York City
long distance -> provided by user
services ------> Windows interface or shell/menu; all IP services
fees ----------> $15/mo. (inc. 5 hrs) or $20/20 hrs or $35 unlimited
email ---------> info@pipeline.com, staff@pipeline.com
voice ---------> 212-267-3636
ftp more info -> n/a


<< portal >>
name ----------> The Portal System
dialup --------> 408-973-8091 high-speed, 408-725-0561 2400bps; 'info'
area codes ----> 408, 415, PDN
local access --> CA: Cupertino, Mountain View, San Jose
long distance -> SprintNet: $2.50/hour off-peak, $7-$10/hour peak; Tymnet:
                 $2.50/hour off-peak, $13/hour peak
services ------> shell, ftp, telnet, IRC, UUCP, feeds, bbs
fees ----------> $19.95/month + $19.95 signup
email ---------> cs@cup.portal.com, info@portal.com
voice ---------> 408-973-9111
ftp more info -> n/a
off-peak ------> 6pm to 7am + weekends and holidays
```

```
<< prairienet >>
name ----------> Prairienet Freenet
dialup --------> (217) 255-9000 'visitor'
area codes ----> 217
local access --> IL: Champaign-Urbana
long distance -> provided by user
services ------> telnet, ftp, gopher, IRC, etc.
fees ----------> Free for Illinois residents, $25/year for non-residents
email ---------> jayg@uiuc.edu
voice ---------> 217-244-1962
ftp more info -> n/a


<< PREPnet >>
name ----------> PREPnet
dialup --------> contact for numbers
area codes ----> 215, 412, 717, 814
local access --> PA: Philadelphia, Pittsburgh, Harrisburg
long distance -> provided by user
services ------> SLIP, terminal service, telnet, ftp
fees ----------> $1,000/year membership. Equipment-$325 onetime fee plus
          $40/month
email ---------> prepnet@cmu.edu
voice ---------> 412-268-7870
fax -----------> 412-268-7875
ftp more info -> ftp.prepnet.com:/prepnet/general/


<< psilink >>
name ----------> PSILink -  Personal Internet Access
dialup --------> North America: send email to classa-na-numbers@psi.com and
          classb-na-numbers@psi.com; Rest of World: send email to
  classb-row-numbers@psi.com
area codes ----> PDN
local access -->
long distance -> [per hour, off-peak/peak] PSINet A: included; PSINet B:
          $6/$2.50; PSINet B international: $18/$18
services ------> email and newsfeed, ftp
fees ----------> 2400: $19/month; 9600: $29/month (PSILink software included)
email ---------> all-info@psi.com, psilink-info@psi.com
voice ---------> 703-620-6651
fax -----------> 703-620-4586
ftp more info -> ftp.psi.com:/


<< psi-world-dial >>
name ----------> PSI's World-Dial Service
dialup --------> send email to numbers-info@psi.com
area codes ----> PDN
local access -->
```

```
long distance -> [per hour, off-peak/peak] V.22bis: $1.25/$2.75; V.32:
        $3.00/$4.50; 14.4K: $4.00/$6.50
services ------> telnet, rlogin, tn3270, XRemote
fees ----------> $9/month minimum + $19 startup
email ---------> all-info@psi.com, world-dial-info@psi.com
voice ---------> 703-620-6651
fax -----------> 703-620-4586
ftp more info -> ftp.psi.com:/
off-peak ------> 8pm to 8am + weekends and holidays


<< PUCnet >>
name ----------> PUCnet Computer Connections
dialup --------> 403-484-5640 (v.32 bis) 'guest'
area codes ----> 403
local access --> AB: Edmonton and surrounding communities in the Extended
        Flat Rate Calling Area
long distance -> provided by user
services ------> shell, menu, ftp, telnet, archie, gopher, feeds, USENET
fees ----------> Cdn$25/month (20 hours connect time) + Cdn$6.25/hr (ftp &
      telnet only) + $10 signup
email ---------> info@PUCnet.com (Mail responder) or pwilson@PUCnet.com
voice ---------> 403-448-1901
fax -----------> 403-484-7103
ftp more info -> n/a


<< realtime >>
name ----------> RealTime Communications (wixer)
dialup --------> 512-459-4391 'new'
area codes ----> 512
local access --> TX: Austin
long distance -> provided by user
services ------> shell, ftp, telnet, irc, gopher, feeds, SLIP, UUCP
fees ----------> $75/year.  Monthly and quarterly rates available.
email ---------> hosts@wixer.bga.com
voice ---------> 512-451-0046 (11am-6pm Central Time, weekdays)
fax -----------> 512-459-3858
ftp more info -> n/a


<< ssnet >>
name ----------> Systems Solutions
dialup --------> contact for info
area codes ----> 302
local access --> Wilminton, Delaware
long distance -> provided by user
services ------> shell, UUCP, SLIP, PPP, ftp, telnet, irc, gopher, archie,
          mud, etc.
fees ----------> full service $25/month $20/startup; personal slip/ppp
        $25/month + $2/hour, $20/startup; dedicated slip/ppp
```

```
        $150/month, $450/startup
email ---------> sharris@marlin.ssnet.com
voice ---------> (302) 378-1386, (800) 331-1386
ftp more info -> n/a


<< sugar >>
name ----------> NeoSoft's Sugar Land Unix
dialup --------> 713-684-5900
area codes ----> 504, 713
local access --> TX: Houston metro area; LA: New Orleans
long distance -> provided by user
services ------> bbs, shell, ftp, telnet, irc, feeds, UUCP
fees ----------> $29.95/month
email ---------> info@NeoSoft.com
voice ---------> 713-438-4964
ftp more info -> n/a


<< teleport >>
name ----------> Teleport
dialup --------> 503-220-0636 (2400) 503-220-1016 (v.32, v.32 bis) 'new'
area codes ----> 503
local access --> OR: Portland, Beaverton, Hillsboro, Forest Grove, Gresham,
            Tigard, Lake Oswego, Oregon City, Tualatin, Wilsonville
long distance -> provided by user
services ------> shell, ftp, telnet, gopher, usenet, ppp, WAIS, irc, feeds,
            dns
fees ----------> $10/month (1 hr/day limit)
email ---------> info@teleport.com
voice ---------> 503-223-4245
ftp more info -> teleport.com:/about


<< telerama >>
name ----------> Telerama Public Access Internet
dialup --------> 412-481-5302 'new' (2400)
area codes ----> 412
local access --> PA: Pittsburgh
long distance -> provided by user
services ------> telnet, ftp, irc, gopher, ClariNet/Usenet, shell/menu,
            uucp
fees ----------> 66 cents/hour 2400bps; $1.32/hour 14.4K bps; $6 min/month
email ---------> info@telerama.pgh.pa.us
voice ---------> 412-481-3505
ftp more info -> telerama.pgh.pa.us:/info/general.info


<< tmn >>
name ----------> The Meta Network
dialup --------> contact for numbers
area codes ----> 703, 202, 301, PDN
```

```
local access --> Washington, DC metro area
long distance -> SprintNet: $6.75/hr; FTS-2000; Acunet
services ------> Caucus conferencing, email, shell, ftp, telnet, bbs, feeds
fees ----------> $20/month + $15 signup/first month
email ---------> info@tmn.com
voice ---------> 703-243-6622
ftp more info -> n/a


<< UUNET-Canada >>
name ----------> UUNET Canada, Inc.
dialup --------> contact for numbers
area codes ----> 416, 905, 519, 613, 514, 604, 403
local access --> ON: Toronto, Ottawa, Kitchener/Waterloo, London, Hamilton,
          QC: Montreal,    AB: Calgary,    BC: Vancouver
long distance -> provided by user
services ------> terminal access to telnet only, UUCP (e-mail/news),
    SLIP/PPP, shared or dedicated basis, from v.32bis to 56k+
fees ----------> (All Cdn$ + GST) TAC: $6/hr, UUCP: $20/mo + $6/hr, IP/UUCP:
    $50/mo + $6/hr, ask for prices on other services
email ---------> info@uunet.ca
voice ---------> 416-368-6621
fax -----------> 416-368-1350
ftp more info -> ftp.uunet.ca


<< uunorth >>
name ----------> UUnorth
dialup --------> contact for numbers
area codes ----> 416, 519, 613
local access --> ON: Toronto
long distance -> provided by user
services ------> shell, ftp, telnet, gopher, feeds, IRC, feeds, SLIP, PPP
fees ----------> (All Cdn$ + GST) $20 startup + $25 for 20 hours off-peak +
      $1.25/hr OR $40 for 40 hours up to 5/day + $2/hr OR $3/hr
email ---------> uunorth@uunorth.north.net
voice ---------> 416-225-8649
fax -----------> 416-225-0525
ftp more info -> n/a


<< Vnet >>
name ----------> Vnet Internet Access, Inc.
dialup --------> 704-347-8839, 919-406-1544, 919-851-1526 'new'
area codes ----> 704, 919
local access --> NC: Charlotte, RTP, Raleigh, Durham, Chappel Hill. Winston
          Salem/Greensboro
long distance -> Available for $3.95 per hour through Global Access. Contact
          Vnet offices for more information.
services ------> shell, ftp, telnet, hytelnet, irc, gopher, WWW, wais,
      usenet, clarinet, NNTP, DNS, SLIP/PPP, UUCP, POPmail
```

```
fees ----------> $25/month individual. $12.50 a month for telnet-in-only.
         SLIP/PPP/UUCP starting at $25/month.
email ---------> info@char.vnet.net
voice ---------> 704-374-0779
ftp more info -> n/a


<< well >>
name ----------> The Whole Earth 'Lectronic Link
dialup --------> 415-332-6106 'newuser'
area codes ----> 415, PDN
local access --> Sausalito, CA
long distance -> Compuserve Packet Network: $4/hour
services ------> shell, ftp, telnet, bbs
fees ----------> $15.00/month + $2.00/hr
email ---------> info@well.sf.ca.us
voice ---------> 415-332-4335
ftp more info -> n/a


<< wariat >>
name ----------> APK- Public Access UNI* Site
dialup --------> 216-481-9436  (V.32bis, SuperPEP on separate rotary)
area codes ----> 216
local access --> OH: Cleveland
long distance -> provided by user
services ------> shell, ftp, telnet, archie, irc, gopher, feeds,
         BBS(Uniboard1.10)
fees ----------> $15/20 hours, $35/monthly, $20 signup
email ---------> zbig@wariat.org
voice ---------> 216-481-9428
ftp more info -> n/a


<< world >>
name ----------> The World
dialup --------> 617-739-9753 'new'
area codes ----> 617, PDN
local access --> Boston, MA
long distance -> Compuserve Packet Network: $5.60/hour
services ------> shell, ftp, telnet, irc
fees ----------> $5.00/month + $2.00/hr or $20/month for 20 hours
email ---------> office@world.std.com
voice ---------> 617-739-0202
ftp more info -> world.std.com:/world-info/description


<< wyvern >>
name ----------> Wyvern Technologies, Inc.
dialup --------> (804) 627-1828 Norfolk, (804) 886-0662 (Peninsula)
area codes ----> 804
local access --> VA: Norfolk, Virginia Beach, Portsmouth, Chesapeake,
```

```
              Newport News, Hampton, Williamsburg
long distance -> provided by user
services ------> shell, menu, ftp, telnet, uucp feeds, irc, archie, gopher,
          UPI news, email, dns, archives
fees ----------> $15/month or $144/year, $10 startup
email ---------> system@wyvern.com
voice ---------> 804-622-4289
fax -----------> 804-622-7158
ftp more info -> n/a


<< xnet >>
name ----------> XNet Information Systems
dialup --------> (708) 983-6435 V.32bis and TurboPEP
area codes ----> 312, 708, 815
local access --> IL: Chicago, Naperville, Hoffman Estates
long distance -> provided by user
services ------> shell, telnet, hytelnet, ftp, irc, gopher, www, wais,
      SLIP/PPP, dns, uucp feeds, bbs
fees ----------> $45/3 months or $75/6 months
email ---------> info@xnet.com
voice ---------> (708) 983-6064
ftp more info -> ftp.xnet.com:/xnet.info/


-----------------------------
```

From: PDIAL -05-
Subject: What *Is* The Internet?

The Internet is a global cooperative network of university, corporate, government, and private computers, all communicating with each other by means of something called TCP/IP (Transmission Control Protocol/Internet Protocol). Computers directly on the Internet can exchange data quickly and easily with any other computer on the Internet to download files, send email, provide remote logins, etc.

Users can download files from publicly accessible archive sites ("anonymous FTP"); login into remote computers (telnet or rlogin); chat in real-time with other users around the world (Internet Relay Chat); or use the newest information retrieval tools to find a staggering variety of information (Wide Area Information Servers, Gopher, World Wide Web).

Computers directly on the Internet also exchange email directly and very quickly; email is usually delivered in seconds between Internet sites. Sometimes the Internet is confused with other related networks or types of networking.

First, there are other ways to be "connected to the Internet" without being directly connected as a TCP/IP node. Some computers connect via UUCP or other means at regular intervals to an Internet site to exchange email and USENET newsgroups, for instance. Such a site can provide email (though not as quickly as a directly connected systems) and USENET access, but not Internet downloads, remote logins, etc.

"email" (or "Internet email", "netmail") can be exchanged with a wide variety of systems connected directly and indirectly to the Internet. The email may travel solely over the Internet, or it may traverse other networks and systems.

"USENET" is the collection of computers all over the world that exchange USENET news -- thousands of "newsgroups" (like forums, or echos) on a wide range of topics. The newsgroup articles are distributed all over the world to USENET sites that wish to carry them (sometimes over the Internet, sometimes not), where people read and respond to them.

The "NSFNET" is one of the backbones of the Internet in the US. It is funded by the NSF, which restricts traffic over the NSFNET to "open research and education in and among US research and instructional institutions, plus research arms of for-profit firms when engaged in open scholarly communication and research." Your Internet provider can give you more details about acceptable use, and alternatives should you need to use the Internet in other ways.

From: PDIAL -06-
Subject: What The PDIAL Is

This is the PDIAL, the Public Dialup Internet Access List. It is a list of Internet service providers offering public access dialins and outgoing Internet access (ftp, telnet, etc.). Most of them provide email and USENET news and other services as well.

If one of these systems is not accessible to you and you need email or USENET access, but *don't* need ftp or telnet, you have many more public access systems from which to choose. Public access systems without ftp or telnet are *not* listed in this list, however. See the nixpub (alt.bbs, comp.misc) list and other BBS lists.

Some of these providers offer time-shared access to a shell or BBS program on a computer connected directly to the Internet, through which you can FTP or telnet to other systems on the Internet. Usually other services are provided as well. Generally, you need only a modem and terminal or terminal emulator to access these systems. Check for "shell", "bbs", or "menu" on the "services" line.

Other providers connect you directly to the Internet via SLIP or PPP when
you dial in. For these you need a computer system capable of running the
software to interface with the Internet, e.g., a Unix machine, PC, or Mac.
Check for "SLIP", or "PPP" on the services line.

While I have included all sites for which I have complete information, this
list is surely incomplete. If you have any additions or corrections please
send them to me at one of the addresses listed in section -10-.

From: PDIAL -07-
Subject: How People Can Get The PDIAL (This List)

EMAIL:

  From the Information Deli archive server (most up-to-date):
    To receive the current edition of the PDIAL, send email containing
    the phrase "Send PDIAL" to "info-deli-server@netcom.com".
    To be put on a list of people who receive future editions as they
    are published, send email containing the phrase "Subscribe PDIAL"
    to "info-deli-server@netcom.com".

  To receive both the most recent and future editions, send both
    messages.

  From time to time, I'll also be sending out news and happenings
    that relate to the PDIAL or The Information Deli. To receive
    the Info Deli News automatically, send email containing the
    phrase "Subscribe Info-Deli-News" to "info-deli-server@netcom.com".
  From the news.answers FAQ archive:
    Send email with the message "send usenet/news.answers/pdial" to
    "mail-server@rtfm.mit.edu". For help, send the message "help" to
    "mail-server@rtfm.mit.edu".

USENET:

  The PDIAL list is posted semi-regularly to alt.internet.access.wanted,
  alt.bbs.lists, alt.online-service, ba.internet, and news.answers.
  FTP ARCHIVE SITES (PDIAL and other useful information):

  Information Deli FTP site:
    ftp.netcom.com:/pub/info-deli/public-access/pdial [192.100.81.100]
  As part of a collection of public access lists:
    VFL.Paramax.COM:/pub/pubnet/pdial [128.126.220.104]
    (used to be GVL.Unisys.COM)

  From the Merit Network Information Center Internet information archive:

```
nic.merit.edu:/internet/providers/pdial [35.1.1.48]
```

As part of an Internet access compilation file:
```
liberty.uc.wlu.edu:/pub/lawlib/internet.access [137.113.10.35]
```
As part of the news.answers FAQ archive:
```
rtfm.mit.edu:/pub/usenet/news.answers/pdial [18.70.0.209]
```

From: PDIAL -08-
Subject: Appendix A: Other Valuable Resources

InterNIC Internet Help Desk

  The US National Science Foundation has funded Information, Registration,
and Directory services for the Internet, and they are available to all
Internet users. The most useful branch for PDIAL readers is Information
Services, which provides all sorts of information to help Internet users.
Contact Information Services by:

```
  voice:   800-444-4345 (US)
  voice:   +1 (619) 455-4600
  fax:     +1 (619) 455-4640
  email:   mailserv@is.internic.net, put "SEND HELP" in body
  email:   info@internic.net
  gopher:  gopher gopher.internic.net / telnet gopher.internic.net
  ftp:     is.internic.net
  postal:  InterNIC Information Services
           General Atomics
           PO Box 85608
           San Diego, CA 92186-9784 USA
```

Internet Guide Books

  Connecting To The Internet; Susan Estrada; O'Reilly & Associates; ISBN
  1-56592-061-9 (A how-to on selecting the right IP provider, from dialup
  to dedicated.)

  A DOS User's Guide to the Internet -- E-mail, Netnews and File Transfer
  with UUCP; James Gardner; MKS; ISBN 0-13-106873-3 ("Internet" in the
  title is misleading -- covers UUCP connections only.)

  The Electronic Traveller -- Exploring Alternative Online Systems;
  Elizabeth Powell Crowe; Windcrest/McGraw-Hill; ISBN 0-8306-4498-9. (A
  good tour of various personal IP and other types of providers, but some
  data is seriously out of date.)

  Internet Basics; Steve Lambert, Walt How; Random House; ISBN
  0-679-75023-1

The Internet Companion; Tracy LaQuey, Jeanne C. Ryer; Addison-Wesley;
ISBN 0-201-62224-6

The Internet Companion Plus; Tracy LaQuey, Jeanne C. Ryer;
Addison-Wesley; ISBN 0-201-62719-1

The Internet Complete Reference; Harley Hahn, Rick Stout; Osborne;
ISBN 0-07-881980-6

The Internet Directory; Eric Brawn; Fawcett Columbine; ISBN
0-449-90898-4 (Phone book style listing of resources.)

The Internet for Dummies; John R. Levine, Carol Baroudi; IDG Books
Worldwide; ISBN 1-56884-024-1 (Lots of useful information, but much
of it is intermediate level, not "dummy".)

Internet: Getting Started; April Marine, Susan Kirkpatrick, Vivian Neou,
Carol Ward; PTR Prentice Hall; ISBN 0-13-289596-X

The Internet Guide for New Users; Daniel P. Dern; McGraw-Hill; ISBN
0-07-016511-4 (Good, very thorough guide for new users.)

The Internet Navigator; Paul Glister; John Wiley & Sons; ISBN
0-471-59782-1 (Good, comprehensive guide for new users.)

The Internet Roadmap; Bennet Falk; Sybex; ISBN 0-7821-1365-6

Internet Starter Kit for the Macintosh With Disk; Adam C. Engst; Hayden
Books; ISBN 1-568300646

The Mac Internet Tour Guide; Michael Fraase; Ventana Press; ISBN
1-56604-062-0

Navigating the Internet; Richard J. Smith, Mark Gibbs; SAMS
Publishing; ISBN 0-672-30362-0

Welcome to... Internet -- From Mystery to Mastery; Tom Badgett, Corey
Sandler; MIS:Press; ISBN 1-55828-308-0

The Whole Internet User's Guide & Catalog; Ed Krol; O'Reilly & Associates;
ISBN 1-56592-025-2 (Good all around guide.)

Zen & the Art of the Internet: A Beginner's Guide; Brendan P. Kehoe;
PTR Prentice Hall; ISBN 0-13-010778-6

Other BBS/Internet Provider Lists

FSLIST -- The Forgotten Site List.
  USENET: alt.internet.access.wanted;
  ftp: freedom.nmsu.edu:/pub/docs/fslist/ or login.qc.ca:/pub/fslist/
nixpub -- public access Unixes. USENET: comp.bbs.mis, alt.bbs;
  email: to <mail-server@bts.com>, body containing "get PUB nixpub.long";
  ftp: VFL.Paramax.COM:/pub/pubnetc/nixpub.long

From: PDIAL -09-
Subject: Appendix B: Finding Public Data Network (PDN) Access Numbers
Here's how to get local access numbers or information for the various PDNs.
Generally, you can contact the site you're calling for help, too. IMPORTANT
NOTE: Unless noted otherwise, set your modem to 7E1 (7 data bits, even
parity, 1 stop bit) when dialing to look up access numbers by modem as
instructed below.

BT Tymnet

For information and local access numbers, call 800-937-2862 (voice) or
215-666-1770 (voice).

To look up access numbers by modem, dial a local access number, hit <cr> and
'a', and enter "information" at the "please log in:" prompt.

Compuserve Packet Network

You do NOT have to be a Compuserve member to use the CPN to dial other
services.

For information and local access numbers, call 800-848-8199 (voice).
To look up access numbers by modem, dial a local access number, hit <cr> and
enter "PHONES" at the "Host Name:" prompt.

PSINet

For information, call 800-82PSI82 (voice) or 703-620-6651 (voice), or send
email to "all-info@psi.com". For a list of local access numbers send email
to "numbers-info@psi.com".

From: PDIAL -10-

Subject: Providers: Get Listed in PDIAL!

NEW SUBMISSION/CORRECTION PROCEDURES:

The PDIAL will be undergoing expansion in both breadth (how many and what kinds of public access providers) and depth (how much information is carried for each provider). To collect the data, I will be emailing a questionnaire to providers already on the PDIAL, and to any providers who wish to be added. Corrections can also be submitted via update questionnaires.

To be listed in the PDIAL, retrieve the PDIAL questionnaire by sending email to <info-deli-server@netcom.com> containing the command "Send PDIAL-Q". The questionnaire will not be available until 15 Dec 1993, but requests received before then will be queued and honored when it is available.
--
Peter Kaminski / The Information Deli

kaminski@netcom.com (preferred)
71053.2155@compuserve.com

End of PDIAL
****

Index

X

Z

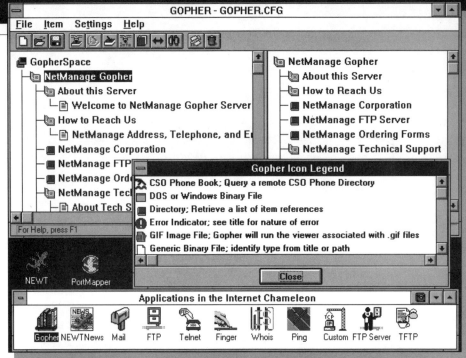